The African Diaspora and the Study of Religion

THE AFRICAN DIASPORA AND THE STUDY OF RELIGION

EDITED BY

THEODORE LOUIS TROST

palgrave
macmillan

THE AFRICAN DIASPORA AND THE STUDY OF RELIGION
Copyright © Theodore Louis Trost, 2007.

First published in 2007 by
PALGRAVE MACMILLAN™
175 Fifth Avenue, New York, N.Y. 10010 and
Houndmills, Basingstoke, Hampshire, England RG21 6XS
Companies and representatives throughout the world.

PALGRAVE MACMILLAN is the global academic imprint of the Palgrave Macmillan division of St. Martin's Press, LLC and of Palgrave Macmillan Ltd. Macmillan® is a registered trademark in the United States, United Kingdom and other countries. Palgrave is a registered trademark in the European Union and other countries.

ISBN-13: 978–1–4039–7786–1
ISBN-10: 1–4039–7786–0

Library of Congress Cataloging-in-Publication Data

The African diaspora and the study of religion / edited by Theodore Louis Trost.
    p. cm.
    ISBN 1–4039–7786–0 (alk. paper)
    1. Africa—Religion—Study and teaching. 2. African diaspora.
I. Trost, Theodore Louis, 1954–

BL2400.A417 2007
200.89'96—dc22   2007019674

A catalogue record for this book is available from the British Library.

Design by Newgen Imaging Systems (P) Ltd., Chennai, India.

First edition: December 2007

10 9 8 7 6 5 4 3 2 1

Printed in the United States of America.

Contents

Illustrations

Series Editor's Preface

Religion/Culture/Critique is a series devoted to publishing work that addresses religion's centrality to a wide range of settings and debates, both contemporary and historical, and that critically engages the category of "religion" itself. This series is conceived as a place where readers will be invited to explore how "religion"—whether embedded in texts, practices, communities, or ideologies—intersects with social and political interests, institutions, and identities.

The African Diaspora and the Study of Religion brings together the work of scholars from a range of disciplines—history, religion, cultural anthropology, literature, and cultural studies—to focus attention on the richness and intricacy of the African diaspora and its engagements with and stagings of religion. The contributors to this volume invite readers to explore the religious cultures and worlds that have emerged out of the complex legacies of enslavement and colonial subjugation. What comes into view is the very transformation of received traditions—whether Christianity, Islam, or indigenous religions— into distinctive iterations of themselves and of religiosity itself. This book explores religion as both a social fact and a mode of representation and signification, as a way of thinking, and as a way of being and doing in the world. Each chapter in the volume stays closely focused on the object of analysis, whether the life of a community lived out ritually or the figurations of diasporic Africa in a literary text or, indeed, the theoretical questions that "diaspora" and "Africa" as organizing terms themselves raise. At the same time, each chapter also challenges its readers to reconsider the boundaries of "religion" as a category of social and cultural analysis and to rethink the work that "religion" does in lives characterized by loss, displacement, and dispersion. *The African Diaspora and the Study of Religion* is a welcome addition to the Religion/Culture/Critique series for its contributions to religious studies, Africana studies, and the places where the two fields so fruitfully intersect.

Elizabeth A. Castelli
Religion/Culture/Critique Series Editor
New York City
May 2007

Preface

This book consists of fourteen chapters focusing on a series of interrelated topics having to do with religion, Africa, and religion in the African diaspora. The problematic of the volume is set forth in the introductory chapter by Wilson Jeremiah Moses, who presents the career of Alexander Crummell as an entrée into the kinds of complexities the other contributors subsequently explore. During the course of his own illustrious career, Moses has devoted a great deal of scholarly attention to Crummell. Raised in New York by his African parents in the early part of the nineteenth century, Crummell was an African American intellectual leader, an Episcopal missionary, and a key figure in the emergence of the state of Liberia, among other things. Despite his many achievements, Crummell remains difficult to classify, as opposed to better-known contemporaries such as Frederick Douglass—a point Moses does not hesitate to press. Crummell's cultural Eurocentrism and his political Afrocentrism, for example, surface everywhere in Moses's account to challenge contemporary constructions of blackness. This theme recurs in a number of chapters in this volume including those by Merinda Simmons, in her study of the mulatto heroine Helga in the novel *Quicksand* and Jonathon S. Kahn, who investigates the famous sermon on blackness in Ralph Ellison's *Invisible Man*.

The first part of the book draws together three chapters under the heading of "Africa in Diaspora." In the aftermath of the Christian missionary enterprise to Africa, Christians have emigrated from Africa to many parts of the world. In his chapter, "Raising Champions, Taking Territories," Afe Adogame presents the Redeemed Christian Church of God (RCCG) as one example of this phenomenon. A Pentecostal organization that originated in Nigeria, the RCCG has been described as wanting to export its own brand of ecstatic worship and moral discipline to the United States, a country its members believe has lost its religious salt. Here a critique of American religiosity arises if not along the lines of Crummell, at least in the same spirit. Meanwhile, the narrative of Pentecostalism itself is being reshaped—a theme that reappears later in this volume in

Matthew Waggoner's chapter on early American Pentecostalism. Adogame's scholarship, reflecting a sociological approach to the study of religion, is based on first-hand accounts of this "new religious movement."

If the RCCG participates in a contest over "authentic" Christianity, the next two chapters examine movements that have competed against various forms of Christianity in African American and Afro-Jamaican contexts during the early and mid-twentieth century. Interestingly, whereas the RCCG "comes from" Africa, the Nation of Islam and the Rastafari "go to" Africa in order to retrieve alternative or suppressed narratives of origin and destiny. In chapter 2, Maboula Soumahoro recounts the emergence of the Nation of Islam and Rastafarianism in relation to the work of Marcus Garvey—thus serving as a bridge and historical link between Alexander Crummell, on the one hand, and the RCCG on the other. In chapter 3, Fatimah Fanusie documents the emergence of the Nation of Islam primarily in the context of the post–World War II jazz scene. Partly on the basis of interviews with people who were centrally involved, Fanusie offers here the first research to document the early relationship in Boston between the Islamic Ahmadi movement, with roots in India, and the Nation of Islam.

The second part of the book looks to creative expressions of African diaspora and religion in music and literature. From a discussion, then, about jazz musicians in Boston, the book turns to the early twentieth century and another musician, R. Nathaniel Dett. In chapter 4, Regennia N. Williams portrays Dett as a gifted composer and arranger of African American sacred choral and instrumental music, a celebrated concert pianist, and a renowned faculty member at several historically black colleges and universities. Dett's story, particularly as it centers on the "proper" presentation of the spirituals or "sorrow songs" and the contest over what constitutes African American "culture," ventures into the complexities introduced by Moses's discussion about Crummell. Significantly, both Crummell and Dett are linked to W. E. B. Du Bois, whose influence is asserted at a variety of places in the book—notably in the chapters by Kahn and Glaude.

The other two chapters in this part of the book focus on novels. In each case, an imaginative site for redemption and wholeness is constructed to counter forms of Christianity that conspire to cause harm, especially to women. Merinda Simmons reads Nella Larsen's 1928 novel *Quicksand* alongside Zora Neale Hurston's *Tell My Horse*, a study of Afro-Caribbean Vodou. Simmons suggests that both authors critique the opposition between body and soul by exposing the tragedy that results when physicality is constrained within a Western, and alien, notion of human wholeness.

Meanwhile, in her study "Candomblé, Christianity, and Gnosticism in Toni Morrison's *Paradise*," Maha Marouan shows how the novel *Paradise* resorts to African heritage and diverse religious practices as a way to counteract white Christian discourse. Marouan draws out the novel's use of the Afro-Brazilian religion Candomblé and the Gnostic mysticism associated with Egypt to make room for an African American consciousness and a sense of identity that stands in opposition to the exclusionary politics of the dominant Christianity.

Part 3 of the volume moves from imaginative reconstructions of "African" religions in African American literature to case studies of practices and politics in Mexico, Cuba, and Brazil. In chapter 7, Angela N. Castañeda uses examples from ongoing ethnographic fieldwork in Veracruz, Mexico, to illustrate how performances involving representations of the African diaspora, and the Afro-Cuban religion of Santería in particular, are shaped and informed by both local and national government funding. Religion appears as a cultural tradition commercialized via festivals into foreign symbols of local identity. She points to the degree of prestige linked with rituals done either by Cubans or in Cuba, which are sharply contrasted with those ceremonies performed by Mexicans or in Mexico. In the eyes of many Mexicans, Cuba takes the place of Africa and thus is viewed as more real, more powerful, and closer to the roots of the "real" religion.

This quest for "authentic religion" is carried on in Cuba as well. In her wide-ranging account of Santería, or the *regla de ocha*, Christine Ayorinde points to efforts in Cuba aimed at the "Yorubization" of Santería—a recovery process that seeks to complete or deepen and extend ritual knowledge. Those who advocate this position believe that religious knowledge was lost either in transmission from Africa or over the centuries in Cuba and that a return to "authentic" African practice ought to be pursued. As in the case of Mexico, meanwhile, the ostensibly unreligious, or even, antireligious Cuban government has discovered a variety of uses for the *regla de ocha*—from supporting national identity to promoting tourism, a theme already developed in Castañeda's work.

In the final chapter of this very rich section, Kelly E. Hayes turns to the Afro-Brazilian religions of Candomblé and Macumba. Her ethnographic research in Brazil leads her to ask why one religious group is generally considered legitimate and the other is seen as nefarious. The ensuing investigation results in a careful interrogation of the classification systems laid down by scholars in the late nineteenth and early twentieth centuries and used by political authorities to distinguish between legitimate and illegitimate. Although she does not refer to Jonathan Z. Smith, her research serves as evidence for Smith's assertion that "religion" is the invention of the scholar's study—an assertion returned to in the chapters by McCutcheon and Glaude.

Part 4 of the book develops along the lines established by Hayes as the collection turns from the field of ethnographic inquiry to the scholar's study and a variety of theoretical considerations that arise there. In chapter 10, Matthew Waggoner interrogates the development of Pentecostalism in America. Challenging the dominant narrative that establishes the early movement as an interracial phenomenon, Waggoner argues that the disavowal of Pentecostalism's blackness was present already in the nascent period of its history. Waggoner performs a visual exegesis of a photograph that includes William J. Seymour, the black founder of the Azusa Street Mission in Los Angeles, among his white colleagues. According to Waggoner's reading, the photograph offers a contradictory scene of desire and power; it stages "a reconciliation that it abstains from fully representing." Here Waggoner finds resonances with W. E. B. Du Bois, who, writing contemporaneously with the emergence of Pentecostalism in America, insisted that the abolition of slavery and Reconstruction did not resolve the dilemmas of race and racism and that the color line would constitute the major problem of the twentieth century.

W. E. B. Du Bois is often considered a profound critic of religion. But in chapter 11, Jonathon S. Kahn uses the category of pragmatic religious naturalism to examine the place of religion in Du Bois's classic work, *The Souls of Black Folk*. After careful consideration of Du Bois's rhetoric, Kahn concludes that *Souls* transforms religious devotion from the need for the supernatural into the need for beauty and inspiration in the sufferings and achievements of black lives. Kahn then applies this observation to a reading and assessment of Ralph Ellison's novel *Invisible Man*. Russell T. McCutcheon's focus in much of his work has been on the manner in which the act of classification betrays social interests—whether those interests are on the political Left or the Right. In his chapter, "Africa on Our Minds," McCutcheon challenges scholars to recognize that their object of study is a product of their own interests and tools. As such, the effort to find an authentic Africa that can then serve as an anchor for social action, for example, is part of a contemporary political program; it tells us very little, McCutcheon argues, about some objective place called Africa.

In his conclusion, Eddie S. Glaude, Jr., elaborates on issues raised in McCutcheon's chapter and elsewhere in the volume. With reference to the discipline of history, Glaude points to the many ways in which the historian shapes the narrative and singles out events and characters with particular purposes in mind. In so doing, the scholar enters into the fray, or the "mess"—of faiths, doctrines, politics, conventions—in an effort to find a form that will make sense of the data, that will, in the words of Samuel Beckett, "accommodate the mess." At the end of the book, Glaude directs attention to the importance of beginnings in narratives about, in particular, African American religions. He calls for new beginnings to these narratives.

Acknowledgments

I would like to thank my colleagues in the Religious Studies Department at the University of Alabama for inventing this project and helping me see it through to completion. Russell McCutcheon was instrumental in envisioning the conference that served as impetus for the book. Steve Jacobs, Catherine Roach, and Kurtis Schaeffer (now of the University of Virginia) carefully read and reviewed these chapters in their earliest stage of composition. A special word of thanks is extended to Tim Murphy, whose well-wrought call for papers has afforded me the privilege of working closely with this book's many writers. I am also grateful to my new colleagues in the department, Steven Ramey and Maha Marouan, who have offered support and occasional commentary.

Betty Dickey and Donna Martin oversaw the arrangements that resulted in bringing people from all over the world to Tuscaloosa in April 2005. Noble assistance was rendered by Samantha Sastre, Kim Davis, Marianne Stanton, and Christine Scott. Sarah Luken's introduction to this project was as transcriber—a role she performed admirably. Many thanks to all of you.

I gratefully acknowledge all who participated in the African Diaspora and the Study of Religion conference. In particular, the comments of Katherine Smith, Josephine Nhongo-Simbanegavi, Amilcar Shabazz, James Hall, Tom Wolfe, and Jennifer Purvis proved helpful in the shaping of this book.

The University of Alabama provided significant financial support for the conference and also arranged for this book's index. Sincere thanks to Robert Olin, dean of the College of Arts and Sciences, and to the University's provost, Judith Bonner.

Heartfelt thanks to Amanda Moon at Palgrave Press for her patience and enthusiasm. For overseeing the project I thank executive editor Farideh Koohi-Kamali. For tireless advocacy, inter-personal skills, and attention to detail I thank Brigitte Shull. For wisdom and guidance at a perplexing moment I am particularly grateful to series editor Elizabeth Castelli.

My own introduction to Africa and African American religions came far too late in life. I am glad that I had such a wonderful teacher when that introduction finally came. This seems a most appropriate occasion to thank James Noel publicly for waking me up. On behalf of all of the contributors, I also thank Professor Noel for his painting "Wading in the Water," which graces the cover of this book.

Finally, Catherine Roach and our two sons, Nathaniel and Benjamin, have lived with this book for as long as I have. I don't have the words right now to express what your love has meant to me during the making of this book, but there will be time to make a song or two about it now that this work has come to an end.

THEODORE LOUIS TROST
May 1, 2007
Tuscaloosa, Alabama

Abbreviations

ABBS	Arab American Banner Society
CONACULTA	Consejo Nacional para la Cultura y las Artes or Federal Cultural Institute
DESR	Departmento de Estudios Sociorreligiosos or Department of Socio-Religious Studies
GED	General Education Development or high school equivalency test
GI bill	Servicemen's Readjustment Act of 1944
IGOC	International Gathering of Champions
INS	Immigration and Naturalization Service
IVEC	El Instituto Veracruzano de Cultura or Veracruz Institute of Culture
KICC	Kingsway International Christian Center
NAACP	National Association for the Advancement of Colored People
NAFTA	North American Free Trade Agreement
NGO	Nongovernmental Organization
NOI	Nation of Islam
RASHAD	The Initiative for the Study of Religion and Spirituality in the History of Africa and the Diaspora
RCCG	Redeemed Christian Church of God
RCCGNA	Redeemed Christian Church of God (North America)

Introduction: Alexander Crummell and the Destined Superiority of African People

Wilson Jeremiah Moses

These remarks were first presented as a keynote address at a conference on the study of religion held at the University of Alabama. As the purpose of the conference was to examine religion in the African diaspora, it seemed appropriate for me to speak on the life and intellectual contributions of the prolific African American author, Alexander Crummell, the subject of a biography that I completed early in 1988. Although the book is still in print with one of the world's most prestigious publishers, its publication did not lead to Crummell becoming a household name. Thus I sieze this opportunity to present again some of the content of that biography, fortified by recent reflections. Since the presentation of this address, my scholarly interests have taken a radically different turn, and I have not been able to revisit the entire trunk-full of scholarly evidence on which this address was based. For erudite readers who may be troubled by the admitted paucity of archival documentation, I recommend several works that I have authored on the subject of this essay over a period of thirty-five years (Moses 1975; 1989; 1991; 1992; 1998; 2004).[1] This chapter represents my most recent reflections, presented in a form hopefully appealing to a more general audience.

Alexander Crummell (1819–1898) an ordained priest of the Protestant Episcopal Church and a scholar of considerable accomplishment, belonged to a minority within a minority. An Episcopal priest, proud of his apparently unmixed black ancestry, he identified himself in the language of his times as a "Negro." His parents were Charity Hicks, a freeborn woman of Quaker heritage, and Boston Crummell, a Christianized African of the Temne people, probably from the region that is now Sierra Leone. Boston Crummell had been first converted, then captured, and finally brought to America as a youth. Taking advantage of the fluid situation in early-nineteenth-century New York, he peremptorily declared himself free, went into business as an oysterman, and, according to early accounts, welcomed the founders of the first African American newspaper into his home to establish *Freedom's Journal* in 1827. Although as a free New Yorker he was able to give his children economic and educational advantages, he never became rich, and left his widow in strained circumstances.

Living in a free household headed by an Africa-born father made Alexander Crummell unique among those African American leaders of his generation who are remembered today.[2] More typical was Frederick Douglass, who never knew his own father. But Crummell had awareness of a patriarchal heritage that included not only his father but also his grandfather. Furthermore, his knowledge of Africa was not dependent on white supremacist perceptions of Africa and its peoples.

> From my early childhood [Crummell wrote] my mind was filled with facts and thoughts about Africa and my imagination literally glowed with visions of its people, its scenery, and its native life. In my boyhood I read the "Arabian Nights Tales," and all you who have read them know how they stimulate the youthful mind. It was just thus with me with regard to Africa. I will tell you how all this came about:
> My father was born in the Kingdom of Timanee. He was stolen thence at about twelve or thirteen years. His burning love of home, his vivid remembrance of scenes and travels with his father into the interior, and his wide acquaintance with diverse tribes and customs, constantly turned his thoughts backward to his native land. And thus it was by listening to his tales of African life, I became deeply interested in the land of our fathers; and early in my life resolved, at some future day, to go to Africa. (Moses 1992: 61)

With a father born in Africa, a mother lacking any signs of white admixture, and a formal education in the North, Crummell differed tremendously in background and appearance from his more famous contemporary Frederick Douglass. But although he never directly experienced the thought and speech, the folklore, the music, or the language of rural plantation slavery, he had more than sufficient experience with racism and violence. He grew up in the often violent Five Points district, within a stone's throw—literally—of the toughest white ruffians in New York. African Americans, regardless of how educated, had little control over the gentility of their surroundings. Charles Dickens described the district in which Crummell was reared with shock and dismay. It was filled with flop houses, crime, prostitution, and child abuse. It had open sewers, pigs wallowing in the streets, and the constant threat of violence from the white lower classes (Dickens 1842: 104).

The occasional racial disturbances that erupted in New York are well-known, and Crummell's religiosity developed in the context of the frequent race riots that disrupted the community. The African American Episcopal Church the Crummell family attended was destroyed by fire in one of these, along with the headquarters of the New York Abolition Society. White children often threw stones at black children on their way to school. One professor at one of America's most prominent universities has actually published a book recently with a distinguished university press stating that Crummell never experienced a race riot. Everyone knows that riots of all sorts, including race riots, were common in New York during Crummell's childhood and thereafter. I do not know how anyone could assert otherwise. Crummell was driven from a school in New Hampshire in a race riot, along with his friends Henry Highland Garnet and Thomas Sipkins Sidney. Let me say a bit about them.

The Crummell family lived next door to George Garnet, a fugitive from slavery, who spoke of himself as "the son of a Mandingo warrior." One day, a band of slave-catchers came to abduct George Garnet, who escaped by leaping out of the back window and running down the street. The younger Garnet, later the Reverend Henry Highland Garnet and Crummell's lifelong friend, on discovering that his father was gone and his family scattered, had to be restrained from stalking the streets of New York with a knife. Garnet died in Africa in 1882, shortly after assuming a post as American consul general and minister to Liberia.

Crummell was never immersed in the patterns of slave culture and never had any respect for it, but he developed a precocious and vastly superior sensitivity to antislavery struggles in the United States, North and South. He was aware of David Walker, a correspondent of *Freedom's Journal*, whose *Appeal to the Colored Citizens of the World* (1829), replete with the language of Christian radicalism, caused a national sensation (as did his mysterious death in 1830). The following year, Crummell and his young friends heard reports of Nat Turner's uprising and reinforced each other's fantasies that they would some day go South to lead a slave revolt. But unlike Frederick Douglass, neither Crummell nor his school chums had any direct knowledge of the daily lives of the black masses of the South. Their heads were filled with romantic notions of creating a black nation, but they viewed many aspects of lower-class culture with contempt.

Some sense of this contempt can be gained from Crummell's "Eulogium on the Life and Character of Thomas Sipkins Sydney," the youth who had accompanied Crummell and Garnet when they were driven by a drunken mob from a boarding school in New Hampshire. What Crummell found remarkable about Sydney was that he represented a certain set of moral and intellectual values that were difficult to maintain even under the best of circumstances. Only a year or two older than Crummell, he represented a variety of tough Christian virtue that the younger boy respected. The following minor incident provides some insight into the past and present cultural problems encountered by African American youth:

> One day when a group of us boys were standing on the street corner, disgracing the Lord's Day with foolish and idol jesting, one of them asked Sydney, why aren't you participating, and Sydney said, "because a fool hath his tongue in perpetual motion but a wise man keepeth his council."
>
> The African American youth said: "Oh, so you think you're wise"; and Sydney replied: "oh, no, but I hope someday to be so." (Moses 1992: 48)

What Crummell described was more than priggish demeanor; it was an illustration of a standing conflict between two concepts of African American culture. Crummell and Sydney were future-oriented and shared a potentially black nationalistic vision. Sydney's critics were present-oriented and stationed on the street corner. Crummell and Sydney were following the lead of David Walker and Lewis Woodson, rejecting what some people today confusedly believe to be the only authentic black culture of "Talley's Corner," "Signifying Monkey," and "Hip-hop."[3] Both boys were recognizing at an early age the differences between the political concepts of being and becoming. It had to do with the idea of rejecting a self-concept of black people based in slave culture and developing one that was based on black nationalist progressivism, or to use Marcus Garvey's later phraseology, "Negro Improvement."

Alexander Crummell consistently assumed the aristocratic, elegant manner of an African prince, and some of us recognize this pattern from the Africans we have known. You do not walk up to an African and say "Hey my man, what's happening?" because he does not really like to be approached in that way; sometimes he can be very put off by African American colloquialisms and vulgarisms. Although I have known some Africans who not only accept, but emulate, the African American vernacular, I have known just as many Africans who do not. You may grin at a person you see walking down the street in Monrovia or Paris and say, "Hey man, what's happening?" and he may stare at you with the iciest contempt. On one occasion, I asked an African on the street in Liberia, "Hey my man, where did you get your hat?" He answered, *"Demandez à une autre personne"* [ask someone else], very haughtily, as if to say, "Don't come up to me with this, 'Hey man, what's happening?' stuff." Many Africans are extremely contemptuous of such an African American proletarian approach.

Crummell, like other contemporary black nationalists, followed his elders in rejecting the African American vernacular. He was not involved with that African American frivolity that David Walker, Lewis Woodson, and other serious black Americans denounced. If you had seen Boston Crummell walking around the streets of New York in 1829, you would not walk up to him and say, "Hey my man, what's happening?" Boston Crummell was very serious and very political. During his childhood, presumably, Alexander Crummell would ask his father: "What was Africa like, Dad?" Crummell's father would tell him about how he and Crummell's grandfather traveled through West Africa; he would describe the different peoples and customs they had encountered. Crummell grew up with something that the average African American leader of that generation did not have. He had first of all a strong male presence in the house, a strong father, right at the center of his conscience. Not only that, but this patrilineality included not only a strong father, but one who talked to him about his own father. He was not dependent on whites for his image of Africa or Africans.

In 1844, after many heartbreaking struggles, Crummell was ordained as an Episcopal clergyman. In 1848, he departed to England in order to raise funds for his congregation, but he soon became active as an abolitionist speaker. Despite these activities he managed to take a Cambridge University degree and decided to become an African missionary. He left for Liberia in 1853 and wrote to a friend at the time that he hoped to bring up his children amid black institutions. Some of his friends and acquaintances found his positions contradictory, for although he had chosen to become a Liberian statesman, he never abandoned his commitment to full citizenship in America for African Americans. Although he was politically a black nationalist, his commitments were to the culture of the Anglo-American elite and the heritage of European civilization. His thinking, like that of most educated clergy, embodied these and other contradictions, which he righteously struggled to resolve. His attitudes concerning religious ritual and elite culture were conservative and Anglocentric; his political black nationalism was radically Afrocentric.

Alexander Crummell arrived in Africa with the suspicion, if not the belief, that pristine Africans were superior to American Negroes in important respects. His writings were often an attempt to confirm this bias. As did his intellectual peers, Edward Wilmot Blyden and Edward J. Roye, he disproved the stereotype of the Americo-Liberian colonizer. The stereotype presents American immigrants as arriving with the goal of establishing a settler state and reducing the indigenous population to a subordinate caste. For many years my work has sought to "problematize" this cliché, which contains elements of both truth and falsehood. Missionary activity, which I define broadly as the attempt to introduce an "alien" religion, ideology, or worldview to a native population, has taken multiple forms in Africa. Missionary Christianity is only one form; it must be evaluated in the context of missionary Islam, missionary capitalism, and missionary communism. Missionaries of every variety have often "discovered" in the indigenous population the very cultural values that they seek to import. They have thus justified their missionary activity with the argument that they are not introducing something alien, only enhancing cultural and moral virtues that were already present in the population.

For example, Crummell observed indigenous traits resembling Victorian sexual morality among African peoples he visited. He also observed indigenous traits of the bustling capitalist ethic. He sought to develop these traits and utilize them in order to develop West Africa into a formidable world power. W. E. B. Du Bois, a century later, likewise discovered traits resembling Victorian sexual mores among West Africans. And where Crummell saw indigenous capitalism, Du Bois discovered an ancient African socialism—proving that the Africans were predisposed to communism. Thus, whether Christian or Communist, the reform of African societies, in the views of Crummell and Du Bois, was really not an attempt to change Africans or to make them white. On the contrary, their missionary activity was truly conservative, for it attempted to conserve and enhance traditional African manners and customs.[4]

I have identified Alexander Crummell with conservatism, and I think this can be demonstrated in several respects. He accepted and nurtured the doctrine of the Conservation of Races articulated by W. E. B. Du Bois and believed in the maintenance of separate black institutions. He was a classicist who aggressively preached the values of elite culture founded in the study of Greek, Latin, and elite British literature. He was a political conservative who accepted the principles of Hamilton, Burke, and the Federalist Papers and viewed government as a means of protecting the rights of all from the democracy of the masses. His absolute commitment to the Episcopal Church is alone sufficient to convince many students that he was conservative. Like most people, however, he was liberal on some things and conservative on others. On the issues of economic and political rights, he was unswervingly and vocally committed to full participation in every aspect of American life. He made no compromises with the conservatism he perceived in Booker T. Washington and expressed vehement hostility to the Tuskegee machine in the months before his death.

Crummell believed in elitist government as a result of his connections to the tradition of Cambridge Platonism, a school of theology that arose at

Cambridge in the seventeenth century and was revived in the nineteenth by the lectures of William Whewell–lectures that Crummell attended. The Cambridge scholar, Henry Moore, had taught that the human species innately possessed the social instinct that we refer to as a "conscience." Conscience was, in his view, more than the result of Pavlovian conditioning. Human beings actually had an organic and inborn conscience. Crummell and Jefferson shared the belief that there was actually an instrumentality in the human soul called conscience, as an inborn a sense. But Crummell rejected the Jeffersonian democratic conception of conscience in one essential respect. He did not believe, as Jefferson and Thomas Paine did, that government and traditional institutions corrupted the natural instincts of natural man. In the tradition of Aristotle, he believed that human beings were naturally social, and like Alexander Hamilton and Edmund Burke, he believed that the state was a natural institution, well suited to the noblest aspirations of the human spirit.

Social institutions such as the church and the state were necessary to human morality because the individual conscience, like all other senses, could be mistaken or deceived. Crummell once delivered a sermon on the necessity of Mosaic law, arguing that even the most sincere Christian needed an external guide to life. But Crummell did not believe that anyone could be saved by a vain attempt to live up to the Bible's moral code. He believed that the Christian was to be saved by a conversion experience and by the blood of Jesus that had atoned for our sins. Nonetheless, he believed that on the day of doom we would all be judged on our deeds, on the basis of our adherence to the law of Moses.

Like most American Protestants of his era, Crummell disapproved of graven images, whether they appeared in African villages or in the Catholic churches of New York. He was shocked by rumors of the erotica in the museums of Italy, and in the Vatican itself. He believed that many of the problems of the black Republic of Haiti stemmed from its Roman Catholicism (Moses 1989: 147–152). And yet Crummell was part of a "strict church" movement in the Episcopal Church, whose theology resembled Roman Catholic doctrine with its endorsement of the "doctrine of works." Crummell shared the Catholic doctrine that a Christian is justified by good deeds rather than by faith alone, and this belief placed him in accord with the strict churchmen rather than the evangelical clergy among Episcopalians and Anglicans (Moses 1992: 12–13, 97–115). Alienated from the enthusiastic religion of the African American masses, he was not inclined toward any practice of religion that relied primarily on the emotion. The idea of "gettin' saved," based on the belief in communication with Jesus or the Holy Spirit after a frenzied dance, or "ring shout," or trancelike possession, seemed to him the height of absurdity.

During his years in Africa, Crummell could sometimes be pragmatically tolerant, though never supportive, of indigenous African religion. He could put up with such traditional practices as polygamy when convenient. On the other hand there is good evidence that he was among the early opponents of female genital mutilation. Recent feminists who have peremptorily denounced him have overlooked his written opinions in this regard. His Christian conservatism displaced his Afrocentric conservatism when it came to some of the traditional practices of African secret societies, and he disagreed with Edward Wilmot Blyden, among others, who defended female genital mutilation (Moses 1998: 80, 113). Christian conservatism promoted a Victorian bourgeois veneration of women and placed a high value on women's education. He was a pioneer advocate for women's higher education, initiating a crusade for the higher education of women at Liberia College; he sent his daughters to Oberlin College in America when that campaign initially seemed fruitless. In later years, he became fast friends with the scholarly Anna Julia Cooper, one of his strongest supporters, after he returned to the United States and became pastor of St. Philips Church in Washington, DC.

The contradiction between Crummell's cultural Eurocentrism and his political Afrocentrism surfaced everywhere. As an inveterate Anglophile, he believed English was superior to any African language. English, in his view, was not only the repository of civilization's highest ideals, it was also the transmitter of those political values that had made Great Britain into a world power. Unlike Edward Wilmot Blyden, who was professor of classics at Liberia College and who is said to have known forty-two African languages, Crummell mastered none, and pointedly disparaged African languages. But Crummell's Eurocentric Afrocentricity was not unique in this respect, for indigenous African intellectuals were equally Eurocentric in their Afrocentricity. Some historians would give the impression that Eurocentrism is peculiar to Crummell and his generation of intellectuals who were born outside the continent.[5] They present the idea that Crummell was in some way unique or that he represents an inescapable alienation or isolation from an African tradition simply because he grew up in North America and not in Africa. Crummell was not unique, however, but representative of educated Africans functioning in Africa at that time. Even in the early twentieth century, persons who identified themselves as nationalists, including the great Caseley Hayford, tended to be infected with that same Anglophilism that is very fundamental to Crummell's thinking. His black nationalism was Eurocentric in the cultural sense, but separatist in the political sense. He really did believe that African Americans had a destiny to build a nation-state in West Africa, to create, in the words of Henry Highland Garnet, "a grand center of Negro nationality."

Alexander Crummell left us three published books and twelve reels of microfilm, which are in the Schomburg collection of the New York Public Library. In addition, there are a number of uncollected published sermons, tracts, and letters—including African correspondence. There are the Crummell papers at Columbia University and materials in the Episcopal Archives of the South West in Austin, Texas. Nevertheless, few people read this author despite the fact that they claim to have read *The Souls of Black Folk*, by W. E. B. Du Bois, which includes a chapter on Crummell.

I suspect that there are at least two reasons for this. Alexander Crummell's narrative is not typically black; this leads to the second point: Alexander Crummell was not typically an American. He was brought up with a strong African consciousness, and in a sense, he never really did become an American Negro. He was always an African, even after he resettled in the United States in 1872.

Crummell's mission to Africa was, admittedly, a "civilizing mission," but he came increasingly to believe that African Americans were in no position to talk about civilizing anyone. He made this position very clear in a speech at the Atlanta Exposition in 1895. He had little faith in the Black Church as it existed in the South. The vestiges of slave religion corrupted the typical black Christians of the South, from his point of view. They would have been better off to have been left in Africa as pagans than to have adopted the travesty of religion that we call Southern Black Christianity. That was how strongly he felt. That was how African he was. Crummell's was a mission of redemption, but he was also attempting to establish in Africa—and in America—a tradition of Afrocentrism as a high culture. Anyone who has ever seen a Mandingo elder in his white robes as he majestically moves along the street in Monrovia or in Paris will realize what it was that Crummell was attempting to recreate—and what he wanted to revitalize both in Africa and in the cities of the Western world.

Late in life, Crummell delivered an address in which he described various African peoples in the most glowing, indeed the most romantic terms. Forty years after first setting foot in Africa, he still retained the impression of his first vision of African people on African soil. In the following passage, he speaks of his encounter with members of the stately Wolof nation.

Their average height was about 6' and 3 or 4 inches. But with their remarkable slenderness they appeared 2–3 inches taller. I was much struck with both the depth and brilliancy of their complexions. Such utter blackness of color, I had never seen in our race, not either the copper or ashy blackness which is common to the Negro of America, but black like satin. With a smoothness and thickness of skin so that you could easily see the blood mantling in their cheeks. (Moses 1992: 62)

It is obvious what he is saying—not only are Africans more refined than African Americans; they are even more elegant in appearance. Their very blackness is purer, more radiant, more pleasing to the eye. Africans are just plain better looking than African Americans, who have been degraded in America, culturally, spiritually, even in terms of our personal bearing and physical appearance, says Crummell. Thus the reclamation of our African elegance is what we are trying to accomplish, what we want to discover again. We have degenerated from what we were in the past. But does this mean that Crummell was backward looking? Did he think, as many conservatives seem to think, that the best values are to be found in the beliefs and ideals of some past generation? Was he calling for Mount Rushmore heroes to be engraved in Africa's black hills with the images of African demigods? Were our grandfathers and our grandmothers better than we are, and must we search the tombs of our ancestors for models of true greatness?

Crummell arrived in Africa in 1853. Even today many people are critical of his migration to Liberia believing, as David Walker maintained in 1829, that it was "a scheme got up by a gang of slaveholders." But, as John Hope Franklin—certainly no friend of colonization—has noted, the goals of the American colonization society and the motives of its membership varied (1998: 155–157). There was more than one reason for the founding of Liberia and more than one set of positions in the American Colonization Society and its founders. The Society was interpreted by some persons as an abolitionist association and by just as many others as a society for the maintenance of slavery. Its organization was loose and variable. Crummell was roundly criticized for his uneasy association with the abolitionist wing of this Society. Crummell also belonged to the American Colonization Society, which should not be confused with the African Civilization Society—an institution with overlapping membership and goals, but which was unequivocally abolitionist.

Crummell was also criticized for becoming a Liberian citizen because that nation was seen as carrying out a policy of colonialism similar to the Indian removal policies of the United States. The charge is a serious one, but in Crummell's defense, he was neither the proponent nor the practitioner of a settler statecraft. Although many Americo-Liberians did, in fact, have the mentality of a settler state, many of them were embarrassed by, and hostile to, such a position. Those who planned to establish an elitist settler-state enclave were often spoken of as the Virginia mulatto faction. In some cases, they were literate and articulate people with a sense of pan-African commitment; but Crummell and Blyden described many of them as haughty and overbearing. Indeed some of them were very conscious of their mulatto status and did attempt to set up an elite based on color and American origin.

Crummell and his associates, including the Liberian president, E. J. Roye and his fellow statesman, Edward Wilmot Blyden, had nothing to do with that party. They were the founders of the True Whig Party, which, during Crummell's sojourn, believed that all Africans were to be one people. Crummell, believing in a strong nationalistic government, saw himself as a Hamiltonian and a Whig. He believed that there was eventually to be a West African state and this would be based very fundamentally on the idea of intermarriage. I think this is the basic difference between Liberia and the other settler states where European immigrants seemed bent on the subordination or displacement of indigenous populations. Liberia was split over the issue, but it has painfully worked towards the still-unachieved goal of ethnic amalgamation. Crummell and Blyden were among those who saw intermarriage as a fundamental aspect of building the new republic, and this was an aspect of their philosophy that spoke very well of them.

Crummell arrived in Liberia in 1853 which was the same year that Commodore Perry made his first stop in Tokyo. We know how that went; Japan was humiliated and obliged to open its doors to foreigners on terms that were not universally favorable. It is important to think about the symbolism of Commodore Perry's military diplomacy, because we are talking about a period when the nonwhite nations really did not have much of a basis for any kind of resistance against European or American imperialism. Those scholars who have attempted to look at Liberia purely in terms of settler-state politics have drawn a far too simplistic picture of what actually happened in Liberia. Some have attempted to justify European colonialism, racism, and slavery by focusing on the abuses and crimes of Africans and Africans Americans and addressing the tragedies of the past two decades purely in those terms. I think that is a total misreading; for while the crimes of the Liberian elite were many, their initial goal of a united, economically independent West Africa was admirable—regardless of how miserable their failures in terms of both ends and means.

In 1872, the first violent takeover of an Africa republic occurred in Monrovia and the government of E. J. Rye was overthrown under the leadership of the mulatto elite. Officially calling themselves the Republican party, they were Jeffersonians, many with Virginia mulatto roots. On returning to the United States, Crummell continued his work as an Episcopal clergyman in Washington, DC. In 1897 he founded the American Negro Academy, which questioned the "industrial education" panacea of Booker T. Washington. Crummell encouraged the intellectual ideals and racial mysticism of the young W. E. B. Du Bois. Two Crummell protégés, John E. Bruce and William H. Ferris, later became senior officials in Marcus Garvey's Universal Negro Improvement Association (UNIA).

Crummell was a man of large intellect, noted for his volatile temperament and sarcastic disposition. His ample writings were not confined to race relations but touched on European and American letters and politics, African missionary work, and a broad variety of political, social, and moral issues. The division between Hamilton and Jefferson ideals, for example, which is so important in American history, is replicated in many aspects of African American culture. As already noted, Crummell saw himself as Hamiltonian. He was appalled by the obvious ability of elites to control masses with a cynical populist rhetoric. The problem with Jeffersonian democracy, as far as Crummell was concerned, was not that its founder was a slaveholder, but that Jefferson had claimed that governments and states were the creations of human beings and that the power of government came from the consent of the governed.

Thanks, in part, to his classical training at the Cambridge University, Crummell was sufficiently an Aristotelian to believe that because human beings were by nature social, government was a part of mankind's natural state, and thus derived from God. He was sufficiently a Platonist to believe that ideal forms of government existed in the mind of God. Was he so much the Platonist as to completely reject the idea of democracy? No, he was not such a purist. He believed in democracy as it exists in the mind of God; but his own experiences with democracy was not the sort that would make him terribly sympathetic to the Jacksonian democracy he had experienced as a boy in New York. Crummell was not a theocrat, but he did believe in government for West Africa based on principles of Christendom. As did most of his black nationalist contemporaries—whether West Indian, African American, or continental African—Alexander Crummell subscribed to the classical linkage of Christianity, Commerce, and Civilization as indispensable elements of African redemption.

Notes

1. With reference to Moses (1992) *Alexander Crummell, Destiny and Race: Sermons and Addresses 1840–1898*: this is an edited teaching text on Crummell. It is often incorrectly cited as if it were his own publication even though Crummell never compiled any work by that title and much of it consists of items that were either incomplete or never intended for publication.

2. Many pages would be required to explain why Crummell's patrilineal heritage was of such importance. For an introduction to the issue of paternity in the context of slavery, see E. Franklin Frazier (1939).

3. Crummell violated, as did most of his Christian contemporaries, the literal interpretation of the first commandment by widely circulating his own photographic

images. Nor was he a fundamental literalist in interpreting the words of the *King James Bible*, which asserted that Jesus had turned water into wine and offered it for consumption at a wedding feast. Crummell believed that the consumption of alcohol was never harmless.

4. Samuel Ajai Crowther (1807–1891), a member of the Igbo Ethnic Group in Nigeria, was the first African to become Anglican "Bishop of Western Equatorial Africa." Crowther was among those who could not accept the sophisticated traditionalist argument of Africans who justified polytheism by insisting that minor gods were only local or particular manifestations of the one supreme Deity whom all peoples worshipped under various different names. See Moses 2004: 95–97, 292.

5. See the index entries in Appiah (1993). For an even more forcefully stated position, see Tunde Adeleke (1998).

Bibliography

Adeleke, Tunde (1998). *Unafrican Americans: Nineteenth-Century Black Nationalists and the Civilizing Mission*. Louisville: University Press of Kentucky.

Appiah, Anthony (1993). *In My Father's House: Africa in the Philosophy of Culture*. New York: Oxford University Press.

Dickens, Charles (1842). *American Notes for General Circulation*. London: Chapman & Hall.

Franklin, John Hope (1988). *From Slavery to Freedom*, 6th edition. New York: McGraw Hill.

Frazier, E. Franklin (1939). *The Negro Family in the United States*. Chicago: University of Chicago Press.

Moses, Wilson Jeremiah (1975). "Civilizing Missionary: A Study of Alexander Crummell," *Journal of Negro History* (April): 229–251.

——— (1989). *Alexander Crummell: A Study in Civilization and Discontent*. New York: Oxford University Press.

——— (1991). "Cambridge Platonism in the Republic of Liberia, 1853–1873: Alexander Crummell's Theory of Culture Transfer." In Wilson J. Moses (ed.), *The Wings of Ethiopia: Studies in African American Life and Letters*, 79–93. Ames: Iowa State University Press.

——— (ed.) (1992). *Alexander Crummell, Destiny and Race: Sermons and Addresses 1840–1898*. Amherst: University of Massachusetts Press.

——— (1998). *Afrotopia: Roots of African-American Popular History*. Cambridge: Cambridge University Press.

——— (2004). *Creative Conflict in African American Thought*. Cambridge: Cambridge University Press.

Part 1

Africa in Diaspora

Chapter 1

Raising Champions, Taking Territories: African Churches and the Mapping of New Religious Landscapes in Diaspora

Afe Adogame

Introduction

The African diaspora as an academic field of study has grown considerably in recent years and scholarship on the subject is burgeoning, particularly in the United States. An emphasis upon the earliest phase of migration dominates the literature. Until recently, however, the contemporary phase of African migration—now described as the second phase of African diaspora—has not attracted much scholarly scrutiny. To what extent can the African communities emerging from this new wave of immigration be described as a new African diaspora? To what extent do classical and contemporary theories provide theoretical and empirical insights toward an understanding of contemporary African migration and the new diaspora?

A survey of the extensive African diasporic and migration literature reveals a lack of theoretical and methodological reflection on the role of religion in the context of contemporary diaspora and migration studies (Kilson 1976; Harris 1993; Okpewho et al. 1999; Arthur 2000). And yet, religious institutions play a key role in diaspora communities. They facilitate the integration process of new immigrants into the host society and serve as both a source of security and a bastion for cultural, ethnic, and religious identity. The role played by religious institutions has significant implications both for the community in diaspora and for religious communities in the homeland, that is, in Africa. As religious communities continue to expand and proliferate in diaspora, a deeper understanding of their role is required. Recently, social scientists and historians of religion have begun to focus on the interconnectedness of religion, diaspora, and migration (Warner and Wittner 1998; Ebaugh and Chafetz, 2000; 2002; Haddad et al. 2003; Vàsquez and Marquardt 2003). But these studies are concerned primarily with North America and the Americas; they hardly ever deal with the various new religious movements from Africa that have contributed to the religious diversification and richness of these new host contexts.

New Immigration Policies and Demographic Shifts: Revisiting Migration Theories

The liberalized provisions in the 1965 Immigration Act, coupled with prevailing economic, social, and political difficulties in other parts of the world, have accelerated the pace of immigration into the United States particularly in the past few decades. As a consequence, the country has experienced a massive influx of newcomers from Latin America, Asia, and the Middle East.[1] Immigrants from Africa have joined in this process though Africa still accounts for a relatively small percentage of the total immigrants in the United States.[2] A new twist has been occurring with the recent establishment of the Diversity Immigrant Visa Lottery in the 1996 Immigration Act. This program allocates visas to countries with a low rate of immigration and has attracted considerable interest from African countries. In 1996 there was a 153 percent increase in visas issued to immigrants from Africa to a total of 28,514 visas—a direct result of many African countries qualifying in the Diversity Visa category.[3] This initiative, the aim of which is to further diversify the American population, has transformed the demographics of African immigrants in the United States. At the same time, it has resulted in an extensive reordering of American religious life (Garber and Walkowitz 1999; Eck 2001).

Zeleza (2002: 13) has demonstrated how African participation in international migration, particularly into Western Europe and North America, has become more pronounced despite the imposition of stringent immigration controls by some of these countries. The adoption of restrictive immigration policies, particularly after 9/11, and the regional policy harmonization imposed through the North American Free Trade Agreement (NAFTA), have partially impeded the flow of regular immigration; but they have also led, indirectly at least, to an increase in illegal immigration. The U.S. Immigration and Naturalization Service (INS) estimated that the total unauthorized immigrant population residing in the United States in January 2000 was 7 million. Previous estimates indicated a progressive rise in figures from about 3.4 million in 1992 and 5 million in 1996.[4] In October 2003, there were about 8 million illegal aliens in the United States, assuming a continuation of the average 350,000 annual net increase that occurred during the 1990s (Larson and Droitcour 2003). African immigrants number themselves among both legal and illegal aliens.

With this influx of immigration, Europe and the United States have experienced a proliferation of new religious communities and an expanding diversification in religious life. There is a preponderance of political and socioeconomic considerations in discourses on transmigration and diaspora; consequently, the religious factors that stimulate and effect such processes are usually glossed over. As we are faced with "space-time compression" and a growing interconnection of local-global spaces, contemporary migratory trends bring to the fore the crucial role religious symbolic systems play in new geocultural contexts. It is necessary to contextualize the place of religion as a "motor" or driving force of African diaspora formation. This approach allows for a consideration of religious identity not only as a by-product of migration, but as a central motivation in the decision-making processes that results in both the departure from the home country and actions pursued during the integration process in the host country (Warner and Wittner 1998; Adogame and Weisskoeppel 2005). It further enables us to situate the various roles and strategies of religious organizations in establishing the "transnational" space between home and host countries and broadens the scale from local, transnational, and global levels (Ebaugh and Chafetz 2002; Vásquez and Marquardt 2003).

Several case studies on immigrant religions in Europe and the United States have noted the importance of religion as a central element for ethnic and religious identity formation, reproduction, and maintenance (Ter Haar 1998a; 1999; Ebaugh and Chafetz 2000; Adogame 2003, 2005; Haddad et al. 2003). A people's religious belonging is not merely part of the cultural heritage they retain when they emigrate. Religious conviction can also be a central motivation for migration or an incentive for organizing places of refuge in exile. Religious identity can also serve as an important resource for invigorating the culture of origin in a host country. Religious institutions provide immigrants with opportunities of central relevance for mixing with people from different cultural backgrounds under the umbrella of a common religion.

In general, Africans have migrated to the United States and elsewhere carrying their religious identities with them. Most often, their sojourn in a different geocultural context has encouraged these immigrants to reconstruct, organize, and identify "their religion(s)" both for themselves and their host environments. Recent scholarship on new African religious communities in Europe and the United States provide useful insights into the significance of the new African religious diaspora while pointing out the urgent need for more critical studies about the role of religion in diaspora. Thus, this chapter maps new African religious communities in the diaspora using the case study of the Redeemed Christian Church of God (RCCG), a Nigerian Pentecostal Church. The chapter explores how and to what extent African churches are reconfiguring global and diasporic spaces; the existing networks between the RCCG in the home (Africa) and diaspora contexts; and the patterns of relationship between African religious traditions of the historical and contemporary diasporas.

Mapping New African Religious Demography in Diaspora

A multitude of African religions has appeared in the United States and Europe especially in the past two decades (Adogame 2004a). The most visible varieties in the contemporary georeligious landscape are the African-led charismatic/Pentecostal churches. Their histories of emergence can be located in three broad categories. The first contains churches that exist in diaspora as branches of a mother church headquartered in Africa. The second consists of churches founded by new immigrants in the United States and Europe; these churches establish their headquarters in the diaspora and from there they are expanding to Africa and elsewhere. Lastly, there are now para-churches: interdenominational ministries with flexible, nonformalized structures in which freelance evangelists embark on frequent visits to a network of churches overseas under the rubric of evangelism and intrareligious networks.

In *The Next Christendom* (2002b), Philip Jenkins quite appropriately calls attention to the shifting contours of Christianity, particularly as they are shaped by the generally neglected religious communities of North America and Europe. As if to echo some of Jenkins's observations, *The New York Times* of October 13 and 14, 2003, featured two stories: "The Changing Church: Faith Fades Where It Once Burned Strong," by Frank Bruni, and "Where Faith Grows, Fired by Pentecostalism," by Somini Sengupta and Larry Rohter (Bruni 2003; Sengupta and Rohter 2003).

Bruni's article focuses on the decline of Christianity in Europe during the past quarter century and the shift in its center of gravity to the Southern hemisphere. As Bruni notes: "Christianity has boomed in the developing world, competing successfully with Islam, deepening its influence and possibly finding its future there. But Europe already seems more and more like a series of tourist-trod monuments to Christianity's past...." Although the focus on church-oriented religiosity in these stories is on Europe, the U.S. situation is only a little different. In the midst of this decline, the article refers to the appearance of African churches in the religious landscape. As Bruni further remarks: "Christianity's greatest hope in Europe may in fact be immigrants from the developing world, who in many cases learned the religion from European missionaries, adapted it to their own needs and tastes, then toted it back to the Continent."

One example used in these reports is the Nigerian-born Matthew Ashimolowo and his Kingsway International Christian Center (KICC) located in East London. The KICC is believed to be the largest single Pentecostal congregation in London with about 3,000 participants in each of the three scheduled Sunday worship services. African churches have also extended their religious reach from Western Europe into the realms of the former USSR. A remarkable example in this respect is the Embassy of the Blessed Kingdom of God for All Nations founded by Sunday Odulaja in Kiev, Ukraine (Brown 2003).[5] More than half the total membership of this exceptional African church is made up of non-African Ukrainians and Russians.

Similar to these new religious developments in Europe, the United States is also currently witnessing a rapid proliferation of African religious influences both within and beyond Christian and Islamic communities. In a *Chicago Tribune* front-paged report, for example, Julia Lieblich and Tom McCann write about the RCCG. The story describes the Nigerian-based Pentecostal church's efforts to spread its evangelistic form of Christianity to America. Lieblich and McCann note: "For years American missionaries brought Christianity to Africa. Now African Christians say they want to export their own brand of ecstatic worship and moral discipline to the United States, a country they believe has lost its fervor" (2002). As Jenkins aptly remarks:

> Many African immigrants...come from nations in which Christianity is enjoying an upsurge of passionate enthusiasm scarcely precedented in the whole history of the religion. Independent and prophetic African churches are now firmly rooted in American cities, from which they plan ambitious evangelistic expansion. To take one critical example that has attracted next to no media attention, consider the thriving Nigerian churches based in Houston, many of which stem from the prophetic healing tradition known as

Aladura. Conceivably, these African-derived churches could soon represent a significant new phase in the history of American urban revivalism. (2002a)

The globalization of African religions has made a significant impact on African traditions, cultural values, and worldviews; at the same time, African religions have proven to be resilient and adaptable while maintaining a relatively high degree of cohesion both within and beyond the African landscape. Consequently, Hunt (2002: 185), among others, has signaled the rise of independent African churches, especially those within a West African setting, as one of the most significant development within the broad Pentecostal movement.

The RCCG: A New African Pentecostal Church in Europe and the United States

The RCCG is an African Pentecostal Church that has spread from Nigeria to about sixty countries. It includes more than 2 million members worldwide in such diverse locales as Africa, America, Europe, Asia, Australia, the Middle East, and other parts of the world. The RCCG was founded in Lagos in 1952 after Josiah Akindayomi received a divine call to a special mission. Akindayomi became popular for his charismatic abilities and healing activities, although the church he founded did not witness any large scale growth under his tutelage. The task of expanding the church fell to Enoch Adeboye, Akindayomi's successor. A former University professor of applied mathematics and hydrodynamics, Adeboye became the general overseer of the church in 1980. Subsequently the church has experienced considerable growth within Nigeria and beyond its borders with an estimated 5,000 parishes worldwide.[6]

RCCG parishes are organized into "areas"; each "area" is subdivided into "zones"; and each zone, made up of several parishes, is administered by a coordinator.[7] For instance, the RCCG North America (RCCGNA) area comprising the United States, Canada, and the Caribbean Islands, is divided into ten zones. At the RCCGNA Annual Convention held in Dallas, Texas, in 2003, more than 120 parishes were listed.[8] The first RCCG parish in the United States was founded in 1992 in Detroit, Michigan. From 1994 onward, new parishes have been established in Florida, Texas, Massachusetts, and several other states. There are more than 150 branches scattered in different parts of Europe with ninety-eight parishes in the United Kingdom alone.[9] The enthusiasm for establishing parishes in Europe and North America is not unconnected with the goals expressed in the RCCG "Mission Statement":

It is our goal to make heaven. It is our goal to take as many people as possible with us. In order to accomplish our goals, holiness will be our life-style. In order to take as many people with us as possible, we will plant churches within five minutes walking distance in every city and town of developing countries; and within five minutes driving distance in every city and town of developed countries. We will pursue these objectives until every nation in the world is reached for Jesus Christ our Lord.[10]

In the case of RCCGNA, the goal of proximity between churches had to be qualified in view of the demographic peculiarities of the North American region. An addendum to the Mission Statement shows how contextual factors can shape the growth of a religious movement and serve as a dynamic for change in a new context. For planting new parishes in North America and Caribbean countries, the location to any existing parish must be at least 30 minutes driving distance. The addendum states: "We believe in positioning our worship centers close to the people, hence in North America we are challenged to establish parishes in every State, County, City and in fact within thirty minutes driving distance."[11] Summarizing the significance of evangelism in the RCCGNA, Pastor Samuel Shorimade, of Cambridge, Massachusetts, said: "The United States was often described in some circles as God's own country, but this country has become very slack morally and spiritually. So God is making us [RCCG] bring worship and praise to them [Americans] as well as in rediscovering God."[12]

Reproduction of Space: The RCCGNA Redemption Camp

The construction of "sacred space" is a significant dimension of religious expression. One way in which the RCCG is gradually imprinting itself on the American geocultural landscape is through the reproduction of the "Redemption Camp" (Adogame 2004a). The Redemption Camp (a.k.a. Redemption City) in Nigeria doubles as RCCG's international headquarters and its most important sacred space. It hosts religious programs such as the massively popular Holy Ghost Congress.[13] As a direct response to space constraints within the former national headquarters, the first plots of land for the Camp were procured in the early 1980s along the Lagos-Ibadan motorway in Nigeria. The Camp now rests on a property of more than 10 square kilometers of land.

The Camp contains a variety of buildings including a large auditorium, a conference center, guesthouses and chalets, and a presidential villa reserved for visiting dignitaries. Also on the site are a maternity center, an orphanage, a post office, a gas station, bookstores, supermarkets, a bakery, and a canteen. Other facilities include two banks, a secondary school, and a Bible school. The significance of the Redemption Camp lies not only in the religious functions that take place there for members and nonmembers alike. The Redemption Camp is also a crossroads: a place where social, economic, cultural, ecological, and political concerns intersect.

Some African churches in the United States and Europe have grown to acquire immense real estate holdings as one way of asserting and inserting themselves in new geocultural contexts. By 2003, the RCCGNA had acquired a multimillion-dollar property of more than 400 hectares of land in Floyd (Hunt County), near Dallas, Texas. The property is being developed along the lines of the Redemption Camp international headquarters in Nigeria.[14] This new Redemption Camp serves as RCCGNA headquarters; it includes the Holy Ghost Ground, chapels, a Bible college, a baptismal pool, a recreational center, an administrative building, a library, banquet and seminar halls, a shopping mall, restaurants, a community center, guesthouses, residential accommodations, and an impressive driveway. The duplication of the original camp is important for many reasons. In particular, it represents the decentralization of church programs that were previously concentrated at the international headquarters across the sea.

Other examples of African churches that are inserting themselves into new geographic spaces in the United States and Europe are the Embassy of the Blessed Kingdom of God for All Nations in Kiev[15] and the KICC in London.[16] In many large cities such as London, Hamburg, Paris, Cologne, Amsterdam, and Berlin, decrepit warehouses, abandoned cinemas, disco halls, and pubs are being bought up and transformed. In this process of acquisition, a renegotiation of space is taking place; "desecrated space" is taken over and re-sacralized for religious ends. Some churches have also acquired fleets of cars and buses to be used by members for official church purposes or for commercial rentals. Business centers, lodging, religious book centers, guidance and counseling services, recreation and rehabilitation centers, cyber cafés, computer training centers, musical halls, video and music shops, and shopping malls are also owned and operated by these churches.[17] The KICC and the Embassy of God are examples of African churches that have even proposed religious banks to "empower God's people economically, and promote the Kingdom of God."[18] Such extrareligious activities no doubt have immense religious, social, and economic import for the church members and for the communities in which these facilities are located. This development suggests that some of these churches have "come of age" in this new cultural environment.

The Transnationalization of New African Churches

One distinguishing feature of the recent trend as compared to previous waves of immigration is the fluid nature of transnational networks that characterize what Castles and Miller described as "the age of migration" (2003). The transnational quality of many African churches in diaspora challenges the assumption that immigrants inevitably cut off ties to the homeland after integration into the new host context. Most new African immigrant churches are rooted locally, with ties to the land of origin, while also maintaining relationships through the intra-communal web that links them with different places across the globe. These communities are connected through religion, economy, friendship, kinship, politics, and increasingly by cell phones and, in particular, the Internet—which has become a key component in the development and maintenance of diasporic identity. Diasporas are webs, and webs consist not only of fibers and ropes but also of the nodes that link them together (Haller 2001: 7). In an article on "New Black Pentecostal Churches in Britain," Hunt and Lightly contend:

[t]he importance of the "new" black African churches within the framework of globalization is not merely with reference to a unique expression of African Christianity. Rather, they are noteworthy in that they constitute international ministries, which have implications on a worldwide scale. As part of an increasing phenomenon of what might be termed "reverse prose-lytization," these new West African churches have systematically set out to evangelize the world. In the case of the RCCG this has meant establishing churches in as far-flung places as India, the Caribbean, Hong Kong, the USA, and Europe. The impact and significance of the exportation of a fiercely evangelical Nigerian church such as the RCCG, driven by a vision of winning converts, is that it offers a unique opportunity to analyze its impact at a local level, in this case the Western context. (2001: 121)

Thus, the place of local and global networks among African churches in both home and host contexts cannot be overemphasized. Such networks assume increasing significance for new African migrants. The range and nature of ties include new ecumenical affiliations, pastoral exchanges

between Africa, Europe and the United States, special events and conferences, prayer networks, Internet sites, international ministries, publications, and audio/video and tele-evangelism. The "flow" is two-directional
with both global and local sending and receiving links. The proliferation
of social ties among new African immigrants, and between immigrant
churches, host churches, and their home bases, has implications that need
to be contextually understood. Some of these groups frequently organize
programs that are local in nature but have a global focus that links the
local church with other churches globally. The mobility and itinerancy of
religious leaders, freelance evangelists, and members between the homeland and diasporic spaces is a complex peregrination that demonstrates the
religious transnationalization of African churches in diaspora.

There is a common tendency to perceive the religious landscape in the
West as a "valley of dry bones," reminiscent of the biblical valley of dry
bones represented in Ezekiel 37. Church leaders also articulate the biblical
conceptions of diaspora and the exigencies of "leaving" and "return" as
recorded in Psalm 68.31: "Princes shall come out of Egypt; Ethiopia shall
soon stretch out her hands unto God." The hermeneutics involved in these
oft-quoted passages gives religious legitimacy, empowerment, and hope to
the sojourners. Thus, most members of new African religious communities
do not see emigration to the West as an end in itself. They believe that this
painstaking decision was reached through divine design and not by acci-
dent. It is the result of a divine initiative whereby the "oppressed" and the
"downtrodden" of the world are charged with a mission to the cultured
despisers of the faith in the West (Olagoke 2002).

The exile metaphor epitomized by the Back-to-Africa Movement or the
American Colonization Society resonates very powerfully among African
Americans. Kalu (2004) asserts that two ideologies, "exile" and "crossing
Jordan," jostle for preeminence among immigrant communities. This rhetoric also finds currency among new African immigrants, although with a
slightly different slant. In Europe and the United States today, African
churches are concerned with what they call "reverse-mission" or "the remis-
sionization of Christianity to a dead West" (Adogame 2004b). The powerful symbol of the biblical "covenant" now becomes a motivating concept
for "exile" and "crossing Jordan" narratives (Kalu 2004). Immigrants are
encouraged not to lament about their past, but to use the past to make
meaning out of the present for the future. As the notions of leaving and
returning characterize exile, many new African immigrants indicate their
intention to return home at the "sunset" of their sojourn. Irrespective of
the duration of stay, virtually all my respondents express a desire to return
at some point. Although this claim of return may just be wishful thinking
for many who leave Africa, or a myth with which to mediate the ambiguity

of the present situation, it nevertheless serves as a source of hopefulness. Still, the resolve to return is contingent upon a number of factors such as improved economic status and the completion of educational programs and vocational training. More interestingly, some African emigrants to Europe claim to be in transit. In this regard, they express desire to migrate from Europe to North America before finally returning home. Figuratively, North America becomes the terminal point of migration for many African emigrants in Europe.

Ireke Versus Guilt: Tropes of "Otherness" Within the African Diaspora

Diasporas are largely defined according to two spatial relations. While some scholars emphasize the relationship of the diaspora to the land of origin (Safran 1991), others focus on the new locality and the host societies in which the diasporic communities are embedded (Clifford 1994). Glick-Schiller et al. (1999) and Levitt (2001) have continued to popularize a transnational analytic framework for understanding global migration. These approaches help to widen the horizon of migration and diaspora scholarship by signaling the complexities of contemporary migration and transnational processes. Another neglected feature is the interrelationship between the historical and contemporary dimensions of African diaspora (Haller 2001). What patterns of relation exist between new African immigrants and African Americans for instance? To what extent do new African churches establish networks and maintain links with African American churches? Do new African immigrants and African Americans operate within similar sociocultural frames of reference? I now turn briefly to these questions.

As new African immigrant religiosity proliferates, so do connections between emigrant communities in the diaspora and religious communities in the homeland. To strengthen these connections, many African churches in the homeland are now consciously engaged in sending missionaries to evangelize Europe, the United States, and other parts of the globe. Many of the African missionaries are commissioned by "home" churches that provide them with financial and material resources. Although this "reverse-mission" initiative cannot be claimed to be a peculiar feature of African Christian movements, these movements are nevertheless engaged in transmitting their religious traditions beyond their immediate geoethnic contexts. Some of their mission objectives suggest an urgency to bridge the gap between Africans and African Americans. However, one characteristic of religion in North America is the ethnic dimension of "denominationalism." Churches are established along ethnic lines leading to the common description of "ethnic-based churches" such as Korean, Irish, German, and African American (black) churches. It seems as if each ethnic-based congregation is operating largely within its own group and without any significant interethnic links and networks.

However, two observations can be made on the relationship between African American churches and churches of new African immigrants. First, there are some levels of institutional networking and ecumenical cooperation between them—especially in the planning and execution of religious programs such as crusades, conventions, and training. For instance, the catchword for the KICC's annual Christian Conference, the "International Gathering of Champions" (IGOC) is "Raising Champions, Taking Territories." The initiative that was started by Matthew Ashimolowo in 1991 gathers more than 180,000 Christians from more than forty nations for what is now known as Europe's premier Christian conference.[19] Local and international evangelists and leaders participate in this ecumenical event. African American evangelists and Pentecostal leaders who have participated in this annual event include Eddie Long, Thomas Jakes, Keith Butler, Juanita Bynum, and Donnie McClurkin. They have appeared alongside African Pentecostal preachers such as Enoch Adeboye, David Oyedepo, Dipo Oluyomi, Mensah Otabil, and Robert Kayanja.[20] Such forums often parade a mix of leaders and members from both constituencies.

The conference is also an avenue for the commodification of sermon texts, gospel music, songs, films, anointing oil, documentaries and programs of participating leaders and churches made into books, diaries, almanacs, souvenirs, and audiovisual products.[21] Whether this kind of association and networking actually extends beyond the particular event is questionable. Essentially, African American church congregations continue to be largely dominated by African Americans while the new African immigrants keep to themselves—although some mixing does occur on occasion. Most respondents in the new African churches indicated that they identified with African American upon their arrival in the United States, but later pulled out to join ranks with, or to establish, new African churches. Reasons adduced for this switching of religious affiliation vary but range from perceived cultural differences and different mentalities to accusations of arrogance, mutual suspicion, and lack of trust.[22]

One concern common to many African immigrants is their experience of a cold reception from the African American community.[23] On the other hand, some African Americans confront new African immigrants with the guilt of selling their ancestors into slavery. African Americans thus label new African immigrants as "primitive people," "our primitive brothers and sisters," or descendants of slave merchants or slave stealers. They also allege that the new African immigrants consider themselves "superior" to their African American counterparts (a notion that arises, even among Africans, as a result of the tendency in the media and elsewhere to profile African Americans negatively). Some new African immigrants fondly refer to their African American counterparts with names like *ireke/onireke* (Yoruban) or *awhedeam/awhedeamni/awhedeamfoo* (Akan)—words that mean literally "sugarcane" and "sugarcane people." These names suggest the plight of slaves who were rudely uprooted and forced to work on sugarcane plantations across the Americas. The tendency toward mutual suspicion and contempt characterizes one level of relationship between the new African immigrants and the African Americans. This mutual, negative perception has led to a somewhat uneasy relationship between the groups, while also polarizing the "black community" in a way that inhibits its ability to become a formidable force within America's sociopolitical and economic systems.

Conclusion

This chapter has demonstrated the increasing import of religion among diasporic communities, showing how new Christian communities are carving out a niche within the African diaspora and contributing to the diversification of the religious landscape. In particular, it has focused on the RCCG, a church that has emerged in the past fifty-five years as the fastest growing Pentecostal movement in Nigeria. Thus, the chapter demonstrates both how Africa is becoming the new center of gravity of Christianity and how this influence has transcended the continent into the African diaspora. The transnational character of this phenomenon suggests a number of significant topics that need further contextualization and analysis. This chapter has considered some of these topics, including: the links to the original home from the diaspora; the peculiarities that arise in the host context; the reverse-mission dynamics as an evolving dimension of the transnational process; and the myriad spheres of mutual exchange, reinforcement, and influence that pertain in the contemporary context of globalization. It is necessary to examine further the relationship patterns between African Americans and the new African immigrants in order to establish the political, social, cultural, economic, religious, and strategic factors that facilitate or inhibit such relationships. Interdisciplinary approaches, and theoretical and methodological discipline are needed to further explore the dynamics of these phenomena, as we come to appreciate the contributions made by diasporic communities to religious and civic life—both "at home" and abroad.

Notes

1. See *The Foreign-Born Population: 2000. Census 2000 Brief,* United States Census Bureau, December 2003, available at: http://www.census.gov/prod/2003pubs/c2kbr-34.pdf. Accessed August 23, 2007.
2. Zeleza (2002: 9) has shown that many Africans who emigrate go to other African countries. He notes that between 1965 and 1990 Africa's migrant population grew at a faster rate than any other region in the world. The continent increased its share of international immigrants from 10.6 percent to 13.1 percent.
3. See the *Triennial Comprehensive Report on Immigration.* Available at: http://www.uscis.gov/portal/site/uscis/menuitem. Accessed August 23, 2007.
4. See "Estimates of the Unauthorized Immigrant Population Residing in the United States: 1990 to 2000" (Office of Policy and Planning, U.S. Immigration and Naturalization Service 2003).
5. Information on the church and its activities is available at: http://www.godembassy.org. Accessed August 23, 2007.
6. See "A Brief History of the Redeemed Christian Church of God," in *Sunday School Manual, The Redeemed Christian Church of God, 2002/2003 Edition,* 127. A conservative list of parishes worldwide is available at the RCCG Internet Outreach: http://main.rccg.org/parish_directory/parish_directory_main.htm. Accessed August 23, 2007. This list is far from complete.
7. The Zonal Coordinator heads a local parish but also performs special functions in matters of doctrine, protocol, finance, legal and immigration affairs, special programs and projects, and so on. See details in the pamphlet "The Structure, Administration and Finance of the Redeemed Christian Church in North America" (Dallas, TX: RCCGNA Headquarters, 2003).
8. "The Latter Rain" in the "7th Annual RCCG North American Convention Program," Dallas, TX, June 2003.
9. See the list of UK parishes at the RCCG Web site: http://directory.rccg.org/uk.htm. Accessed August 23, 2007.
10. See RCCG official Web site: http://www.rccg.org created and maintained by the RCCG Internet Project, Houston, TX.
11. See "Addendum—Our Poise" in The Redeemed Christian Church of God, North America and Caribbean Statement of Fundamental Truths, a publication of RCCGNA, n.d.: 39–40.
12. Author interview with Dr. Samuel Shorimade at the RCCG Cornerstone Worship Center for All Nations parish, Cambridge, Massachusetts, November 23, 2003. Pastor Shorimade is the founder and current pastor of the parish.

13. The Holy Ghost Congress attracts over two million participants, thus leading some observers to describe the religious festival as the largest Christian gathering on earth. See Grady (2002).
14. Author's interview with Pastor (Dr.) Ajibike Akinyoye at the RCCGNA Headquarters, Dallas, TX, March 9, 2004. Cf. Laolu Akande, "Multimillion Dollar Redemption Camp Underway in U. S." *The Guardian*. April 8, 2003. Also available at: http://www.rccgna.org/rcnews/templates/news.asp? articleid =9&zoneid=2 Accessed August 23, 2007.
15. See full details at the church Web site available at: www.godembassy.org/eng/ projnewbuild_e.shtm. Accessed March 2, 2005.
16. See church Web site available at: http://www.kicc.org.uk/. Accessed August 23, 2007.
17. Cf. The Vifezda "Mercy House" initiative of the Embassy of God. The charitable fund "Vifezda" (translated from the Greek to mean House of Mercy) was organized in 1999 as a result of the outreach for homeless children. For further details, see Web site: http://www.angelfire.com/ms2/mercyhouse/. Accessed August 23, 2007.
18. See Christian Bank Project of the Embassy of God: www.godembassy.org/ eng/projsbank e.shtm. Accessed March 3, 2005; and KICC's Vision at http:// www.kicc.org.uk/. Accessed August 23, 2007.
19. See KICC official Web site at: http://www.kicc.org.uk/events-igoc.asp. Accessed August 23, 2007.
20. See profiles of invited church leaders and evangelists at the IGOC 2003 and 2004 at: http://www.kiccdev.org.uk/igoc2003/main.asp? and http://www. kiccdev.org.uk/igoc2004/main.asp respectively. Accessed March 2, 2005. Other renowned American evangelists include Mike Murdock, Robb Thompson, and Peter Daniels.
21. See IGOC 2004 Conference products at: http://www.kiccdev.org.uk/igoc 2004/main.asp?location=products. Accessed March 3, 2005.
22. Author's interview with Cornelius Oyelami and Pastor (Dr.) Ajibike Akinyoye at the RCCGNA Headquarters, Dallas, Texas, March 9, 2004. Most of my informants in Boston and Texas indicated one or more of these reasons for switching religious affiliation.
23. Author's interview with Cornelius Oyelami at the RCCGNA Headquarters, Dallas, Texas, March 7, 2004. Virtually all my informants corroborated this view.

Bibliography

Adogame, Afe (2000). "The Quest for Space in the Global Religious Marketplace: African Religions in Europe," *International Review of Mission* 89/354: 400–409.
———— (2002). "Traversing Local-Global Religious Terrain: African New Religious Movements in Europe," *Zeitschrift für Religionswissenschaft* 10: 33–49.

Adogame, Afe (2003). "Betwixt Identity and Security: African New Religious Movements and the Politics of Religious Networking in Europe," *Nova Religio: The Journal of Alternative and Emergent Religions* 7/2: 24–41.

——— (2004a). "Contesting the Ambivalences of Modernity in a Global Context: The Redeemed Christian Church of God, North America," *Studies in World Christianity* 10/1: 25–48.

——— (2004b). "Engaging the Rhetoric of Spiritual Warfare: The Public Face of Aladura in Diaspora," *Journal of Religion in Africa* 34/4: 493–522.

——— (2005a). "African Christian Communities in Diaspora." In Ogbu Kalu (ed.), *African Christianity: An African Story*, 495–514. Pretoria, South Africa: University of Pretoria.

——— (2005b). "African Instituted Churches in Europe: Continuity and Transformation." In Afe Adogame (ed.), *African Identities and World Christianity in the Twentieth Century*, 225–244. Wiesbaden, Germany: Harrassowitz.

——— (2005c). "To Be or Not to Be? Politics of Belonging and African Christian Communities in Germany." In Afe Adogame and Cordula Weisskoeppel (eds.), *Religion in the Context of African Migration*, 95–112. Bayreuth, Germany: Bayreuth African Studies.

Adogame, Afe and Cordula Weisskoeppel (eds.) (2005). *Religion in the Context of African Migration*. Bayreuth, Germany: Bayreuth African Studies.

Akyeampong, Emmanuel (2000). "Africans in the Diaspora: The Diaspora and Africa," *African Affairs* 99: 183–215.

Arthur, John (2000). *Invisible Sojourners: African Immigrant Diaspora in the United States*. Westport, CT: Praeger.

Basch, Linda, Nina Glick-Schiller, and Cristina Blanc-Szanton (eds.) (1994). *Nations Unbound: Transnational Projects, Postcolonial Predicaments, and Deterritorialized Nation-States*. New York: Gordon and Breach.

Braziel, Jane and Abita Mannur (eds.) (2003). *Theorizing Diaspora*. Oxford: Blackwell.

Brettell, Caroline and James Hollifield (eds.) (2000). *Migration Theory: Talking across Disciplines*. New York and London: Routledge.

Brown, Frank (2003). "Taking Kiev by Surprise: Europe's Biggest Church," *Charisma and Christian Life* 28/11 (June): 88–94.

Bruni, Frank (2003). "The Changing Church: Faith Fades Where It Once Burned Strong," *New York Times*. October 13: A1.

Castles, Stephen and Mark Miller (2003). *The Age of Migration*, 3rd edition. New York: The Guilford Press.

Clifford, James (1994). "Diasporas," *Cultural Anthropology* 9/3: 302–338.

Cohen, Robin (1997). *Global Diasporas: An Introduction*. London: UCL Press.

Ebaugh, Helen and Janet Chafetz (2000). *Religion and the New Immigrants: Continuities and Adaptations in Immigrant Congregations*. Walnut Creek, CA: Altamira Press.

——— (eds.) (2002). *Religion across Borders: Transnational Immigrant Networks*. Walnut Creek, CA: Altamira Press.

Eck, Diana (2001). *A New Religious America: How a Christian Country Has Now Become the World's Most Religiously Diverse Nation*. San Francisco: HarperCollins.

Garber, Marjorie B. and Rebecca L. Walkowitz (eds.) (1999). *One Nation under God: Religion and American Culture*. New York: Routledge.

Glick-Schiller, Nina, Linda Basch, and Cristina Szanton Blanc (1999). "Transnationalism: A New Analytic Framework for Understanding Migration." In Steve Vertovec and Robin Cohen (eds.) (1999). *Migration, Diasporas and Transnationalism*, 1–24. Cheltenham, UK: Elgar Press.

Grady, Lee (2002). "Nigeria's Miracle: How a Sweeping Christian Revival Is Transforming Africa's Most Populous Nation," *Charisma and Christian Life* 27/10: 38–41.

Haddad, Yvonne, Jane Smith, and John Esposito (eds.) (2003). *Religion and Immigration: Christian, Jewish, and Muslim Experiences in the United States*. Walnut Creek, CA: Altamira.

Haller, Dieter (2001). "Transcending Locality: The Diaspora Network of Sephardic Jews in the Western Mediterranean," *Anthropological Journal on European Cultures* 9/1: 3–31.

Harris, Joseph E. (ed.) (1993). *Global Dimensions of the African Diaspora*, 2nd edition. Washington, DC: Howard University Press.

Hunt, Stephen (2002). "A Church for All Nations: The Redeemed Christian Church of God," *PNEUMA: The Journal of the Society for Pentecostal Studies* 24/2: 185–204.

Hunt, Stephen and Nicola Lightly (2001). "The British Black Pentecostal Revival: Identity and Belief in the New Nigerian Churches," *Ethnic and Racial Studies* 24/1: 104–124.

Jenkins, Philip (2002a). "A New Religious America," *First Things* 125 (August/ September): 25–28. Available at: http://www.firstthings.com/article.php3?id_ article=2052. Accessed August 23, 2007.

————— (2002b). *The Next Christendom: The Coming of Global Christianity*. New York: Oxford University Press.

Kalu, Ogbu (2004). "The Andrew Syndrome: Models in Understanding Nigerian Diaspora." Unpublished paper presented at the University of California at Davis (December 4): 13. To be published in Olupona, Jacob (ed.) (forthcoming). *Religion and African Migration*.

Kilson, Martin L. (ed.) (1976). *The African Diaspora: Interpretive Essays*. Cambridge, MA: Harvard University Press.

Larson, Eric M. and Judith A. Droitcour (2003). "Estimating the Illegal Alien Population in the United States: Some Methodological Considerations." Available at: http://www.un.org/esa/population/publications/secoord2003/ GAO_Paper17.pdf. Accessed March 3, 2005.

Lieblich, Julia and Tom McCann (2002). "Africans Now Missionaries to U.S.," *Chicago Tribune*. June 21: A1.

Levitt, Peggy (2001). *The Transnational Villagers*. Berkeley: University of California Press.

Okpewho, Isidore, Carole Boyce Davies, and Ali Mazrui (1999). *The African Diaspora: African Origins and New World Identities.* Bloomington: Indiana University Press.

Olagoke, Ezekiel (2002). *Pan Africanism and the New Diaspora: African Christians in the United States.* Unpublished PhD Dissertation, University of Denver and Iliff School of Theology.

Safran, William (1991). "Diasporas in Modern Societies: Myths of Homeland and Return," *Diaspora* 1/1: 83–100.

Sengupta, Somini and Rohter Larry (2003). "Where Faith Grows, Fired by Pentecostalism." *The New York Times.* October 13: A5.

Smith, Peter and Guarnizo Luis (eds.) (1998). *Transnationalism from Below.* New Brunswick, NJ: Transaction Publishers.

Ter Haar, Gerrie (1998a). *Halfway to Paradise: African Christians in Europe.* Cardiff UK: Cardiff Academic Press.

———— ed. (1998b). *Strangers and Sojourners: Religious Communities in the Diaspora.* Leuven: Peeters.

———— (1999). "Imposing Identity: The Case of African Christians in the Netherlands," *DISKUS* 5: 1–5. Also available at: http://web.unimarburg.de/religionswissenschaft/journal/diskus/haar.html. Accessed August 23, 2007.

Vásquez, Manuel and Marie Marquardt (2003). *Globalizing the Sacred: Religion across the Americas.* New Brunswick, NJ: Rutgers University Press.

Vertovec, Steve and Robin Cohen (eds.) (1999). *Migration, Diasporas and Transnationalism.* Cheltenham, UK: Elgar Press.

Warner, Stephen and Judith Wittner (eds.) (1998). *Gatherings in Diaspora: Religious Communities and the New Immigration.* Philadephia: Temple University Press.

Zeleza, Paul (2002). "Contemporary African Migrations in a Global Context," *African Issues* 30/1: 9–14.

Chapter 2

Christianity on Trial: The Nation of Islam and the Rastafari, 1930–1950

Maboula Soumahoro

Introduction

The Afro-Jamaican Rastafarians and the African American Nation of Islam (NOI) are two nationalist religious groups that both emerged in urban centers in the Americas during the early 1930s. Following the activities of Marcus Garvey and the Universal Negro Improvement Association (UNIA), both groups adopted religious approaches to the sociopolitical issues of the era. According to historian Michael Gomez, the black populations of the Americas during this period included three different groups that could be distinguished by their positions in relation to Christianity:

> The first [group] extended a process that began with the African initial contact with European Christianity, whereby the religion was steadily Africanized both liturgically as well as theologically. The second...also continuing from previous periods, involved practices developed in Africa and transferred to the Americas, where they were renewed with some alteration but remained identifiably African. The third saw the creation of new religions, typically taken from the fabrics of Islamic-Judeo-Christian traditions, and woven into entirely novel patterns, informed by a vision of Africa as a historical power and, at least in one instance, a future destination. (Gomez 2005: 170)

The NOI and the Rastafarians have held this third position since the 1930s—although the "historical power" involved in their cases has not necessarily turned out to be African (as shall be explained in greater detail through the beliefs of the NOI).

Marcus Garvey and the Black God of Ethiopia

The African American "Great Migration" from the South to the North in the United States and massive peasant migration from the rural to the urban areas of Jamaica (and to other foreign destinations) provided the context of relocation out of which the two religious groups emerged.[1] In the United States, for instance, more than a million African Americans left the South for the North between 1916 and 1930 to escape from poverty, racism, and lynching (Gomez 2005: 166). In these newly inhabited environments in the North, a significant encounter took place between African Americans and people from the Caribbean diaspora—in particular, Jamaicans.[2] A certain "religious creativity" was nurtured in this historically and numerically novel environment. Two significant illustrations of this phenomenon are Marcus Garvey's enterprise and the Noble Drew Ali's Moorish Science Temple of America. Of these, Marcus Garvey best exemplifies the creative link between religion and politics.

Marcus Garvey arrived in the United States from Jamaica in 1916. Seven years later, in 1923, he was arrested and charged with mail fraud and conspiracy in relation to the methods employed to advertise the Black Star Line. Found guilty in 1925 and sentenced to five years in a Georgian prison, Garvey was granted a pardon by U.S. president Calvin Coolidge in 1927. He was deported upon his release from prison to Jamaica. Once there, Garvey decided to campaign for a seat on the Jamaican Legislative Council, but he was arrested and found guilty of sedition. After a second release from prison, he left Jamaica for England where he resided until his death in 1940.

Garvey established the UNIA in Jamaica in 1914. When he arrived in the United States in 1916, the headquarters of the UNIA moved to Harlem, in New York City, in an effort to launch his program on a wider scale. At the time, Harlem was intellectually and culturally in full swing. A place where people of the African diaspora gathered and interacted, it was the home of Harlem Renaissance or the New Negro movement. Marcus Garvey's activities in Harlem provide the crucial context out of which developed the worldviews of both the Rastafarians and the NOI. Garvey's ambitions were grand. The UNIA ventured nothing less than to organize the black people of the world (as emphasized by the use of the word "universal" in the name of his organization). Toward that end, Garvey published his newspaper the *Negro World*; he set up black businesses; he created The Black Star Line, a shipping line, with the goal of linking the United States, the Caribbean, and Africa in a manner that would profit black people; and he endeavored to secure Liberia as the destination for his back-to-Africa movement.

In addition to all this, Garvey established the African Orthodox Church. Among its noteworthy features, the church incorporated the worship of the Black Christ and popularized the representation of the Black Madonna and Child. The rationale for this iconography was that the black people of the world were in need of a God who resembled them physically. Garvey articulated this point in a discourse on "the image of God":

> If the white man has the idea of a white God, let him worship his God as he desires. If the yellow man's God is of his race let him worship his God as he sees fit. We, as Negroes, have found a new ideal. Whilst our God has no color, yet it is human to see everything through one's own spectacles, and since the white people have seen their God through white spectacles, we have only now started out (late though it be) to see our God through our own spectacles. The God of Isaac and the God of Jacob let Him exist for the race that believes in the God of Isaac and the God of Jacob. We Negroes believe in the God of Ethiopia, the everlasting God—God the Father, God the Son and God the Holy Ghost, the One God of all ages. That is the God in whom we believe, but we shall worship Him through the spectacles of Ethiopia. (Garvey 1986: 44)

This excerpt draws attention to the prevailing dichotomy between idealism and pragmatism. Indeed, while Garvey acknowledges the ultimate "colorlessness" of God, he still sees the clear connection between race, Christianity, and power. Positioning himself as a racial essentialist, he claims Africa—the shorthand for which in this instance is Ethiopia—as the place of origin for black people and the lens through which they envision their theologies. Thus the "New Negroes" do not need to fully reject Christianity but rather to mold it to their particular needs and interests. Each race is intrinsically different, consequently each needs it own distinct God. As far as religious principles are concerned, they remain identical and genuinely universal. Therefore, the Christian God can be universal. What cannot be universal, however, is *how* this God is represented. In this manner Marcus Garvey sought racial empowerment through a positive and meaningful representation of God.

Garvey's ideas came from a black nationalist tradition that existed throughout the Americas (Moses 1996). However, Garvey's novelty

originated in the strong international orientation he gave to his activities as
well as the wide range of issues that his organization attempted to cover.
Garvey's endeavors aimed to embody the variety of languages, experiences,
and geographical orientations that pertained among the people of the African
diaspora. The goal was a lofty one, even if Garvey's conception of race and
racial solidarity eventually had the effect of concealing the crucial social differences in the population he was addressing. The following lines taken from
the UNIA anthem bring the Garveyite project into clear focus:

> Ethiopia, thou land of our fathers;
> Thou land where the gods love to be,
> As storm cloud at night suddenly gathers
> Our armies come rushing to thee.
> We must in the fight be victorious
> When swords are thrust outward to gleam;
> For us will the vict'ry be glorious
> When led by the red, black and green. (Van Deburg 1997: 29–30)

This passage depicts Ethiopia as heaven and home: the place of origin and
the ultimate destination for all the black people of the world. It therefore
implies that happiness for dislocated Africans cannot be found in diaspora.
What is good for blacks exists outside of the Americas. The African continent, meanwhile, appears as good, logical, and divinely ordained.[3]

Although Christians made up the primary religious group to which
Garvey appealed, the "God of Ethiopia" was not limited to Christianity.
Consequently, the UNIA sought to cooperate with other religious groups
as well. Tony Martin provides a description of the organization that reveals
an openness toward the Black Jews of Harlem, for example, and the
Ahmadiyya (Muslim) Mission.[4] Other groups, such as Noble Drew Ali's
Moorish Science Temple of America, openly expressed their respect for
Garvey's activities and managed to attract many American UNIA members after Garvey's deportation from the United States. Significantly, an
active member of the UNIA was reported to have been a member of Elijah
Muhammad's staff in Chicago and Detroit (Martin 1976: 74–77). Richard
Brent Turner, distancing himself from Tony Martin's reference to "active
participation," only mentions Elijah Muhammad's knowledge of Garvey's
activities and the fact that Elijah Muhammad attended one UNIA event
in Chicago probably in 1919 (Turner 1997:154–155). In any case, the leader
of the NOI was clearly aware of Garvey's activities.

As far as the Rastafari are concerned, Garvey's near-prophet status is
accounted for by the legendary statement Garvey is said to have made just
prior to his departure from Jamaica to the United States in 1916. He

advised those in attendance to look to the East for the crowning of a Black King: that day, he prophesied, would herald the coming liberation of all black people. When Ras Tafari was crowned emperor of Ethiopia in 1930, Garvey's words resurfaced—or were refashioned—in concert with the emergence of the Rastafarian movement (Barret 1977; Chevannes 1994; Erskine 2005).

Rastafarianism and the NOI emerged from the socio-theological ferment inaugurated by Marcus Garvey. To this day, the NOI and Rastafarianism are examples of Afro-Caribbean and African American[5] religions that emphasize active political resistance to white hegemony. Both groups look for their true identities beyond the borders of a white-dominated society. The NOI relates itself to a color-blind, or at least nonwhite, Muslim world. Rastafarians use a similar process of religious territorialization to assert a strong black identity within and beyond national borders. In equating the African continent with blackness, Rastafarianism constitutes a form of pan-Africanism in which blackness itself takes on religious significance.

Rastafarianism and the NOI develop a kind of theology that reveals both the roots of and the routes to liberation.[6] Perhaps most significantly, both groups share in common an overall assessment of Christianity as the identified enemy of black people. To the NOI and to Rastafarians, the oppression of displaced Africans in the Americas has been total, including religious. To them, no plan of complete black liberation can afford to overlook the religious question. Christianity is apprehended with great suspicion because the oppressed and the oppressors cannot be conceived as sharing the same God. Since Christianity was effectively used by slaveholders to pacify the slaves, descendants of slaves now need to utterly turn away from Christianity thereby putting an end to the cycle of oppression. Christianity is understood as an active political force that needs to be first acknowledged then countered, controlled, and eventually shunned.

The NOI and Rastafarianism are secular and religious movements that find themselves in opposition to a kind of Christian nationalism that has, in various guises, fused religious and political power since the "discovery" of the Americas. Their centers of interest cannot be analyzed as strictly social, political, or religious. While it is understood that these two long-lasting movements have undergone significant changes and transformations over time, I have chosen to consider briefly their early years between 1930 and 1950. My interest in this specific period is focused on the attempt to identify the first priorities of these two groups as they emerge from, and respond to, Marcus Garvey's initiatives. My aim in making a transnational comparison between Rastafarianism and the NOI is to reflect upon the function of "religion" in the African diaspora of the Americas. By venturing

along the fine line that perhaps separates the sacred from the secular, I wish
to demonstrate the role religion plays in the identity politics of African
diasporic people in Jamaica and the United States.[7]

NOI: From Racial Trauma to Color-Blindness

The NOI, a separatist, black nationalist, religious organization, was
founded in 1930 in Detroit by the mysterious W. D. Fard and was developed subsequently by his most trusted lieutenant Elijah Muhammad (born
Elijah Poole, 1897–1975). Its members accept W. D. Fard Muhammad as
the reincarnation of Allah and Elijah Muhammad as his prophet (messenger). The organization advocates black mental and physical resurrection
consisting in self-help experiments and rhetorical opposition to white
America. The ideology of the NOI that attracted Elijah Muhammad and
eventually tens of thousands of other blacks to Fard and his legacy is
heavily influenced by Christianity as well as orthodox Islam. The prophet
Muhammad ibn Abdullah ("slave of Allah")—honored as the last prophet
by orthodox Muslims—is portrayed in the early NOI theology as the
emissary to Europe whose task was to reintroduce Islam to whites. Contrary
to "orthodox" Islam (while sharing certain affinities with Ahmadiyya), the
prophet Muhammad is neither the final messenger of Allah nor the most
important one: Fard reserved those distinctions for himself and later for
Elijah Muhammad.

  Scholars have noted in early NOI theology the influence of traditional
black nationalism, Marcus Garvey, the Moorish Science Temple of
America of Noble Drew Ali, the Jehovah's Witnesses, and black freema-
sonry (Fauset 2001; Gomez 2005). The central tenet of this theology is a
belief in a black god. This faith serves two purposes. First, it affirms that
African American history extends back far before the period of slavery to
a time of black creation and creativity. Second, the portrait of God as a
flesh and blood human being with the ability to construct the universe
conveys the idea that black people have the power to affect their own environment for better and for worse. The dialectics formulated by the religious organization articulates a reciprocal system of identification whereby
the God of black people is human and blacks themselves are divine.

  The Myth of Yacub depicts the NOI's understanding of the creation of
the world. In a nutshell, this cosmology presents whites as a degenerate
race. Black Muslims, on the other hand, are the original people of the
earth: divine and Asiatic. The principal consequence of the theogony of

black gods and the original people is that African Americans are linked to a glorious and pristine past. Therefore, without distancing itself too far from the Judeo-Christian and Quranic worldviews, the cosmology of the "Black Muslims" was attractive to black Christians who found the racial core of the story inspiring and the biblical shell of the message encouraging. Through symbols and rhetoric, the myth of Yacub portrayed all whites as subhuman and even as "devils." These "facts of origin" explained both white racism in the present and the past abuses of blacks by Europeans; it also exploited fomenting nationalist sentiments in the African American community. In the cosmic scheme of things, hell emerged as a geographic location, Europe, and its historical extension—the United States. Most significantly, this theology gave black people hope: African Americans were the victims of evil; but this evil was a temporary phenomenon that could be opposed.

During the 1930s, the city of Detroit was an important destination for African Americans determined to escape the enduring and brutal racism of the South. The failure of Reconstruction coupled with the rapid industrialization of the northern United States triggered the Great Migration, mentioned above, that brought millions of African Americans to northern cities. However, adjusting to urban industrial life proved highly stressful and disorienting for the newly arrived immigrants. Amid this disorientation, ascetic and secret societies had a certain appeal. Fard's group was one of these: it rationalized the predicament of the black race as the result of an ancient white conspiracy and promised a new and alternative identity for those African Americans willing to withdraw culturally from a doomed America.

Eschatology is part and parcel of the NOI teachings. Drawing upon the Book of Revelation, America is equated with the mighty and corrupt Babylon—which served as predecessor and code for the Roman Empire that vexed early Christians at the time of John's apocalyptic vision. By appealing to this familiar mythology, the NOI positioned itself in a fashion conducive to the recruitment of disenchanted black Christians. These newcomers to the North found themselves severed from their Southern roots and economically endangered because of the Depression, the competition against European immigrants, racial discrimination in the work place, and race riots in the streets.

The NOI turned to the Bible as a common authority among African American people. It was the repository of "some truths" while the Quran was conceived as the "seal" of biblical prophecy: an enhancement, not a negation, of the Bible. According to Eddie S. Glaude, Jr. (2000), the African American community's identification with the biblical Exodus dates back to the nineteenth century. Naturally, the narrative about an escape from slavery imposed by the Pharaoh resonated with the African American experience of slavery. However, the failure of the Exodus—that is to say, Emancipation—to bring real freedom to the ex-slaves gave rise to an interest in eschatological theology. Wayne Taylor notes that "eschatological theology reached its zenith in the African American community in the times of its greatest perils." He refers in particular to the popularity of the apocalyptic in light of the failures of Reconstruction (2005: 53).

Although appeals were made to the Bible, the NOI's relationships to it and to the Quran were ambiguous. Indeed, in the early years of the Nation, the Quran seems hardly to fit into the movement's preaching and teaching at all. Even though many scholars have pointed to the Muslim heritage of the enslaved Africans imported in the United States, that heritage seems not to have had a direct influence on the NOI's choice to develop its Muslim identity as an alternative identity in the context of African America (Turner 1997; Clegg 1997; Gomez 2005). Rather, what seems of significance is the *idea* of Islam as it represented an alternative to the "master" narrative of American religious history. In short, Islam was appealing because it stood outside of and apart from that (white) history.

If the temper of the times was eschatological, the time was also ripe for an alternative myth of origin, a different sense of personhood not under white control. Here the founding Myth of Yakub played a key role in explaining the creation of the world and the place occupied by African Americans in time and space. It offers the primary illustration of the NOI's view of history. For the NOI, the "Original Man" was the "Asiatic Man," the Black Man from the tribe of Shabazz—whose descendants inhabited both the Nile Valley of Egypt and region around Mecca in Saudi Arabia. Upon closer inspection, then, one discovers that the racial identification at the core of the Nation's belief system advances a particular sense of the black race. It includes not only black Africans or persons of African descent; it also includes other Asiatic, that is to say, non-white, people. According to this perspective, Elijah Muhammad distinguished his movement from others, such as Garvey's, that emphasized the importance of Africa in the construction of black identity in America. Illustrating this in *The Fall of America*, Elijah Muhammad wrote:

> …we must realize that whereas the Black man in Africa is our brother our central responsibility is with the Black man here in the wilderness of North America. For us to expend our energies pleading for the cause of Africa is like a blind man pleading that his fellow blind man be given eyes while he continues to stumble in darkness. (1997 [1973]: 17)

At the time of its emergence in the 1930s, then, the NOI kept its focus strictly on African Americans and national issues. The role played by the Quran and Islamic tenets per se were not central in the founding years of the NOI. What truly had a stronger impact was the visible difference that this newly articulated Muslim identity put forward in terms of language, diet, and social behavior. Nevertheless, strategically speaking, the NOI had no other practical choice than to acknowledge the significance of the Bible in African American culture. The Christian text was therefore called into service, but it was approached as both poisonous and necessary to attract a deeply Christianized African American community. Meanwhile the eschatological vision of the Nation, originating as it did during hard economic times, did not look to Africa—or, for that matter, to Mecca—for salvation; rather it sought solidarity, and indeed resurrection, among black people in what Elijah Muhammad called the wilderness of North America.

The Rastafari: The Spectacles of Ethiopia

Rastafarianism, more of a "livity" than an organization, did focus on Africa as a source of identity.[8] Its name is derived from the Ethiopian word "Ras" (meaning prince or head) "Tafari" and refers to Ras Tafari Maknonnen who, in November 1930, was crowned "His Imperial Majesty Haile Selassie I" with an accompaniment of additional titles including: King of Kings (Negusa Negast), Lord of Lords, Conquering Lion of the Tribe of Judah, Elect of God, and Light of the Universe. The Rastafarian movement made its appearance in the impoverished areas of Kingston in Jamaica, then still under the rule of Great Britain. Among the principal early Rastafarian leaders were Leonard Howell, Joseph Hibbert, Arhcibald Dunkley, and Robert Hinds. Around the same time in 1930, these four men began preaching independent of one another about the divinity of Haile Selassie. Each of these four men developed his own community of followers (Chevannes 1994). The words Marcus Garvey is said to have uttered before leaving Jamaica for New York in 1916 were judged prophetic by the four men. At a time in history when the entire African continent—with the exception of Ethiopia—was under European rule, the greatly publicized coronation of the Ethiopian Emperor took a peculiar signification in Jamaica.

Rastafarians consider Haile Selassie the returned Messiah; Ethiopia, meanwhile, is Zion, the *axis mundi* or center of the Rastafarian world. The divinity of the Ethiopian Emperor Haile Selassie, fully accepted by early Rasta leaders, was supported with references taken from Ethiopian history and politics. Meanwhile, Psalm 68:31 from the King James Version of the

Bible, with its explicit mention of Ethiopia, added a biblical dimension to Haile Selassie's authority. "Princes shall come out of Egypt," the Psalmist declares; "Ethiopia shall soon stretch out her hands unto God." Through the coronation name he adopted in 1930, Emperor Haile Selassie positioned himself as the last Ethiopian Solomonic king. The Makonnen dynasty and other parts of Ethiopia nobility had, since at least the Middle Ages, claimed descent form King Solomon of Jerusalem and Queen Sheba of Ethiopia or Yemen.

The Ethiopian religious text *Kebra Nagast*, or "the Glory of Kings," tells the story of King Solomon of Jerusalem, a Jew, and Queen Makeda or Sheba of Ethiopia (Brooks 1995). The Queen of Sheba ventures to Solomon's court to witness his great wisdom and to increase her own personal knowledge. After a most pleasant stay in Solomon's palace, the Queen converts to the King's faith. Afterwards Solomon seduces the Queen and impregnates her before her departure. Solomon's aim, the text suggests, is to spread his seeds all over the world so that all people, through his children, would convert to his God. Raised in the land of his mother, Menlyelek or David II, the son of Sheba, returns one day to Jerusalem to meet his father. After their encounter, the prince leaves Jerusalem and takes the Ark of Covenant with him to his homeland. Gomez comments:

> The Ark, symbol of Yahweh's presence and Israel's unique status, henceforth rests, according to this tradition, in Ethiopia, thereby transferring to the Ethiopians the honor of "God's chosen people." Likewise, the kings of Ethiopia are descendants of Solomon, each a "lion of Judah." (2004: 23)

The Rastafarians' relationship to the Bible is multidimensional. Rastas interrogate the royal decree of 1611 that fixed the English translation of the text and delineated the canon of the Bible. According to the Rastafarians, the King James Bible was the result of a concerted editing process that kept out a number of books that would have given Africa, and particularly Ethiopia, a more central position in the story of God's encounter with human beings. Consequently, Rastafarians look upon the Bible with suspicion deeming it somewhat acceptable though corrupted and incomplete. Other texts must be read alongside the Bible, they argue, to get a more comprehensive picture of the story of black people and to render the world's history closer to "reality." These books include: *The Promised Key* (published in 1933 in Ghana) by Leonard Howell; Shepherd Robert Athlyi Rogers's *The Holy Piby: The Blackman's Bible* (published in the United States in 1924); and *The Original Maccabees Bible: The Royal Parchment Scroll of Black Supremacy* by Balantine Pettersburgh.

While looking to extra-canonical sources in addition to the Bible for written authority, Rastafarians still equated Ethiopia with Africa and Africa with blackness. No ambiguity is to be found among them regarding racial conception and self-perception. This search for essentialism, purity, and racialism stands in stark opposition to the hybridity of the Caribbean (and more generally American) space. As such, Rastafarianism does not constitute an "authentic" African religion, but is, rather, an example of creolization. It is a prime example of how Africanness and blackness have been claimed and created in the Americas in the aftermath of slavery.

Conclusion: Using the Bible and the Quran to Establish God's Color

In the context of the African diaspora in the Americas, the effort to uncover or manufacture a history and to include others in that history has functioned as a source of group agency and political power. Religion also makes meaning and makes the world meaningful: it can be used to explain life and to account for the hardships faced by black people in the Americas. Indeed, religion—when controlled by black communities—has served the purpose of opposing the horror of the slave trade and the resulting institutionalization of slavery, offering what one scholar calls "a way out of no way" (Coleman 2000). However, as Marx observed, in the hands of the dominant class, religion brings moral legitimacy to the established order. For both the NOI and Rastafarianism, to challenge Christianity has necessitated the reimaging of God including the reimagining of the color God. Christianized people of African descent in the Caribbean and the United States were thus encouraged to cast off the religion of their former masters and present oppressors and to embrace a God who looked like them.

One of the major differences between Rastafarians and the NOI lies in the conceptualizing of God: the Asiatic identity of the NOI contrasts with the African and black identity of the Rastafarians. Both groups add to this process of representation with concerns about territorialization. Rastafarians look to Ethiopia and the African continent for community while the Nation turned first to Asia, then to the United States, and finally today to the *Ummah*—the color-blind community of Muslims, based on the Muslim taboo over image and color (race) representations of both Allah and the human beings he created. As with Marcus Garvey, this belief that God has no color is maintained despite a strong emphasis on blackness and race within the boundaries of the United States of America. For the NOI both the wilderness and the Promised Land are located inside American borders. Rastafarians and members of the NOI are respectively centering and decentering the African continent, in nearly exact opposite directions, in the construction of their respective identities.

The NOI and Rastafarians both honor gods whose orientation is this-worldly. They were embodied in the figures of two black males—W. D. Fard and Haile Selassie—who were alive at the time of the emergence of each group. Each in its own way, both Rastafarianism and the NOI remind us that the colonizers did not limit themselves to the realm of history: they also colonized religions. The colonizers managed to master time in both the present and the afterlife. The colonized found themselves locked in a preestablished discourse and a fixed worldview with no escape routes from a preordained and meager existence. Both the NOI and Rastafarianism provide black people with an alternative, emancipatory discourse, in others words: a counter-narrative.

Rastafarian beliefs posit that the liberation of peoples of African descent necessitates the reappropriation of the continent of origin. This differenti-ates them from the NOI who maintain that too close an association with the continent of origin (still under almost total colonial rule in the early creation of the religious organization) is damaging to the community. Both groups rewrite, reread, look for alternative books, create new books. Their knowledge of themselves as a racial community simply cannot be accounted for by the Bible alone. Put on trial, then, by the NOI and the Rastafarians, Christianity has been found guilty of furthering the racial, political, and social oppression experienced by the descendants of enslaved Africans in the Americas.

Notes

1. One example of these foreign destinations was Panama where the construction of the Canal from 1904 to 1914 attracted great numbers of workers from the Caribbean.
2. On this topic see James (1998).
3. On the topic of Ethiopianism, see Scott (1978).
4. For more on the Ahmadiyya, see chapter 3 in this volume by Fatimah Fanusie.
5. I use the term "African American" with reference to people and movements in the United States of America as opposed to the American continent in general.
6. Although "liberation theology" arose in the context of Latin American Roman Catholicism in the 1960s, the term can be applied to a variety of historical circumstances. One thinks of liberation theology in relation to the work of James Cone in the United States, for example, or Desmond Tutu in South

Africa. It is slightly anachronistic but not at all inaccurate to apply the term to the underlying emphases in both Rastafarianism and the NOI.

7. With respect to Rastafarianism, at least, this matter is considered in some detail by Noel Leo Erskine (2005).

8. "Livity" means "a way of life" in Dread or Rasta talk according to Velma Pollard (2000). The term, in my view, may also be a direct reference to the biblical book of Leviticus that contains the laws concerning diet and health that Rastafarians observe.

Bibliography

Barret, L. E. (1977). *The Rastafarians: The Dreadlocks of Jamaica*. London: Sangsters and Heinemann.

Brooks, Miguel F. (ed.) (2001) [1995]. *Kebra Nagast (the Glory of Kings): The True Ark of the Covenant*. Kingston, Jamaica: LMH.

Chapman, Mark (1996). *Christianity on Trial: African-American Religious Thought Before and After Black Power*. Maryknoll, NY: Orbis Books.

Chevannes, Barry (1994). *Rastafari: Roots and Ideology*. Syracuse, NY: Syracuse University Press.

——— (ed.) (1995). *Rastafari and Other African-Caribbean Worldviews*. London: Macmillan.

Clegg, Claude Andrew (1997). *An Original Man: The Life and Times of Elijah Muhammad*. New York: St. Martin's Press.

Coleman, Will (2000). *Tribal Talk: Black Theology, Hermeneutics, and African/American Ways of "Telling the Story."* College Park, PA: Pennsylvania University Press.

Curtis, Edward E. IV (2002). *Islam in Black America: Identity, Liberation, a Difference in African-American Islamic Thought*. New York: State University of New York Press.

Edmonds, Ennis Barrington (2003). *Rastafari: From Outcasts to Culture Bearers*. New York: Oxford University Press.

Erskine, Noel Leo (2005). *From Garvey to Marley: Rastafari Theology*. Gainesville: University of Florida Press.

Essien-Udom, E. U. (1971). *Black Nationalism: A Search for an Identity in America*. Chicago: University of Chicago Press.

Fauset, Arthur Huff (2001) [1944]. *Black Gods of the Metropolis: Negro Cults in the Urban North*. Philadelphia: University of Pennsylvania Press.

Gardell, Mattias (1996). *In the Name of Elijah Muhammad: Louis Farrakhan and the Nation of Islam*. Durham, NC: Duke University Press.

Garvey, Amy Jacques (1986) [1923]. *The Philosophy and Opinions of Marcus Garvey or Africa for the Africans*. Dover, MA: Majority Press.

Glaude, Eddie S. Jr. (2000). *Exodus! Religion, Race, and Nation in Early Nineteenth-Century Black America*. Chicago: University of Chicago Press.

Gomez, Michael A (2004). *Reversing Sail: A History of the African Diaspora.* Cambridge: Cambridge University Press.

———— (2005). *Black Crescent: The Experience and Legacy of African Muslims in the Americas.* Cambridge: Cambridge University Press.

Hill, A. Robert (2001). *Dread History: Leonard P. Howell and Millenarian Visions in the Early Rastafarian Religion.* New York: Research Associates School Times Publications.

James, Winston (1998). *Holding Aloft the Banner of Ethiopia Caribbean Radicalism in Early Twentieth America.* New York: Verso.

Lincoln, Eric C. (1994) [1960]. *The Black Muslims in America.* Grand Rapids, MI: Eerdmans.

Marsh, Clifton E. (1996). *From Black Muslims to Muslims: The Resurrection, Transformation, and Change of the Lost-Found Nation of Islam in America, 1930–1995.* New York: The Scarecrow Press.

Martin, Tony (1976). *Race First: The Ideological and Organizational Struggles of Marcus Garvey and the Universal Negro Improvement Association.* Westport, CT: Greenwood.

Moses, Wilson Jeremiah (1996). *Classical Black Nationalism.* New York: New York University Press.

———— (1998). *Afrotopia: The Roots of African American Popular History.* Cambridge: Cambridge University Press.

Muhammad, Elijah (1965). *Message to the Blackman in America.* Chicago: Muhammad's Temple Number 2.

———— (1997) [1973]. *The Fall of America.* Chicago, IL: Secretarius Memps Publications.

Pollard, Velma (2000). *Dread Talk: The Language of Rastafari.* Montreal, Canada: McGill-Queen's University Press.

Scott, William (1978). "And Ethiopia Shall Stretch Forth Its Hands: The Origins of Ethiopianism in Afro-American Thought 1767–1896," *Umoja* 2/1 (Spring): 1–14.

Taylor, Wayne (2005). "Premillennium Tension: Malcolm X and the Eschatology of the Nation of Islam," *Souls: A Critical Journal of Black Politics, Culture, and Society* 7/1 (Winter): 52–65.

Turner, Richard Brent (1997). *Islam in the African-American Experience.* Bloomington: Indiana University Press.

Van Deburg, William L. (1997). *Modern Black Nationalism: From Marcus Garvey to Louis Farrakhan.* New York: New York University Press.

Chapter 3

Ahmadi, Beboppers, Veterans, and Migrants: African American Islam in Boston, 1948–1963

Fatimah Fanusie

Introduction

When Muhammad's Temple Number 11 of Boston, Massachusetts, was formally organized in 1954 it was heir to forty years of Islamic development in African America.[1] This forty-year development produced a movement markedly different from the mainstream Black Church. Fard Muhammad's peculiar amalgam of Islam, Garvey-styled black nationalism, and vintage African American Masonic symbolism found fertile ground within the mixture of Ahmadiyya, Sunni, and Moorish Science Islam that black musicians, returning servicemen, and Southern and Caribbean immigrants brought to Boston immediately after World War II. In particular, the African American musicians who established Temple Number 11 were attracted to the mystic nature of the Nation of Islam's (NOI) theology as well as its practical program for individual and community growth. Although the "Lost Found Nation of Islam" had been fashioned in the 1930s Midwestern heartland of America, innovations that would propel its growth through the civil rights era took their form in this northeast corner of the country. Boston's Temple Number 11 represents a departure from the depression-era temples of the Midwest that previous scholars of the NOI have focused on and serves as a case study for the unique role of local musicians as both transporters and innovators of twentieth century religious and cultural ideas.

An increase in African American migrants to Boston following World War II overwhelmed the city's institutions and altered the racial consciousness of black Bostonians who previously saw themselves as being different, Northern, and distinct from the broader African American population due to their position within an elitist New England environment (Thernstrom 1973: 178–182).[2] African American veterans of the post–World War II era brought a new, enterprising spirit that would set the tone for a more lively black culture in the city that celebrated the breaking of Jim Crow barriers. Boasting the pride of the Tuskegee Flyers and the first African American marines unit, black veterans of the Second World War had lived and fought in North Africa, the Pacific Islands, France, Russia, Japan, and China. The ranks of these veterans were quickly buttressed by Korean Conflict veterans who were the first U.S. soldiers to fight in the desegregated armed forces in battles against Mao Tse Dung's new Chinese Communist government (Dalfiume 1969). Enterprising veterans arriving in Boston in order to take advantage of the funds provided for educational training by the new GI bill (Servicemen's Readjustment Act of 1944) included a sizeable number of aspiring musicians, drawn to the city by its plethora of academic institutions including the New England Conservatory of Music, the Berklee School of Music, Harvard University, and Boston State College. In the wake of World War II, Boston offered a cosmopolitan environment and a crossroads for religious and cultural influences that would rejuvenate black life.

During the pre–World War II period, musicians and clergymen formed the largest number of African American "professionals" in Boston (Thernstrom 1973: 199). Residing in a world with extremely permeable boundaries, the musicians' urban night life concealed a multilayered milieu that was at once an incubator of social activism, racial consciousness, and spiritual awakening. Jazz artists of the 1930s and 1940s prebop and bebop eras were embracing pan-African and pan-Asian political ideology, particularly as shaped by an increasingly connected anticolonial and religious-reformist global network. By the 1940s, musicians rising from the working-class echelons began to assume a more definitive role as cultural transmitters in contrast to the period before the Harlem Renaissance, when black middle-class institutions shaped by the sensibilities of Victorian America drove African American society and culture. Renaissance artists like Countee Cullen, Langston Hughes, Alain Locke and others who had drawn inspiration from, and elevated the status of, African American popular culture paved the way for bebop artists in the 1940s and 1950s such as Dizzie Gillespie, John Coltrane, Ahmad Jamal, Miles Davis, Sun Ra, McCoy Tyner, Art Blakey,

Idris Sulieman, Lynn Hope, Yusuf Lateef, Thelonius Monk, Ahmed Abdul-Malik, and Khadijah, and Steve Davis (L. Porter 1999: 95–96, 107, 257; see also: Davis 1989; Gillespie 1979: 291; O' Connor 1993: 58–59). These artists actively merged new forms of social consciousness and activism and delved into eastern religions, contributing in no small measure to the popularization of Islamic growth among African Americans. Increasingly alienated and disenchanted African American working-class men and women in the 1940s admired the professional jazz, blues, and big band artists who provided a forum for the theatrical emergence of jazz and blues. Music, as spiritual as it was cultural, gradually displaced the role of religion in the lives of many urban blacks. Jazz artists by this time were experimenting with Bahai' ism, Islam, Hinduism, and other Eastern and alternative religious practices (Kelley 1994: 35–36; Malcolm X 1965: 43–52; E. Porter 1999; Jones 1963: 188; Deveaux 1977).

Between 1945 and 1954, this environment nurtured the lives of Boston residents like Steven Peters, Malcolm Little, Alfred Sutton, Charles Williams, Lloyd Williams, Jimmy Diamond, Charles O'Neil, Evelyn Williams, and Jack Byat. Their conversions and subsequent mobilization were instrumental in cultivating Islam among the city's African American population. Connected in their affinity for jazz music, these residents were eventually transformed by the new Islamic identity introduced by musicians who embraced Islam as taught by Ahmadiyya and NOI representatives (Abdul-Tawwab 2001: 27 n67; Szwed 1997: 4; 70; 105–106; Malcolm X 1965: 49–50; 110–111).[3]

Musicians and Ahmadi in Boston

Boston's artistic climate fostered a vibrant social life that would eventually connect residents with exciting forms of cultural innovation (Turner 1997: 138–146; Akbar 1996; S. Mahmoud 1998). Massachusetts Avenue and Columbus Avenue were at the heart of Boston's jazz scene with establishments such as the IIi Hat, Wally's Jazz Club, and the Savoy earning the South End neighborhood the nickname of "Harlem" during the 1930s and 1940s. At the Hi-Hat, one could hear the sounds of Fats Waller misbehaving, Lionel Hampton flying home, Count Basie jumping at the Woodside, and Duke Ellington taking the A Train. Jazz musicians and jazz lovers alike enjoyed the entertainment in Boston's renowned Rainbow Room where Lester ("Prez") Young, Buck Clayton, and Cootie Williams were featured. The Big Bands of Benny Goodman, Jimmy Lunceford, Charlie Barnett, and Woodie Herman kept throngs of Bostonians dancing all night long at the South End's Roseland Ballroom and the Raymor-Playmor Ballroom on Huntington Avenue.

The first African American Bostonians to convert to Islam did so after being exposed to Ahmadiyya Islam; they remained fixtures in this South End scene even after converting, providing an important link to Islam for the city's musician population. Formally established in 1889 by Mirza Ghulam Ahmed as an Islamic modernist response to Empire in British India, the Ahmadiyya movement used complex strategies to subvert European Christian dominance in the late nineteenth and early twentieth centuries and to establish Islam in the Christian West (Friedmann 1989: 3–10; Lavan 1974: 93).[4] While the global Islamic community's record for spreading Islam in the West was scant in the modern era, Indian Ahmadiyya Muslims focused on this task and began to officially disseminate Islam in America in 1920 with the arrival of Mufti Muhammad Siddiq in New York City. Ahmadiyya missionaries were active in the United States, notably among supporters of Marcus Garvey's Universal Negro Improvement Association (UNIA) and also among African American musicians (Turner 1997: 127–130; Simpkins 1989: 39–40; 115; E. Porter 1999: 423–429). Amina McCloud observes that Ahmadiyya converts to Islam drew heavily from jazz musicians and created a distinctly Islamic culture that was highly visible in African American urban centers between 1917 and 1960. According to McCloud, "... these musicians were major propagators of Islam in the world of jazz even though the subject of music was often a source of debate with the subcontinent Ahmadis. Some even developed a distinct jargon—a unique blend of bebop and Arabic" (Mc Cloud 1995: 20–21). For musicians traveling and playing on the East Coast, particularly New York City, Philadelphia, and Boston, the impact of the Ahmadiyya Muslims was considerable (Weinstein 1993: 51–54; Gillespie 1979: 291–293).

By 1945, the Ahmadiyya missionaries had established a beachhead among African Americans in Boston. Bashir Ahmad, a Philadelphia native and devout Muslim, was a vocal advocate of Islam for the Ahmadiyya movement in Boston (S. Mahmoud 1998; Williams 2000; Abdul-Tawwab 2001).[5] Adorned in Pakistani robe and headpiece, Ahmad's highly visible proselytizing paid high dividends when jazz pianist Stephen Peters embraced Islam later that year (S. Mahmoud 1998; K. Mahmoud 1994).[6] Changing his name to Khalil Mahmoud, Steven Peters used his jazz world connections to establish Islam as a viable alternative for African American musicians in Boston. Throughout the 1940s Mahmoud held Ahmadiyya meetings and Islamic study groups at his parents' Chilton Street home in Cambridge while still frequenting the South End to spread the message in his old haunts. In 1946, Mahmoud's close friend, musician Blazely Perry, introduced him to a young aspiring trumpet student named Malcolm Jarvis. In addition to expressing interest in learning more about Islam, Jarvis arranged to bring his friend, Malcolm Little, to meet Mahmoud (Hill 1999; Williams 1999; Perry 1991: 119; Bailey 1998: 116). Although not a musician, Little represented the growing number of African American urban men, disenchanted with Christianity and religion as they knew it, yet almost hypnotized by the singers and artists of jazz, blues, and bebop. For many of these individuals, the religious void was often unconsciously filled by the deeply spiritual and secular climate of the musicians' world. Unfortunately for Jarvis, he and his buddy Malcolm Little were both arrested and consequently convicted for burglary before the meeting with Mahmoud ever came to pass. These early musician-turned-Muslims were highly visible on account of their name changes, dress, behavior, and dialogue; they enjoyed significant stature among jazz and bebop musicians, a community whose cult-like characteristics and closeness encouraged cultural and religious replication among its members (Mc Cloud 1995: 21).

Khalil Mahmoud was prepared to launch an enthusiastic campaign to transform African Americans into Ahmadiyya Muslims. Between 1947 and 1952 an increasing number of the city's musicians began embracing Islam as taught by the venerable missionary. Jack Byat set an example when he converted and changed his name to Jahmid Ahmad Bashir. Lenny Grahm of the Savy Louis Band initially was exposed to Islam by Ahmadiyya in Boston in 1945; he embraced Ahmadi Islam while on the road in New York the following year. The new convert followed his predecessors, adopting the Islamic name of Idris Suleiman. Women working as artists and staff in the nightclub scene were equally exposed to Islam. Ahmadiyya musicians playing at the Savoy captivated bartender Eleanor Jumper, who credits her conversion to Islam while visiting with musician friends in New York City to her Boston-based Islamic acclimatization (Jumper 1999). During the early 1950s, Wilbur Lucas, known on the streets of Boston as "Crazy Wilbur," changed his name to Waji Lateef after embracing Ahmadi Islam (Williams 2000). As a devout Muslim, Khalil Mahmoud also spent significant time with the Arab Muslims of Quincy Point, providing an Ahmadiyya bridge between African American musicians and orthodox Islam.

Prior to 1950, the presence of traditional Islam in Boston was insignificant. Boston's first "orthodox" Islamic community traces its roots to the early portion of the twentieth century and the history of a community of immigrant Muslims fifteen minutes away from Dorchester in Quincy, Massachusetts. Although the majority of the Syrian and Lebanese immigrants who entered the United States between 1875 and 1912 were Arab Christians, seven families arriving in Massachusetts were

Muslim (Lahaj 1994: 293). In 1934 the Muslim Arabs joined with other Syrians and Lebanese to form the Arab American Banner Society (AABS) in an effort to retain their culture as Arab Americans. Outside of social gatherings and informal discussions, these Muslims made little effort to practice Islam or to pass it on to their children. A generation later, in the aftermath of World War II, the children of the seven Muslim families were completely assimilated into American culture. Many of the families could no longer speak or read the native Arabic language and even fewer possessed the ability or inclination to understand and adhere to Islamic practices.

Oriented toward establishing a cultural norm for AABS members as Arab Americans, the second generation of the Syrian and Lebanese Muslim families had only begun to organize an identifiably Islamic community in Quincy by 1950. In 1952 businessman Aziz Abraham served as the society's president alongside Sam Hassan. Fatima Allie, a teacher and school principal served as treasurer and secretary for a decade. According to one chronicler of the community's history, these adults initiated Islamic development after Christian Americans wondered aloud why these Arab American children did not attend any church. Although these overtures forced the Muslim Americans to initiate efforts to build a mosque, it was only after the emergence of an Islamic community among African Americans that these Muslim Americans made any active effort to propagate Islam in the larger society (Lahaj 1994: 294–298).

Contrasting sharply with the lethargy of Boston's orthodox Muslim community, Ahmadiyya and NOI Muslims vied with each other in a spirited race to propagate Islam among the city's African American population. Elijah Muhammad's syncretistic Islam introduced a third strand of Islamic development into Boston's jazz and bebop community. New York City musicians were among the first to transmit the NOI's ideology to Boston. As Khalil Mahmoud crusaded for Ahmadi Islam, Alfred Sutton, a World War II veteran and trumpeter infatuated with the new jazz of the bebop era, migrated to Boston from Ohio with the intention to study music at the Berklee School of Music on the GI bill (S. Mahmoud 1998; Akbar 1996). Although NOI doctrine differed dramatically from Ahmadiyya or orthodox interpretations of Islam, its members asserted the concept of an Islamic identity and perceived themselves as the true purveyors of Islam for black men and women. NOI ambassadors "fishing for souls" (the process of seeking converts) among musicians in Boston discovered an alert ear in the talented Sutton, who accepted his identity as a "righteous Muslim" in 1948. Sutton's conversion was as notable for its swiftness as for its sincerity and commitment. Pledging a support that would remain true for over forty years, Alfred X served as secretary of the

Boston Temple until 1973, during which time he forged a reputation for unstinting honesty and integrity within the local and national NOI communities (Akbar 1996; S. Mahmoud 1999).

Whereas Khalil Mahmoud suffered waning enthusiasm for his efforts to convert Bostonians to Ahmadi Islam, Alfred X began to draw increasing numbers. The promise of "a religion for the black man," a religion that liberated men and women spiritually, mentally, and economically, struck many Boston musicians as a more relevant and practical version of the spiritual wisdom they were already drawn to through Ahmadiyya missionaries. The teachings of the NOI are best understood as a perceptive and sagacious blend of mythology and masonry; a judicious and satirical commentary on American racism pointing to Islam as the solution. Khalil Mahmoud's newfound responsibilities of propagating Islam for the growing Ahmadiyya mission did not go unchallenged; armed with the NOI's powerful antidote for white supremacy, Alfred X Sutton proved to be a vigorous competitor in the rapidly developing race to claim followers of Islam in Boston.

At the same time, in the nearby Massachusetts Correctional Center, a young prisoner named Malcolm Little was brought into the NOI by direct correspondence from his Muslim brothers and the Honorable Elijah Muhammad himself. A personal friend of Billie Holiday, Malcolm had been part of the New York jazz scene prior to his incarceration (Malcolm X 1965: 128). Audacious, articulate, and well-informed, Malcolm affected the Boston scene from his prison cell.

Charles X Organizes the Early Community

On October 27, 1950, Charles X O' Neil walked out of the Massachusetts Correctional Institute at Norfolk a free man for the first time in seven years. Energized by Malcolm X Little, O' Neil was prepared to assist Alfred X Sutton in the race for converts. Approaching Bostonians with two self-assembled books—compilations of pictures and articles from *National Geographic* magazines chronicling archeological discoveries in Asia and Africa and labeled as "a history of the black man"—O' Neil's method was dramatic and immediately successful. A man of intense passion and competing interests, Charles O' Neil was known primarily for his love of music. Until his appearance on the scene, the majority of Bostonian musicians involved with Islam were Ahmadiyya. But from 1950 until Malcolm Little's release in 1952, O' Neil labored at the twin tasks of pointing

Bostonians to question the appropriateness of Christianity for black Americans and to join the NOI.

O' Neil directly transformed the spiritual character of the musicians' scene in Boston. His active proselytizing at social activities and progressive organizations in the South End during the 1950s exposed Charles Williams, an aspiring jazz pianist in the style of bebop innovator Bud Powell, to the NOI. Although Williams was exposed earlier to Islam through Ahmadi musicians, he opted for the NOI instead, attributing his decision to O' Neil's strong sense of self as an *African American* Muslim. By 1952, Northeastern University student Rodney Smith had joined Boston's NOI community (Williams 2000). Despite Smith's premature death, his conversion had important ramifications. As one of the most prominent young saxophonist in Boston, Smith's conversion influenced a number of local musicians including the talented young Louis Eugene Walcott, who succeeded Malcolm X as minister of the Boston Temple in 1957. Smith's esteem among the musicians also led to the conversion of William Bell, a socially conscious and progressive Afro-wearing artiste personally committed to actively targeting Boston youth by capitalizing on the connection of avant-garde jazz artists to young men and women who were influenced by the new music. One young musician who converted to Islam at this time described the attraction of aspiring young artists to Islam this way:

> Musicians were open to... ideas that are out of the ordinary for the masses. You know, there's this right-left brain theory; they claim that the musicians think on the right side, that's the creative side, where the left side is more logical. Well the musicians have a tendency because of the art in music... to have what you might consider... esoteric opportunities with information, knowledge, and therefore, you know most of the musicians... at that particular time were more interested in [Islam] or converted to Islam. So, there was an attraction because as a musician, I would be curious as to what it was about Islam that caused this Muslim to convert. (S. Mahmoud 1998)

With the conversion of drummer Charles Hester in 1951, a coalition of uprooted migrants, veterans, and musicians formed the structural backbone of the NOI's Temple Number 11 in Boston. Dubbed the "Musicians Five," the group emerged as a formidable opponent to the spread and growth of Ahmadiyya Islam among African Americans in Boston (Karim 1992).

The South End's Chicken Lane restaurant provides a microcosmic view of the Islamic culture that developed among musicians in the Northeast. Owned and operated by Syvalia Hyman, Sr., on Massachusetts and Columbus Avenue in the South End, it served as a social and leisure establishment and became an alternative to the Church for the budding African American Islamic community (Hyman 1999).[7] Mr. Hyman accommodated the dietary restrictions of the growing number of Muslim patrons by replacing oil that had been used to cook pork products with fresh oil to fry fish. Both NOI and Ahmadiyya members congregated at Chicken Lane, making the restaurant an important congregating center and fertile environment for both musicians and Muslims of Boston between 1948 and 1958.[8]

Malcolm X Returns

Despite the looming specter of McCarthyism and the rampant ignorance of Islam among the general populace, several factors combined to cultivate Islam among a skeptical but comparatively well-read youthful population of African American Bostonians between 1952 and 1954. Released on parole in 1952, Malcolm X Little headed to Chicago to meet Elijah Muhammad in person (Malcolm X 1965: 191).[9] By 1953, a reformed and zealous Malcolm Little was anxious to return to the scene of his social and moral undoing. In December Elijah Muhammad sent Malcolm back to the East Coast and Boston to propel development there. Arriving in Boston, Malcolm was met by the tiny but determined nucleus of believers intent on building lives based on their new identity as "righteous Muslims." Malcolm's presence energized the embryonic Muslim community and stimulated an intellectual awakening among receptive Bostonian youth (Karim 1994; Brown 1999; S. Mahmoud 1998; Robertson 1999; Gardell 1996: 119).

A spirit of camaraderie and intensive zeal transmitted the nascent movement throughout untouched corners of the northeast, with newly Islamicized musicians assuming the role of Islamic ambassadors. Liberated by the fervent work of Boston's Musicians Five, vigorous assistance from Malcolm X, and a rapidly growing number of new Muslims, Charles X O' Neil felt free to leave Boston and proselytize in other cities. Setting out for Atlantic City, O' Neil prepared to focus on an agenda of aggressive recruitment to the NOI instead of furthering his own career as a professional musician. Quickly finding work in a music store owned by African American Muslims, O' Neil was instrumental in organizing Atlantic City's NOI community, which received its official number in 1953. Thus it was primarily among musicians that the Atlantic City NOI Temple was established. The first informal interest sessions for Temple Number 10 were held in the Muslim owned music shop on Arctic Avenue (Karim 1994). As a traveling minister, Charles X worked closely with Malcolm X and Osborne Thaxton, another prison convert and promising musician. Early organizational efforts in Boston centered on formal biweekly meetings held at the South End apartments of various believers. Instrumental in assisting NOI affiliates in the New England and mid-Atlantic region, O' Neil, Little, and Thaxton spent the next two years in Boston; Springfield, Massachusetts; Atlantic City; and points in between, helping the Muslims everywhere—and particularly Boston's "Musicians Five"—to formally organize (Karim 1994; S. Mahmoud 1998; Malcolm X 1965: 212–215).

Although his duties did not allow him to remain solely in Boston, Malcolm X served as regional minister over all the formative East Coast Temples until a permanent minister was approved. During this time he worked closely with the musicians, training and preparing them to establish themselves as a Muslim community in affiliation with the philosophy and teachings of the Honorable Elijah Muhammad. Although there was no official minister in residence in Boston at this time, Lloyd Williams [a trumpet player], served as an unofficial minister of sorts underneath Malcolm in 1953 and 1954. While Malcolm X was out of town, Lloyd X often spoke from the rostrum as Minister, with Charles 2X, Charles X, or any of the other young men opening the meetings for him. Due to the informal organizational structure of the community prior to induction in 1954, formal tittles simply did not exist. At this time, meetings were being held in Lloyd Williams's residence on Wellington Avenue in Boston's Roxbury neighborhood. As an individual familiar to the community, Lloyd X was viewed as a leader in Malcolm's absence. In the absence of a representative from Chicago, the musicians of Boston did provide the informal leadership structure for the community at this time (Malcolm X 1965: 211–215; Karim 1992: 43–44; Magida 1996 34–35).[10]

Temple Number 11 grew from five men to approximately fourteen individuals by 1953 and exhibited a spirit of camaraderie that magnetized other musicians toward the movement. In Boston, a connection based on the love and study of music is clearly visible in stories of the city's pioneer African American Muslim population. Illustratively, Charles O' Neil, William Bell, Rodney Smith, Charles Hester, and Charles Williams met at a dormitory styled house on Massachusetts Avenue that served as the residence of unmarried women students attending school in the Boston metro area. Evelyn Williams, the younger sister of Charles X Williams, resided there while studying opera at the New England Conservatory. Other residents included Coretta Scott, an opera student at Boston University, and Boston University student Lucille Rosary. While Scott was a devout Christian who began dating Martin Luther King, Jr. (then a young doctoral student at Boston University's School of Theology), her roommates Williams and Rosary were attracted to the teachings of Islam as administered by O' Neil and his circle. Through Malcolm's proselytizing efforts, Evelyn Williams became one of the first women converts to embrace the teachings of Elijah Muhammad in Boston. By the close of 1954, the community gained formal status when Elijah Muhammad sent Ulysses X from Chicago to guide the community's development as dictated by NOI organizational and structural components (Williams 2000; Robertson 1999).

Intra-Islamic Showdown

The presence of the NOI posed a challenge to the further growth of Boston's Ahmadiyya Islamic community. Saxophonist James Diamond experienced this intra-Islamic tension firsthand. Diamond's eventual acceptance of Elijah Muhammad's Islam is illustrative of three separate yet related strands affecting many of the early Muslims in Boston: the dynamics of the social influence of musicians; the presence of Ahmadiyya Muslims; and the undeniably powerful impact of the up and coming Minister Malcolm X. Diamond aspired to stardom at the age of 16, after bebop legend Charlie Parker directly praised his saxophone playing. The Boston high school student was first exposed to Islam through an invitation by Khalil Mahmoud to attend an Ahmadi meeting in Cambridge. Khalil Mahmoud was intent on convincing the spiritually seeking musicians that while Islam truly liberated the oppressed, it was universal and best understood within the context and approach of the Ahmadiyya Muslims (S. Mahmoud 1999).

At the same time, Alfred Sutton labored with equal persistence in Boston's South End. Numbered among Sutton's prospective converts, Mahmoud humorously described his efforts to dodge the dogged Alfred X Sutton while attempting to frequent South End musician circles. As this strategy proved futile, he finally agreed to visit the makeshift NOI Temple on Wellington Avenue. On his sixth visit Mahmoud resolved his hesitancies; he recalled later: "Eventually I was satisfied because Malcolm at that time could answer the questions that I posed to him." Convinced of the "truth" of the teachings of the NOI, he stood and proceeded to "accept his own" by joining the NOI (S. Mahmoud 1998).[11]

Efforts undertaken by Charles X O' Neil, Alfred Sutton, Charles Hester, Charles Williams, Lloyd Williams, Rodney Smith, and William Bell continued to multiply with result as more Bostonians, young and old, began joining the ranks of the city's NOI members. Adnan Shabazz, Diamond's best friend, had "accepted his own" a month earlier. A native Bostonian, the young high school student was an avid reader and budding intellectual. Other new recruits included Frederick Young and Jordan Smith (both pseudonyms), who were coworkers at a local factory. Smith in turn successfully encouraged his wife Elizabeth, and in-laws Alberta and Paul Pope, to embrace the religion in 1953. Sisters Elizabeth and Alberta were both raised by strong Garveyite parents who had migrated to Boston from Jamaica shortly after World War I (Smith 1999; Young 1999). Young Jimmy X Diamond and Charles X Williams recalled visiting nearly every African American church in the city. According to both men, the African American city churches would allow the young NOI ambassadors to speak before congregations on topics of African American and African history as well as the teachings of the Honorable Elijah Muhammad. As their numbers steadily increased, Muslims felt they were on their way to revitalizing their city and awakening their slumbering peers.

By 1954, Boston beat Philadelphia in an intense race to be formally incorporated into the national movement. Due to hard work and the unflagging efforts of the Musicians Five, the Boston community received its official number: "11." As the community continued to expand, so did the need for larger quarters. Collectively raising the funds to rent an old fish market on Columbus Avenue, the community transformed the building into headquarters that served as home until 1955. As the locus of the African American community began to shift from the South End to other parts of Roxbury and Dorchester, the Muslims shifted their hunt for a home as well. Less than a year later, the faithful were renting a space in the Grove Hall section of Blue Hill Avenue, virtually a three-minute walk from their future and final home at 35 Intervale Street (S. Mahmoud 1998). The community's expansion and moves throughout the city also illustrate its increasing impact on the surrounding African American communities. The areas were consequently "cleaned up" to a certain degree as the Muslims did not allow drug sales, prostitution, or other social ills to continue in those areas they considered home (Williams 2000).

The Boston Temple established meetings for the general public on Sundays at 2 PM, as well as Wednesdays and Fridays at 8 PM, *every single week of the year.* It was almost impossible to be an African American resident of the city without at least hearing of, if not attending, a meeting. The closely knit group was indeed "cult-like" in its organization during these years; this sense of community served as a powerful attraction for other young African American Bostonians (S. Mahmoud 1998; Williams 2000).

Boston's NOI community was distinct for several reasons. Temple Number 11 boasted a membership that was educated both academically and culturally. Whereas the historic membership of NOI temples in the

Midwest had been composed of semiliterate to illiterate working-class individuals, Boston's intellectual climate fostered a group more proportionately representative of an educated segment of the African American population (Abdul-Tawwab 2001: 34, 62). NOI teachings gave community members a strong moral code with a mythology purportedly originating from the East that promoted images of an era when the Western world lived in primeval conditions and the religion called Islam civilized an ancient world. Decidedly harsh, uncompromisingly strict, and intent on satirizing the racist and imprisoning rhetoric that loomed over the political, religious, educational, and economic institutions of African Americans, the program of the NOI called first and foremost for black men and women to assume a new identity. Not based on money, stature, or (surprisingly enough) race, this identity was that of a righteous Muslim. Preceding the emphasis on recapturing and redefining African American history as advocated by the Black Power Movement activists of the 1960 and 1970s, the NOI in its early decades attempted to uncover and promote glorious aspects of black history (Abdul-Tawwab 2001: 44–46).

Native Son Louis Comes In

The formative community was rapidly on its way to becoming a viable and longstanding entity within Boston's African American community. Few were aware of the full impact that the still rather small group of African American adherents to the Honorable Elijah Muhammad's teachings would have on the city. Conspicuous in dress, proud in their mission, and calm in their approach, the fledgling community was prepared to bring remarkable social and economic changes to an African American community in Boston that was ready for new leadership. The political and economic prominence enjoyed by black Bostonians in the last quarter of the nineteenth century had faded to political impotence and economic invisibility by the middle of the twentieth century. Temple Number 11 provided a blueprint that attracted both industrious migrants and the offspring of Garvey's Black Legionnaires. By the mid 1960s, even the cultured heirs of Booker T. Washington's National Negro Business League, William Monroe Trotter's protest tradition, and Mary Evans Wilson's National Association for the Advancement of Colored People (NAACP), would have been affected by the leadership of Minister Malcolm, his understudy Minister Louis, and their new Temple Number 11.

Temple Number 11 was a center of religious, cultural, and ideological activity during the two decades that bridged the jailhouse conversion of

Malcolm Little and the Memphis assassination of Martin Luther King, Jr. While the 1955 Montgomery Bus Boycott provided a theater for the emergence of the youthful Martin Luther King, Jr. and Ralph David Abernathy, the 1954 incorporation of Boston's Temple Number 11 launched the equally youthful duo of Malcolm X (later Shabazz) and Louis Farrakhan. As the Boston affiliate of the NOI, Temple Number 11 provided an important positive recasting of what it meant to be black and assumed a pivotal role in the emergence of an Islamic community in Boston.

At a local night club in Chicago, the Bostonian and saxophonist Rodney X Smith ran into another old friend from Boston, a charismatic Calypso singer by the name of Louis Gene Walcott. Smith introduced Walcott to NOI teachings and invited him to hear the Honorable Elijah Muhammad speak. While Walcott did not embrace the teachings then, he did agree to visit the Temple back in Boston upon his return. A few months later, during 1956, Walcott applied for his X in Boston. Working closely with Minister Malcolm, and building upon the artistic heritage of the pioneer group, Walcott provided the leadership that would culminate in Temple Number 11's stature as a community institution for Boston's African American population. These talented Muslim artists channeled their creative ability into strengthening the spiritual, cultural and economic life of Boston's African American community.

Adeptly blending the artistic culture of his middle-class upbringing while tapping into the calypso, jazz, and bebop legacy of his short-lived career as a musician, Minister Louis melded the uncompromising morality and clear social agenda of Elijah Muhammad's NOI into music and art that could be enjoyed by a wide spectrum of Bostonians. To this end, Minister Louis worked with other talented men and women, particularly the educators who flocked into the community over the next twelve years, in writing and performing plays, recording albums, and promoting independent thought and cultural expression in Boston. The plays were entitled *Orgena* and *The Trial*. *Orgena* is "A Negro" spelled backwards. Utilizing scripts written by a local Boston educator who had embraced the NOI's teachings, Minister Louis helped produce the two plays.

The plays were significant because they were among the first modern attempts of African Americans in Boston to publicly challenge the blatantly racist depictions of African Americans ingrained in all levels and institutions of American society. Indeed, the population of Temple Number 11 did increase after the Boston debut of both plays at the John Hancock Hall. The critical point here is that "Boston Negroes were those within the movement who dramatized it" (Edwards and Morris 1961: 87).[12] Members of the original cast asserted that the play, which debuted to sell-out audiences at the John Hancock Hall, had a tremendous recruitment influence in Boston and other cities where it purportedly sent "shock waves through" Boston's African American community while delivering aspects of the Honorable Elijah Muhammad's teachings in a manner that could not be ignored (Abdul-Tawwab, 2001, 112–115; Al-Mahdi, 1999; Ilyas 1999). One Muslim living in Boston during this period later said that the play inspired local Christian ministers to respond more directly to the practical needs of the city's African American population by prompting many preachers to "change the way they were teaching in Church [and make their teachings] less spooky" (Al-Mahdi, 1999; Ilyas 1999).[13]

The play depicted a nobler image of African culture which belied the stereotypical roles often portrayed in American films and theatre of the time. The play opened with the Islamic call to prayer, highlighting the fact that the first *mu'athen* (one who gives the call to *salat* or prayer) in Islam was Bilal ibn Rabah, a former enslaved Abyssinian and companion of the Prophet Muhammad (Abdul-Rauf 1977: 1, 63–66). Brother Hendricks X Van Leesten, a talented vocalist played the role of the *mu'adhin*. Van Leesten's *adhan* (call to prayer) was so stirring and perfect in accent, pitch, and tone that Arab viewers in the audience swore he was an Arab (Abdul-Tawwab 2001: 112–113). *Orgena* attempted to change the public's narrow-minded stereotypes of Islam, or at the very least, challenge them. The NOI tapped an important and well-kept secret in hinting at the illustrious heritage of Africans prior to the Atlantic slave trade, along with the Islamic roots of many enslaved Africans. For many, the play succeeded in linking a religious past to African Americans outside of a purely Christian or tribal context (Ilyas 1999).

The Trial was always shown on the same bill as *Orgena*. It depicted the "black man" bringing a white defendant to trial for all of the oppressive sins waged against African Americans by the engineers of American society. The all-black jury returned a "guilty" verdict on all charges and the play ended, to its viewers' delight, with the white defendant being dragged off stage "loudly protesting his innocence and enumerating all he had done for the nigra people" (Robertson 1999; Abdul-Tawwab 2001: 113–114). Young African American viewers were alternately shocked, delighted, and intrigued at the ideas presented in the plays—particularly the notion that the true identity of the African American was as a "righteous Muslim" who, upon restoring that true identity, would hold the previously unaccountable white man for heinous crimes against black Americans and their ancestors.

Minister Louis also wrote and recorded a ten and a half-minute song entitled "The White Man's Heaven is the Black Man's Hell" in 1958, which he performed live for the first time at that year's "Saviours' Day Convention." The songs and plays both assisted in stirring the consciousness of African Americans throughout the Nation. By 1962, *Orgena* and *The Trial* had attracted thousands of Bostonians and "The White Man's Heaven is the Black Man's Hell" was well-known among youth on the streets of Roxbury and Dorchester. Under the innovative leadership of Minister Louis, who skillfully tapped into the artistic background of the Bostonian Muslims, Temple Number 11 gave the NOI and its philosophy more exposure in the Boston area than even Malcolm had.[14]

Elma Lewis, a prominent arts educator and founder of the Elma Lewis School of Fine Arts and the Museum of the National Center for African American Artists, was likely influenced by the arts activity facilitated by the NOI in Boston. A longtime friend of Minister Louis, Elma Lewis grew up performing at cultural events and recitals with the young Louis Walcott in the Afro-Caribbean community of Boston's Saint Cyprian's Church. From the1960s through the 1980s she was responsible for establishing the annual production in Boston of the Langston Hughes Christmas spectacular, *Black Nativity*. While her performances were more subtle than the audacious and exciting "Black Muslim" cultural productions of the late 1950s and early 1960s, it is likely that the publicized and stirring plays of her childhood stage partner had some impact of the direction of Ms. Lewis's own subsequent productions. This African American rendering of the story of Christ's nativity challenges white racism and promotes black identity in a manner reminiscent of (and indeed—not seen on Boston stages prior to) Louis X's *Orgena* and *The Trial*.

Conclusion

Ahmadiyya engagement among Boston musicians introduced Islam to African Americans and led to Islam's acceptance among members of this small yet critical segment of the city's African American population. It engendered a climate and culture that was conducive to Islamic growth among other musicians and musically inclined African Americans in Boston. These Boston-based artists, veterans, and migrants of the World War II generation secured their reputations as progenitors of consciousness-raising and social activism in the tradition of their predecessors during the New Negro Movement that spawned the Harlem Renaissance. Upon embracing Islam, these artistically inclined individuals dedicated their lives to community building, establishing Islam, and promoting increased African American pride and self-knowledge. Their artistic programs forced the general public to confront the ideology of Elijah Muhammad by presenting it in a palatable and entertaining mode. In their late teens and early twenties, the Boston artists also foreshadowed the youth who would give birth to the revolutionary sounds of rap during the late 1970s and early 1980s. As the initial transmitters of both Ahmadi Islam and Elijah Muhammad's proto-Islamic teachings, the musicians planted Islamic roots within the African American population of Boston.

Notes

1. The Nation of Islam (NOI) was officially established in 1930 by W. D. Fard Muhammad in Paradise Valley in Detroit, Michigan (Beynon 1938: 896). The first proto-Islamic organization established among African Americans was the Moorish Science Temple of America. Recent scholarship lists "either 1912 or 1913" as the probable year that Noble Drew Ali established the Canaanite Temple in Newark, New Jersey. Aside from official Moorish doctrine however, no evidence has surfaced to establish a Moorish presence prior to the organization's 1926 official incorporation in Chicago, Illinois, as the "Moorish Holy Temple of Science" (Gomez 2005: 206, 215).

2. While Thernstrom (1973) argues that the majority of African American Bostonians were *not* significantly better off than their Southern migrant counterparts in Boston, this does not nullify the fact that many African Americans born and raised in "Freedom's Birthplace" understood their own status as superior to the more recent Southern arrivals. Bostonians interviewed by the author as late as 1999 vividly recalled examples of a perceived distinction among themselves (as second or third generation Bostonians) and newer migrants arriving in the aftermath of World War II. See Abdul-Tawwab (2001: 28–29); Daniels (1914); Malcolm X (1965: 40–41); Cromwell (1994: 171–172); and Jamal (1972: 109).

3. Though Malcolm X did not come directly to Islam through musicians, his autobiography contains illustrations of his close contact with numerous African American musicians. Moreover, his close friend and running buddy Malcolm Jarvis (also an aspiring musician) had been invited to the Ahmadiyya Mosque in Cambridge by Khalil Mahmoud. See K. Mahmoud (1998); S. Mahmoud (1998); Hill (1998); Williams (1998).

4. Owing to a doctrinal position that seemed to challenge the finality of Muhammad's prophethood, the Ahmadiyya were considered a heretical sect by most of the Islamic world.

5. To date the interviews of contemporaries are the only evidence for Ahmadiyya presence in the city prior to 1940.

6. Endowed with considerable talent, young Steven was trained in the piano from an early age. Despite remarkable brilliance and academic aptitude, Peters dropped out of high school to pursue his musical aspirations. By the 1930s, Peters had quickly become a household name among local Boston musicians,

a name he subsequently changed. Abandoning his career as a professional musician, Khalil Mahmoud obtained his GED, or high school equivalency diploma, before enrolling as a freshman at Boston University. Following his graduation from Boston University, he continued his academic journey, receiving MA and PhD degrees in Montreal at McGill University. Traveling around the world as an Ahmadiyya missionary and educator, Mahmoud spent time living in London as well as West Africa. In London Mahmoud and theologian Howard Thurman met by chance. The meeting impressed young Thurman so greatly that he recorded it in his autobiography (Thurman 1979: 198). Thurman may have given an incorrect name for Mahmoud or attempted to use an alias. Khalil Mahmoud's career culminated as librarian and professor of religion in the Department of Religion and Langston Hughes Memorial Library's Special Collections, Lincoln University. Mahmoud was also the author's professor while an undergraduate student at Lincoln University, 1993–1997.

7. The Chicken Lane restaurant, owned by Mr. Syvalia Hyman, is listed in *City Directories of the United States* (1946: 903).

8. In interviews with the author, several older Boston men signaled the presence of Muslims from the Moorish Science Temple. This connection deserves further research.

9. While in Chicago, he began the formal stage of his ministerial training. Under the tutelage of his elder brother Wilfred, the Honorable Elijah Muhammad, and Minister Lemuel Hassan, Malcolm quickly rose to the position of assistant minister in Detroit. Within a year, the young Muslim had learned enough to be of greater use to the organization elsewhere. During this time, Malcolm kept in close contact with the brothers back in the South End.

10. Between 1952 and 1954, Malcolm worked to revive the membership in Detroit. Working with local northeastern believers, Malcolm initiated the formation of official Temples in Philadelphia, Boston, Springfield, Hartford, and Atlantic City. In Boston, Malcolm would often deliver lectures in the apartment at 5 Wellington Avenue in the South End.

11. Before his conversion to Islam, Mahmoud's name was James (Jimmy) Diamond. Mahmoud later became the Resident Imam of Boston's Masjid Muhammad (the renamed Temple Number 11).

12. Very few could remain ignorant of the plays after Mike Wallace's sensational media coverage of the Muslims, which opened with the closing scene from *The Trial*. Excerpts from the play were transmitted to television viewers who watched "The Hate That Hate Produced," a national television special that aired in 1959 with Mike Wallace and journalist Louis Lomax. See Lincoln (1994: 69).

13. Even for those Bostonians who did not actually attend the play, wide circulation of the *Muhammad Speaks* newspaper allowed them to read about it. Readers learned that celebrities such as singer Nancy Wilson had seen, and were profoundly influenced by, the play. One commentator observed: "One could hardly argue with the major truth of the theme of injustices which

it [the two plays *Orgena* and *The Trial*] presents. After *Birth of a Nation*, Jim Crow minstrel shows, and *Amos and Andy*, Minister Louis X's play was quite revolutionary for Boston" (Al-Mahdi 1999). According to one Bostonian, "*Oregena* [and *The Trial*] had [a] dramatic impact on the black community. Keep in mind: it was bold. Nobody ever heard of putting the white man on trial and finding him guilty" (Al-Mahdi 1999; Ilyas 1999).

14. However, Elijah Muhammad was wary of the complexities involved in American entertainment life. Despite the success of the shows, he asked Minister Louis to choose between show life and ministry within the NOI. Keeping in line with the strict rules governing a NOI minister, Louis X ceased public productions of both *Orgena* and *The Trial*. Illustrative of the specific agenda of Muhammad's NOI, the career of Minister Louis, while not developing as an entertainer per se, would take flight as a religious leader and community activist. As Muhammad recognized the value of channeling the creative energies of his members into further development of the NOI agenda, the Muslims were still allowed to perform the play for all-Muslim audiences.

Bibliography

Published Works

Abdul-Rauf, Muhammad (1977). *Bilal Ibn Rabah: A Leading Companion of the Prophet Muhammad*. Burr Ridge, IL: American Trust Publications.

Abdul-Tawwab, Fatimah (2001). "'Doing for Self!': The Nation of Islam's Temple # 11 and Its Impact on Social and Economic Development of Boston's African-American Community, 1948–1968." MA Thesis, Tufts University.

Bailey, A. Peter (1998). *Seventh Child: A Family Memoir of Malcolm X*. Secaucus, NJ: Carol Publishing Group.

Beynon, Erdmann Doane (1938). "The Voodoo Cult among Negro Migrants in Detroit," *The American Journal of Sociology* 43 (May): 894–907.

City Directories of the United States 1936–1960. Boston, MA. Library of Congress 1946 Reel 11: 903.

Cromwell, Adelaide M. (1994). *The Other Brahmins: Boston's Black Upper Class 1750–1950*. Fayetteville: The University of Arkansas Press.

Dalfiume, Richard M. (1969). *Desegregation of the U.S. Armed Forces: Fighting on Two Fronts, 1939–1969*. Columbia: University of Missouri Press.

Daniels, John (1914). *In Freedom's Birthplace: A Study of the Boston Negroes*. New York: Houghton Mifflin.

Davis, Miles with Quincy Troupe (1989). *Miles: The Autobiography*. New York: Simon and Schuster.

Deveaux, Scott (1977). *The Birth of Bebop: A Social and Music History*. Berkeley: University of California Press.

Edwards, Rheable M. and Laura B. Morris (1961). *The Negro in Boston*. Boston: Action for Boston Community Development.

Friedmann, Yohan (1989). *Prophecy Continued: Aspects of Ahmadi Religious Thought and Its Medieval Background*. Berkeley: University of California Press.

Gardell, Mattias (1996). *In the Name of Elijah Muhammad: Louis Farrakhan and the Nation of Islam*. Durham, NC: Duke University Press.

Gillespie, Dizzie (1979). *Dizzie Gillespie, To Be or Not…to Bop: Memoirs*. Garden City, NY: Doubleday.

Gomez, Michael (2005). *Black Crescent: The Experience and Legacy of African Muslims in America*. Cambridge: Cambridge University Press.

Hayden, Robert C. (1991). *African-Americans in Boston: More than 350 Years*. Boston: Trustees of the Boston Public Library.

Jamal, Hakim (1972). *From the Dead Level: Malcolm X and Me*. New York: Random House.

Jones, LeRoi (Amiri Baraka) (1963). *Blues People: Negro Music in White America*. New York: Quill.

Karim, Benjamin (1992). *Remembering Malcolm: The Story of Malcolm X from Inside the Muslim Mosque by His Assistant Minister Benjamin Karim*. With David Gallen and Peter Skutches. New York: Carroll and Graf.

Kelley, Robyn D. G. (1994). *Race Rebels: Culture, Politics, and the Black Working Class*. New York: The Free Press.

Lahaj, Mary (1994). "The Islamic Center of New England." In Yvonne Y. Haddad and Jane I. Smith (eds.), *Muslim Communities in North America*, 293. New York: SUNY Press.

Lavan, Spencer (1974). *The Ahmadiyya Movement: A History and Perspective*. New Delhi, India: Manohar Book Service.

Lincoln, C. Eric (1994) [1961]. *The Black Muslims in America*. Trenton, NJ: African World Press.

Magida, Arthur (1996). *Prophet of Rage: A Life of Louis Farrakhan and His Nation*. New York: Basic Books.

Malcolm X (1965). *The Autobiography of Malcolm X as Told to Alex Haley*. New York: Ballantine.

McCloud, Beverly Aminah (1995). *African-American Islam*. New York: Routledge.

O' Connor, Thomas (1993). *Building A New Boston: Politics and Urban Renewal, 1950–1970*. Boston: Northeastern University Press.

Perry, Bruce (1991). *Malcolm: The Life of a Man Who Changed America*. New York: Station Hill Press.

Porter, Eric (1999). "Dizzy Atmosphere: The Challenge of Bop," *American Music* 17/4 (Winter): 422–446.

Porter, Lewis (1999). *John Coltrane: His Life and Music*. Ann Arbor: The University of Michigan Press.

Simpkins, Cuthbert Ormand (1989). *Coltrane: A Biography*. Baltimore, MD: Black Classic Press.

Szwed, John F. (1997). *Space Is the Place: The Lives and Times of Sun Ra*. New York: Da Capo Press.

Thernstrom, Stephan (1973). *The Other Bostonians: Poverty and Progress in the American Metropolis, 1880–1970.* Cambridge, MA: Harvard University Press.
Thurman, Howard (1979). *With Head and Heart: The Autobiography of Howard Thurman.* New York: Harcourt Brace Jovanovich.
Turner, Richard Brent (1997). *Islam in the African-American Experience.* Bloomington: Indiana University Press.
Weinstein, Norman (1993). *A Night in Tunisia: Imaginings of Africa in Jazz.* New York: Limelight Editions.

Recorded Interviews/Cassette Tapes

All cassette tapes and interview transcripts are in the personal collection of the author.
Al-Mahdi, Abu-Kufu (1999) and Author. Boston, MA.
Austin, Saladin (2000) and Author. Boston, MA.
Brown, Evelyn (1999) and Author. Boston MA.
Hyman Jr., Syvalia (1999) and Author. Boston, MA.
Ilyas, Na'imah (1999) and Author. Mattapan, MA.
Jumper, Eleanor (pseudonym) (1999) and Author. Boston, MA.
Mahmoud, Shakir (1998) and Author. Brockton, MA.
Robertson, Arlene (1998) and Author. Mattapan, MA.
Smith, Jordan (pseudonym) (1999) and Author. Boston, MA.
Williams, Charles (2000) and Author. South End, Boston, MA (September 18; September 20).
Young, Frederick (pseudonym) (1999) and Author. Boston, MA.

Telephone Interviews and Unrecorded Interviews

Hill, Marilyn (1998); (1999) and Author. Telephone Interviews.
Mahmoud, Khalil (1994); (1998) and Author. Lincoln University, PA.
Williams, Beverley (1998); (1999) and Author. Telephone interviews.

Interview Transcripts

Akbar, Rafiq (1996) and Author. Boston, MA.
Karim, Rashida Ali (1994) with Qasim Abdul-Tawwab. Boston, MA.

Part 2

Diaspora in Literature and Culture

Chapter 4

Robert Nathaniel Dett and African America's Christian Kingdom of Culture, 1926–1932

Regennia N. Williams

> *For my people everywhere*
> *singing their slave songs repeatedly*
>
> —*Margaret Walker Alexander, For My People*

Introduction

"My interest in art and history began, almost imperceptibly, on hearing R. Nathaniel Dett's 'Listen to the Lambs' being sung one evening around the piano in the front room of my grandparents' house in Memphis." This confession by Sterling Stuckey, professor emeritus of history and religious studies at the University of California, Riverside, is the opening line in the Preface to *Going through the Storm: The Influence of African American Art in History*, a collection of essays on the history and culture of people in the North American region of the African diaspora. Stuckey's statement reflects more than personal reminiscence alone; it also suggests something about the centrality of African American sacred music—and a particular music maker—in the life of a community. Stuckey goes on to say of Dett's composition:

> It was so much a part of the young men and women who sang it, so much a
> joy to all who heard it, that, as young as I was, I was dimly conscious of a
> shared richness in our lives. Not long thereafter, while listening to poetry
> that was anchored in deep currents of reality, I came to realize that the con-
> juncture of art and history was as natural as that between the lives we lived
> and the flow of historical time. (1994: vii)

The spiritual that inspired Robert Nathaniel Dett's "Listen to the
Lambs" is part of the body of sacred songs created by enslaved men and
women in the antebellum American South. These songs are at once among
the most popular and most controversial cultural expressions to come out
of the Christian religious experiences of the people of the African diaspora.
Although this is not a new revelation, a thorough discussion of the contro-
versy in which the music was sometimes ensnared is frequently omitted
from scholarly discussions about the musical expressions of the diaspora.
Knowing that omissions, if not addressed, can result in historical erasure,
this chapter is offered in part as a historical corrective designed to promote
a better understanding of the social context in which the music and the
music makers emerged. It focuses on Robert Nathaniel Dett (1882–1943),
one of the twentieth century's most prolific African American musicians.
This study of Dett's life, work, cultural politics, and legacy seeks to
contribute to a rich and growing body of knowledge on the history of the
African diaspora.

Dett sought to establish a permanent place for the religious expressions of
African American Christians in academic and concert arenas that were
divided along racial lines. To borrow the words of William Edward Burghardt
Du Bois, Dett wanted to be a "co-worker in the kingdom of culture." He
strove to become an artist of the highest order. He was proud of his ancestry
and anxious to use the religious folk songs of his people as inspiration for a
variety of concert music settings. His efforts did not go unnoticed.

During his lifetime, Dett was recognized as a gifted composer and
arranger of African American sacred choral and instrumental music, a
celebrated concert pianist, and a renowned faculty member at several
historically black colleges and universities. Among his peers in the African
American community, he established an enviable record of service as one
of the leading early-twentieth-century intellectuals of his race. Dett's
efforts to institutionalize his ideas about sacred "race music," especially
works based on nineteenth-century spirituals, are evidence of a significant
aspect of African American culture. Unfortunately, like the larger subject
of spirituals in historical studies of the diaspora, Dett's name is frequently
omitted in scholarly studies of early-twentieth-century African American
cultural history.

These obvious omissions raise a number of important questions for anyone interested in studying the intersections of race, religion, and uplift ideology. Among the most important questions are: What was Dett's philosophy on the use of African American cultural expressions as source material for his work as a composer of sacred music? Why should Dett be viewed as an opinion leader in the African American community? Did he face any opposition or criticism in his efforts to use art as a tool to uplift and inspire members of his race? If so, how did Dett answer his opponents and critics? Finally, how might a closer examination of his religious works in relation to those of secular artists of his day yield new information on the social and religious cultural history of African Americans and the relationship of their culture to others in the Atlantic world? This chapter begins to answer some of these questions and sheds new light on the influence of African American religious music outside the church.

This analysis is based upon information in several collections in academic and public libraries. Sources include letters and other primary documents related to the life of Robert Nathaniel Dett and published works on Dett and diasporic Africa. This overview of Dett's professional activities begins in 1926, the year in which he was appointed director of the music program at Hampton Institute and received the honorary Doctor of Music degree from Oberlin College. The study ends in 1932, when Dett earned his Master of Music degree from the Eastman School of Music and resigned (under fire) from his position at Hampton.[1] The end of the Hampton era coincided with the closing years of the Harlem Renaissance and the year in which Democrat Franklin D. Roosevelt was elected to the presidency of the United States for the first time. It was the beginning of the era of the Great Depression, when millions of Americans, including those in the "kingdom of culture," were especially hard-hit by the nation's economic downturn, and poverty was widespread on both sides of the color line.

Black Souls, Black Music, and Black Authenticity in the Diaspora: A Review of the Literature

William Edward Burghardt Du Bois, who is often credited with being the father of pan-Africanism and Black Studies in the academy, published in 1903 a collection of essays under the title *The Souls of Black Folk*. This work reveals that Du Bois understood better than many intellectuals of his day the many burdens, including psychological ones, borne by African

Americans living in a racist and racially polarized society. Ninety years after the book's publication, Paul Gilroy described *Souls* as "a key text," because

> it underpins all that follows it, and its importance is marked by the way Du Bois places black music as the central sign of black cultural value, integrity, and autonomy.... *The Souls* is the place where slave music is signaled in its special position of privileged signifier of black authenticity. (1993: 90)

As Gilroy subsequently remarks, this idea of "black authenticity" surfaces again and again in studies of early-twentieth-century African American art. This is certainly the case with much of the criticism of Dett's work.

In *Souls*, Du Bois also uses the idea of "double consciousness" or "two-ness" in an effort to explain the tensions felt by persons living within "The Veil": his term for the separate and inferior position to which African Americans were relegated, even if this veiled existence kept authentic cultural expressions alive. In describing these tensions, Du Bois states: "One ever feels his two-ness: two thoughts, two souls, two longings, two unreconciled strivings in one dark body, whose dogged strength alone keeps it from being torn asunder" (Du Bois 1986 [1903]: 364–365; compare Hubbard 2003). The circumstances in which the black masses found themselves were indeed dire. Even as he described these problems, however, Du Bois also sounded a note of cautious optimism by suggesting that the tensions associated with the "strivings" would be resolved when the African American became "a co-worker in the kingdom of culture," thereby escaping "both death and isolation," and earning the right to "husband his best powers and his latent genius" (365). Du Bois remained convinced that race and racism would be problematic for the foreseeable future, concluding famously: "The problem of the twentieth century is the problem of the color line." In the closing chapter of *Souls*, however, another cautious note of optimism is sounded when Du Bois suggests that "America shall rend the Veil and the prisoned shall go free." The key to this future freedom, according to Du Bois, is rooted in "the hope that sang in the songs of [his enslaved] fathers" (359, 545)."[2]

At first glance, Du Bois appears to be an unlikely music critic. With degrees in history and philosophy from Fisk and Harvard, and advanced studies in the emerging discipline of sociology from the University of Berlin, Du Bois confessed his ignorance concerning the technical aspects of the music that he thought so highly of:

> What are these songs, and what do they mean? I know little of music and can say nothing in technical phrase, but I know something of men, and knowing them, I know that these songs are the articulate message of the slave to the world. (538)

At other points in *Souls* he describes the songs as "the most beautiful expression of human experience born this side of the seas" and "the greatest gift of the Negro people" (536–537). His laudatory statements on the importance of the spirituals were frequently associated with the performances of the Fisk Jubilee Singers. Beginning in 1871, this group of African American college musicians began a series of fundraising tours in the United States and Europe, performing spirituals in concert settings and sharing African American sacred music with white audiences, many of which were hearing these songs for the first time (see Ward 2001).

It is clear from his discussion that Du Bois, although lacking the training that would have allowed him to offer a formal analysis of the music, certainly understood the value of this religious art form to social historians and social scientists interested in chronicling the activities of ordinary African American people, including the college students who enjoyed the extraordinary opportunity to travel and perform authentic African American music abroad. Du Bois's contemporary, Alain Locke, agreed with Du Bois about the importance of the spirituals. Paul Gilroy points to Locke's seminal work, *The New Negro*, written in 1925. Locke shares his thoughts on the spirituals while, at the same time, he heralds the beginning of the Harlem Renaissance or New Negro Movement. To Locke's mind, the spirituals were "really the most characteristic product of the race genius as yet in America...uniquely expressive of the Negro [and] at the same time deeply representative of the soil that produced them" (Gilroy 1993: 91). Addison Gayle's anthology, *The Black Aesthetic*, appeared in 1971, at the peak of the Black Arts Movement and exactly 100 years after the Fisk Jubilee Singers' first tour. Its authors came to conclusions similar to those of Locke concerning the importance of the spirituals.

Gilroy's *The Black Atlantic: Modernity and Double Consciousness* was released to critical acclaim a generation after Gayle. In the chapter "Jewels Brought from Bondage: Black Music and the Politics of Authenticity," Gilroy insists that in the final analysis the Fisk Jubilee Singers were more than mere entertainers. They were living examples of Du Bois's double consciousness in action: African Americans offering serious interpretations of the sacred songs of their enslaved ancestors. In an age when African Americans struggled against the tendency of black-faced minstrel performers to parody even sacred musical expressions, this was no small accomplishment. As Gilroy argues:

> Black people singing slave songs as mass entertainment set new public standards of authenticity for black cultural expression. The legitimacy of these new cultural forms was established precisely through their distance

from the racial codes of minstrelsy. The Jubilee Singers' journey out of America was a critical stage in making this possible. (90)

Gilroy's study makes a very important point about the keepers of the cultures of the Black Atlantic: hybrid cultures created in the diaspora are not self-contained, since they shape and are shaped by Europeans and others in the global community. The dynamics of these cultural exchanges and ongoing debates about authenticity are especially relevant for the present discussion of Dett's struggles, but they are also part and parcel of the intellectual work shaping the historiography of the African diaspora. In one of the earliest anthologies, *Global Dimensions of the African Diaspora*, editor Joseph Harris reminds readers that "issues related to assimilation and identity are basic to an understanding of the African Diaspora" and "all the chapters confirm" this idea, including St. Clair Drake's important chapter, "Diaspora Studies and Pan-Africanism," which focuses on the cultures of Africans in the Americas (1982: 8–9).

Michael A. Gomez advances a similar argument in his discussion of African agency and conscious decisions related to acculturation in *Exchanging Our Country Marks: The Transformation of African Identities in the Colonial and Antebellum South*:

> It is the synthesis that best characterizes the activity within the volitive realm of acculturation. In music, art, folklore, language, and even social structure, there is sufficient evidence to conclude that people of African descent were carefully selecting elements of various cultures, both African and European, issuing into combinations of creativity and innovation. Such a process is consistent with the nature of viable cultures; that is, they have the capacity to change and adapt when exposed to external stimuli. (1998: 10)

These themes are repeated in many other studies of the African diaspora (Holloway 2005; Gomez 2005; Walker 2001). Together the analyses provided by these scholars suggest that Dett's activities, rather than being unusual, were in direct keeping with choices that millions of Africans in diaspora had made in earlier generations. The tasks associated with collecting, arranging, and then interpreting both the musicality and the ideology of the spirituals, however, was left to Robert Nathaniel Dett and his generation. With his extensive knowledge of music, and the ability to say many things in *technical phrase*, he would, in the decades immediately following the publication of *Souls*, address Du Bois's lingering questions about the meaning of the "Sorrow Songs" and the power of culture to build bridges of understanding between African Americans and others in the global community.

Robert Nathaniel Dett at Home and Abroad

Dett's achievements were rare but not unprecedented among African Americans in the late nineteenth and early twentieth centuries. Dett's education and accomplishments placed him within the ranks of an elite group, referred to by one historian in the title of his book as the "aristocrats of color" (Gatewood 1990). Members of this group were much more likely than others of their race to have access to education and white-collar employment at home and opportunities for travel and study abroad. Dett's life history makes for an interesting case study of an African American man whose experiences were binational—almost from the time of his birth—and whose renown was international at the time of his death in 1943.

Born in Drummondsville, Ontario, Canada, in 1882, Robert Nathaniel Dett spent most of his formative years in Niagara Falls, New York. He was the third of four children born to Robert Dett, a native of Maryland, and Charlotte Dett, who was born in Drummondsville. Both parents either sang or played musical instruments. In the first half of the nineteenth century, the community of Drummondsville had been a popular destination for African American slaves escaping a life of bondage in the United States and crossing the Canadian border to live a life of relative freedom. Drummondsville became part of the city of Niagara Falls, Ontario, when it was incorporated in 1904 (Simpson 1993). Although the slave spirituals would become an integral part of his mature compositions, it does not seem that they played a major role in his early musical education. Dett recalled, for example, that his maternal grandmother, Harriet Washington, a U.S.-born woman who migrated to Drummondsville before the Civil War, often sang the spirituals while he was a child. In describing the years following his grandmother's death when he was approximately ten years old, Dett said very little about the influence of these songs on his early life. He did state, however, that his mother's insistence that he take piano lessons as a child led to his formal introduction to the world of music (Spencer 1991b: 1).

Dett's personal history was shaped in a binational environment. After his family crossed the Canadian border and settled in Niagara Falls, New York, in 1893, Dett became very active in the music programs of his church. Following his graduation from the Niagara Falls Collegiate Institute in 1903, Dett enrolled in the five-year composition program at the Oberlin (Ohio) College Conservatory. With its ties to the Congregational churches, nineteenth-century abolitionism, and liberal politics, Oberlin had a long history of offering coeducational and interracial education;

nevertheless, Dett became the first African American to complete the composition program when he graduated in 1908 (Simpson 1993; Lerma and Mc Brier 1996).

Rather than pursue a career as a concert pianist, Dett chose to become an educator. He held a series of teaching positions, including work at Lane College in Jackson, Tennessee, and Lincoln Institute in Jefferson City, Missouri. He also continued to compose music, primarily for piano and voice. Dett's most productive years as a musician and educator were those spent at Virginia's Hampton Institute from 1913 to 1932. Under his direction, the Hampton Institute Concert Choir toured the United States and, in the spring of 1930, several countries in Europe. They won the acclaim of audiences and critics alike for their performances of spirituals and other songs (Gray 1984: 8, 11; DPO; DPH).

The second decade of Dett's tenure at Hampton is significant for other reasons. It coincides with the era of the Harlem Renaissance—a cultural movement among African Americans in the 1920s and 1930s during which time New York served as a major center of activity for the so-called New Negro Movement. Many studies of the era stress the leading role that literary artists played in the renaissance, while others focus on the secular music-makers of this 1920s "Jazz Age." Less attention has been given to African American religious expressions of the day, which, thanks in part to Dett, were abundant (see Perry 1982).

W. E. B. Du Bois encouraged this great outpouring of sacred and secular cultural expressions by African American artists. In his editorials for *Crisis*, the magazine of the National Association for the Advancement of Colored People's (NAACP), and during his many public speaking engagements, Du Bois challenged African Americans to define their own aesthetic. He told his African American audiences:

> The ultimate judge has to be you, and you have got to build yourselves up into that wide judgment, that catholicity of temper, which is going to enable the artist to have his widest chance for freedom. (Du Bois 1986 [1926]: 1001)

Dett accepted Du Bois's challenge and tried to define a black aesthetic for sacred concert music. A devout Presbyterian, Dett saw religion as one of the greatest assets of the race, and he considered it to be a powerful force in history (Spencer 1991a; 1991b; 1997). His essays demonstrate his knowledge of the anthologies of Negro Spirituals published by Hampton long before he joined the faculty—although these resulted from the work of folklorists rather than historians. In his 1927 "Religious Folk-Songs of the Negro: As Sung at Hampton Institute," Dett expressed his concern about the paucity of serious studies of this music and offered the following critique:

> Were it not for this tendency on the part of historians to omit or ignore the influence of religion on the events which their annals are intended to record, such a classification as the one presented here might have appeared long ago. (Dett 1991: 56)

While the historians of the day may have been lax in their duties, certainly the essayists among the Harlem Renaissance writers offered their own commentary on religious influences in life and art. In his 1926 piece, "The Negro Artist and the Racial Mountain," Langston Hughes, for example, "praised the Lord" for both the "low down folk" of the African American masses, "whose religion soars to a shout," and African American folk music, which, "having achieved worldwide fame, offer[ed] itself to the genius of the great individual American composer who [was] to come" (Hughes 1997: 1271).

It appears that Dett's approach to his work had much in common with several of the most-celebrated male writers of the Harlem Renaissance era. Throughout his career, Dett insisted that expressions of African American folk culture, particularly the spirituals, provided endless inspiration for "racial artists" who were interested in creating works of religious art that were truly American, and not imports or imitations of art from other countries (Spencer 1991b: viii). According to Gilroy's analysis of the spirituals and other African American music, Dett's arrangements of concert spirituals

> ...are modern because they have been marked by their hybrid, creole origins in the West, because they have struggled to escape their status as commodities and the position within the cultural industries it specifies, and because they are produced by artists whose understanding of their own position relative to the racial group and of the role of art in mediating individual creativity with social dynamics is shaped by a sense of artistic practice as an autonomous domain reluctantly or happily divorced from the everyday life-world. (1993: 73)

Dett's own writings reflect his determination to use his conservatory and university training to "elevate" the folk music and culture of African American people, and in the process to uplift the race. Dett also believed that "Negro school[s]," like Hampton Institute, would continue to play a special role in the preservation of African American music:

> It is in the Negro school for the most part that the songs of the race have been most carefully preserved. It is in the Negro school that these folk

songs, especially the "spirituals" have been used to create and intensify the atmosphere of religion, which is, as their name implies, their best and most natural office...so it is that now only in the Negro school is the ideal presentation of Negro music to be found; —more ideal one may unblushingly say than in the Negro church.... (1927: 304–305)

In choosing to engage in this kind of discourse on uplift ideology, Dett was frequently at odds with artists and intellectuals of the Renaissance Era. Folklorist and novelist Zora Neale Hurston, for instance, found much to criticize in what she perceived as Dett's elitism and an assimilationist approach to his work. While Hurston agreed with Langston Hughes's assessment of the value of folk spirituals, she cared little for the "neo-spirituals" arranged by Dett and others for choral or solo performances; she believed that they were lacking in authenticity and were so severely arranged that they were hardly recognizable to the folk who created the music (Hurston 1967: 15–17; compare Gilroy 1993: 91–92).[3]

For his part, Dett did not deny that the spirituals were transformed. In the 1970s, Lawrence Levine would write that Dett and others "Europeanized" African American spirituals (1978). And indeed, Dett took great pride in using folk spirituals as the basis for "musical forms associated with the European style of composition." An example of this is seen in "The Ordering of Moses," the oratorio submitted as his master's thesis at the Eastman School of Music and based on the spiritual "Go Down Moses" (Mc Brier 1977: 69). Dett constantly defended the right of African Americans, and others, to engage in this kind of work:

> The argument is sometimes made that when one takes a Negro theme as the basis for an anthem, a suite or a choral work it robs the music of its original charm—that it is no longer characteristic, that it does not truly represent the old plantation melodies. Yet, no one argues that the music of Tchaikovsky is not typically Russian, and Tchaikovsky's work forms one of the finest examples we have of the use of folk tunes in the more elaborate phases of art-form development. (Spencer 1991b: 15)

As Kevin Gaines shows in *Uplifting the Race*, James Weldon Johnson (poet, author, well-known NAACP leader, and co-editor with his brother Rosamond of two volumes of spirituals in the 1920s) was, like Dett, "well acquainted with black bourgeois values"; he joined Dett in striking a balance between retaining the basic folk melodies and vernacular speech of the spirituals, while using the formal arrangements as respectable alternatives to Vaudeville's "coon" songs and other misinterpretations of African American music. While some critics questioned the need for elaborate settings of the spirituals, extant evidence suggests that the audience response to concert performances of the music was overwhelmingly positive, at home and abroad (Gaines 1996: 186). In 1927, Dett was included in "Who's Who in Colored America" for his work as a musician and composer.[4] The Harmon Foundation awarded him the first prize in music in 1928. He was selected to receive the $400 prize and a medal in recognition of his being "one of the greatest Negro composers of music."[5] In 1928, Dett and the Hampton Choir also performed at Carnegie Hall and Washington, DC's First Congregational Church. The choir presented the same program at both venues, and the selections included "Sacred Songs of the Early Church," "Russian Liturgical Anthems," "Religious Compositions by American Composers," and the "Negro Melodies" and "Negro Idioms in Motets and Anthems" for which Dett is best remembered.[6]

The crowning achievement of Dett's tenure at Hampton came in 1930, the year of the choir's European tour. George Foster Peabody, Hampton Institute Trustee and Investment Committee member, helped secure major underwriting for the six-week tour with contributions made by philanthropists Arthur Curtiss James and John D. Rockefeller, Jr., among others. The purpose of the tour was to "promote the interests of the Negro of Africa through influential white people of Europe who are interested in colonial and native affairs."[7] Peabody believed that Dett, through the exemplary performances of his student choir, "might have a beneficial effect upon European attitudes toward Negroes in foreign possessions" (Simpson 1993: 168–170).

Despite the philanthropists' dubious racialist motives, Dett agreed with board members that the experience abroad would provide wonderful educational opportunities for his students. Forty select Hampton choristers, Dett, his mother, and three other adults sailed from New York on the morning of Wednesday, April 23, 1930. The group landed in England on May 1 and on the following day gave its first European concert in London. Concerts were also given in Paris, Hamburg, and Vienna, among other cities. By all accounts—including Dett's—the tour was a phenomenal success.

Glowing reviews appeared in European papers and, thanks to wire services, American papers, including the *New York Times*. One publication in Dett's hometown, the *Niagara Falls Gazette*, included the following information in its May 21, 1930, edition:

> The choir sang a group of negro spirituals to the great delight of their hearers who included the Austrian Chancellor, Johann Schober, several members of the cabinet with their wives and other distinguished personages. By request the choristers concluded with "Were You There When They Crucified My Lord?" and then were entertained at tea.

The instructor and director of the Hampton choir is Dr. R. Nathaniel Dett, son of Mrs. Charlotte Dette [sic], 362 Second Street, who was born in Niagara Falls, Ont, and spent his boyhood and youth there and in this city. Dr. Dett is directing the choir on its European tour and his mother is accompanying him. Dr. Dett's work as a composer of music has attracted worldwide attention. He is composer of a number of negro [sic] spirituals that have received praise from the highest musical critics.[8]

On May 14, 1930, a *New York Times* editorial declared,

> For they went to sing not for profit, nor alone for pleasure, but to raise up their race in the esteem of a world which had enslaved their ancestors, and to prove in freedom that it is capable of making a special contribution to the happiness of mankind.[9]

Information wired to the *New York Times* from Vienna stated: "the success which the Hampton Choir of colored students enjoyed in London, Brussels and elsewhere was duplicated in Vienna tonight.... [Audience members] were enthusiastic over the chorus work of the visitors, especially in Negro spirituals."[10]

Dett's own feature article, "A Musical Invasion of Europe," was published in the December 1930 issue of the NAACP's *Crisis* magazine. It appears that on land and sea, the adults from Hampton, the manager of the tour, and European curiosity-seekers, carefully scrutinized everything from the singers' deportment to the choir's repertoire. Dett wrote

> I doubt if any group of people were ever more stared at by Europeans of all classes than was the Hampton Choir. Of course with the more cultured, there was an effort to cover the glance somewhat, but the universal curiosity was undisguisable, and, on taking thought, I would add, excusable; for the glance of the continental European, when looking at Negroes, is of an entirely different nature generally from that of the average American under the same circumstances. In Saltzburg, impressed by our impromptu exercises at the tomb of Mozart, a man who himself had been a choral conductor and a director of a symphony orchestra, volunteered his services as guide about the city. In the Cathedral of Saltzburg, he remarked that the acoustics of the building were possibly the best in Europe, whereupon I said it would be pleasant to sing under such ideal circumstances.... "You may sing," our guide urged, "but," he added, lowering his voice, "please don't sing any jazz." (Dear readers, please remember that we were in a cathedral!)
>   Signaling the choir into formation we sang an "Ave Maria" in Latin. (1930: 405–407, 428)

One reader's response to Dett's story "Classic Music and Virtuous Ladies: A Note on Colored Folks' Prejudices," appeared in the January 1931 issue of *The Crisis*. The writer, Benjamin Stolberg, was bothered by Dett's "deliberate omissions of the racial unpleasantnesses the Choir encountered in Europe" and the director's unwillingness to include more spirituals on the choir's programs. Stolberg also wrote

The Hampton Choir, he'll have you know, sings "only classic music."...Now no sensible person doubts that well trained musicians of any race can play and sing any kind of music. But what's wrong with the Spirituals?...Are the Messers Dett and company ashamed of them?...If the Hampton Choir cannot sing spirituals and even play jazz, the worse for its musicianship. It would be much better off without classical "religious" songs, anyway. What the American Negro needs least is "religion," especially the "liberal" religion which is sneaking in on all of us just when the old religion, thank goodness, is beginning to show the first signs of disintegration. Dr. Dett's whole attitude reeks with a "refined" inferiority feeling and all its correlative of racial shame and racial prejudice. (Stolberg 1931: 23–24)

During his tenure at Hampton, Dett often found it necessary to defend his right to freedom of expression, even to university administrators: to Hampton University's President, Arthur Howe, for example; to the institution's principal, George Phenix; and to a well-to-do benefactor, Wade H. Cooper, president of the Commercial National Bank of Washington, DC, who repeatedly expressed concerns about Dett's programming decisions. In a letter critiquing a March 21, 1931 concert, Cooper offered the following:

While the audience was pleased, I think it was very much disappointed in not hearing more soul-stirring music. Dr. Dett did his work well, but his trouble is that he is trying to have the Choir sing more from Bach, Tschaikowsky, and Gretchaninoff, than he is of the character of music expected to be heard by the audience.[11]

In response, Dett wrote to Cooper on April 1, 1931, requesting that he "state definitely what [he] mean[t] by 'the character of music expected to be heard by the audience.'"[12] Dett received a reply from Cooper's secretary. In two short paragraphs, the letter instructed Dett to read the other letter again and to perform the following songs in the Chapel service on the next Sunday: "America the Beautiful," "When the Saints Go Marching In," and "Onward Christian Soldiers." These three "inspiring songs" would, hopefully, help Dett understand Cooper's concerns.

Principal George Phenix had been even more explicit in a "warning" letter sent to Dett at the start of the European tour:

> …A folk song to be real must be sung as it is sung by the "folk." These folk songs can of course be harmonized differently and modified and the material they contain be utilized in the most sophisticated sort of compositions, but when this is done they have ceased to be folk songs…[13]

Hampton's next Principal, Arthur Howe, agreed with his predecessor. Howe requested Dett's resignation and eventually received Dett's letter, effective January 1932—just one year shy of the composer's twentieth anniversary at Hampton (Simpson 1993: 212).

Conclusion

In hindsight, it appears that if anyone had earned the right to be called a "co-worker in the kingdom of culture," certainly Robert Nathaniel Dett had. His record of achievements is undisputed. The one thing that he was not able to achieve by 1932, however, was the fulfillment of what Du Bois suggested was the wish of everyone facing the challenges posed by the twentieth century "color line." Dett's personal struggles at Hampton were reflective of a larger struggle to resolve the dilemma posed by the reality of the "double consciousness" in African America and the difficulty associated with trying to "make it possible for a man to be both a Negro and an American, without being cursed and spit upon by his fellows, without having the doors of Opportunity closed roughly in his face" (Du Bois 1986 [1903]: 365). For Dett, the closed doors frequently included those that would have allowed him access to the "Christian Kingdom of Culture" and the freedom to decide for himself which songs were appropriate. Unfortunately for him, as Hurston's negative criticism suggests, many of those trying to close other doors of opportunity were also the dark children of the diaspora.

Fortunately for Dett, however, Du Bois remained loyal to him. Thus in July 1933, Du Bois reminded readers of the NAACP's *Crisis* magazine that although Dett's personal battles at Hampton had ended, the war to secure and protect the right to perform "our music" was still being fought:

> If a trained Negro singer gives a concert in New York, or a trained colored chorus sings there or elsewhere in the North, there is a type of comment, always made concerning their singing which is stereotyped and inevitable and repeated from year to year.…Olin Downes, of *The New York Times*,

voiced it after hearing the Fisk University Choir at Carnegie Hall; and asks the listener to "compare last night's singing of spirituals with the manner of the singing in the drama of 'Porgy'.... Or let him attend a real religious revival in Harlem.... He will hear hymns and spirituals, but they will have an emotion that was not to be felt last night...." All this is to our humble opinion pure and unadulterated nonsense. What it really means is that Negroes must not be allowed to attempt anything more than the frenzy of the primitive, religious revival. "Listen to the Lambs" according to Dett, or "Deep River," as translated by Burleigh, or any attempt to sing Italian music or German music, in some inexplicable manner, leads them off their preserves and is not "natural." To which the answer is, Art is not natural and is not supposed to be natural. And just because it is not natural, it may be great Art. The Negro chorus has a right to sing music of any sort it likes and to be judged by its accomplishment rather than by what foolish critics think that it ought to be doing. *It is to be trusted that our leaders in music, holding on to the beautiful heritage of the past, will not on that account, either be coerced or frightened from taking all music for their province and showing the world how to sing.* (Du Bois 1986 [1933]: 1236–1239; emphasis added)

Notes

1. Grateful acknowledgment is hereby given to the librarians at the Oberlin College Conservatory, the Hampton University Archives, and the Local History Division of the Niagara Falls, New York, Public Library System for assistance in obtaining information from their extensive holdings on R. Nathaniel Dett.
2. For a detailed discussion of Du Bois's assessment of the value of the spirituals, especially as they relate to African American ideas about death, see Williams (2007).
3. Other artists whose works Hurston placed in this negative category included Harry T. Burleigh, Rosamond Johnson, Lawrence Brown, Hall Johnson, and John W. Work.
4. Notice of the award was published in the *Niagara Falls Gazette* (Niagara Falls, New York), May 27, 1927 (DPNF).
5. *Niagara Falls Gazette* (Niagara Falls, New York), January 16, 1928 (DPNF).
6. Program for "Concert by the Hampton Institute Choir (A Capella), Directed by Dr. R. Nathaniel Dett," Carnegie Hall, New York, April 16, 1928; and program for "Concert by the Hampton Institute Choir (A Capella), Directed by Dr. R. Nathaniel Dett," First Congregational Church, Washington, DC, April 17, 1928 (DPNF).
7. Peabody's "Statement to the Hampton Institute Board of Trustees from the Administrative Board," October 29, 1929 (DPH).
8. *Niagara Falls Gazette*, May 21, 1930: 1 (DPNF).

9. *New York Times,* May 14, 1930: 26.
10. *New York Times,* May 21, 1930: 21.
11. Wade H. Cooper to Arthur Howe (copy to R. Nathaniel Dett), March 27, 1931 (DPH).
12. R. Nathaniel Dett to Wade H. Cooper, April 1, 1931 (DPH).
13. George Phenix to R. Nathaniel Dett, April 21, 1930 (DPH).

Bibliography

Published Works

Anderson, Paul Allen (2001). *Deep River: Music and Memory in Harlem Renaissance Thought.* Durham, NC: Duke University Press.

Baker, Houston A. (1987). *Modernism and the Harlem Renaissance.* Chicago: University of Chicago Press.

Burleigh, Harry T. (1984). *The Spirituals of Harry T. Burleigh.* Miami, FL: Belwin Mills.

Crouch, Stanley and Benjamin Playthell (2002). *Reconsidering the Souls of Black Folk.* Philadelphia, PA: Running Press.

Dett, R. Nathaniel (1927). "As the Negro School Sings," *Southern Workman* 56 (July): 304–305.

———— (1930). "A Musical Invasion of Europe," *The Crisis* 37/12 (December): 405–428.

———— (1936). *The Dett Collection of Spirituals, First Group: Originals, Settings, Anthems and Motets.* Chicago: Hall & McCreary Company.

———— (1937). *The Dett Collection of Negro Spirituals, Second Group: Originals, Settings, Anthems and Motets with Essay "Understanding the Negro Spiritual."* Chicago: Hall & McCreary Company.

———— (1938). *The Dett Collection of Negro Spirituals, Third Group: Originals, Settings, Anthems and Motets with Essay "The Authenticity of the Spiritual."* Chicago: Hall & McCreary Company.

———— (1939). *The Dett Collection of Negro Spirituals, Fourth Group: Originals, Settings, Anthems and Motets with Essay "The Development of the Negro Spiritual."* Chicago: Hall & McCreary Company.

———— (1991) [1927]. "Religious Folk Songs of the Negro: As Sung at Hampton Institute." In Jon Michael Spencer (ed.), *The R. Nathaniel Dett Reader: Essays on Black Sacred Music,* 56–67. Durham, NC: Duke University Press.

Du Bois, W. E. B. (1986) [1903]. *The Souls of Black Folk.* In Nathan Huggins (ed.), *Du Bois: Writings.* New York: The Library of America.

———— (1986) [1926]. "Criteria of Negro Art." In Nathan Huggins (ed.), *Du Bois: Writings,* 1001. New York: The Library of America.

———— (1986) [1933]. "Our Music." In Nathan Huggins (ed.), *Du Bois: Writings,* 1238–1239. New York: The Library of America.

Fitch, Nancy-Elizabeth (ed.) (2000). *How Sweet the Sound: The Spirit of African American History.* Fort Worth, TX: Harcourt Brace.

Floyd, Samuel A. (1990). *Black Music in the Harlem Renaissance: A Collection of Essays.* New York: Greenwood Press.

——— (1995). *The Power of Black Music: Interpreting Its History from Africa to the United States.* New York: Oxford University Press.

Gaines, Kevin K. (1996). *Uplifting the Race: Black Leadership, Politics, and Culture in the Twentieth Century.* Chapel Hill: University of North Carolina Press.

Gatewood, Willard B. (1990). *Aristocrats of Color: The Black Elite, 1880–1920.* Bloomington: Indiana University Press.

Gayle, Addison (1971). *The Black Aesthetic.* Garden City, NY: Doubleday.

Gilroy, Paul (1993). *The Black Atlantic: Modernity and Double Consciousness.* Cambridge, MA: Harvard University Press.

Gomez, Michael Angelo (1998). *Exchanging Our Country Marks: The Transformation of African Identities in the Colonial and Antebellum South.* Chapel Hill: University of North Carolina Press.

——— (2005). *Reversing Sail: A History of the African Diaspora.* New York: Cambridge University Press.

Gray, Arlene E. (1984). *Listen to the Lambs: A Source Book of the R. Nathaniel Dett Materials in the Niagara Falls Public Library, Niagara Falls, N.Y.* Ridgeway, Canada: Smith-Davison.

Hare, Maud Cuney (1967). "The Source." In Lindsay Patterson (ed.), *The Negro in Music and Art. The Association for the Study of Negro Life*, 19–30. New York: Publishers Company.

Harris, Joseph E. (ed.) 1982. *Global Dimensions of the African Diaspora.* Washington, DC: Howard University Press.

Holloway, Joseph E. (2005). *Africanisms in American Culture.* Bloomington: Indiana University Press.

Hubbard, Dolan (ed.) (2003). *The Souls of Black Folk: One Hundred Years Later.* Columbia: University of Missouri Press.

Hughes, Langston (1997) [1926] "The Negro Artist and the Racial Mountain." In Henry Louis Gates, Jr. (ed.), *The Norton Anthology of African American Literature*, 1267–1271. New York: W. W. Norton.

Hughes, Langston and Arna Bontemps (eds.) (1958). *The Book of Negro Folklore.* New York: Dodd/Mead.

Hurston, Zora Neale (1967). "Spirituals and Neo-spirituals." In Lindsay Patterson (ed.), *The Negro in Music and Art, The Association for the Study of Negro Life*, 15–17. New York: Publishers Company.

Johnson, James Weldon and James Rosamond Johnson (eds.) (1969). *The Books of American Negro Spirituals, Including The Book of American Negro Spirituals (1925) and The Second Book of Negro Spirituals (1926).* New York: Da Capo Press.

Kaplan, Carla (ed.) (2002). *Zora Neale Hurston: A Life in Letters.* New York: Doubleday.

Landrine, Hope and Elizabeth A. Klonoff (1996). *African American Acculturation: Deconstructing Race and Reviving Culture.* Thousand Oaks, CA: Sage.

Lerma, Domininique-Rene de and Vivian Flagg Mc Brier (eds.) (1996). *The Collected Piano Works of R. Nathaniel Dett*. Miami, FL: Warner.

Levine, Lawrence W. (1978). *Black Culture and Black Consciousness: Afro-American Folk Thought from Slavery to Freedom*. New York: Oxford University Press.

Lewis, David Levering (1993). *W. E. B. Du Bois: Biography of a Race*. New York: Holt.

———— (2000). *W. E. B. Du Bois: The Fight for Equality and the American Century, 1919–1963*. New York: Holt.

Loker, Donald E. (n.d.). "R. Nathaniel Dett, Doctor of Music: A Biographical Sketch." DPNF.

Lovell, John Jr. (1972). *Black Song: The Forge and the Flame*. New York: Paragon House.

Maultsby, Portia K. (2000). "Africanisms in African-American Music." In Floyd W. Hayes III (ed.), *A Turbulent Voyage: Readings in African American Studies*, 158–178. San Diego, CA: Collegiate Press, 2000.

Mc Brier, Vivian Flagg (1977). *R. Nathaniel Dett: His Life and Works (1882–1943)*. Washington, DC: Associated Publishers.

McCaskill, Barbara (2003). "Anna Julia Cooper, Pauline Hopkins, and the African American Feminization of Du Bois's Discourse." In Dolan Hubbard (ed.), *The Souls of Black Folk: One Hundred Years Later*, 70–94. Columbia: University of Missouri Press.

Patterson, Lindsay (ed.) (1967). *The Negro in Music and Art*. The Association for the Study of Negro Life. New York: Publishers Company.

Perry, Margaret (1982), *The Harlem Renaissance: An Annotated Bibliography and Commentary*. New York: Garland.

Rampersad, Arnold (1976). *The Art and Imagination of W. E. B. Du Bois*. New York: Schocken.

Simpson, Anne Key (1993). *Follow Me: The Life and Music of R. Nathaniel Dett*. Metuchen, NJ: The Scarecrow Press.

Smith, Lucy Harth (1935). "Negro Musicians and Their Music," *Journal of Negro History* 20/4: 428–432.

Southern, Eileen (1983). *The Music of Black Americans: A History*. New York: Norton.

Spencer, Jon Michael (1991a). "Introduction," *Black Sacred Music* 5/2 (Fall): 1–19.

———— (ed.) (1991b). *The R. Nathaniel Dett Reader: Essays on Black Sacred Music*. Durham: Duke University Press.

———— (1996). "The Black Church and the Harlem Renaissance," *African American Review* 30/3 (Fall): 453–460.

———— (1997). *The New Negroes and Their Music: The Success of the Harlem Renaissance*. Knoxville: University of Tennessee Press.

Stolberg, Behjamin (1931). "Classic Music and Virtuous Ladies: A Note on Colored Folks' Prejudices," *The Crisis* 38/1 (January): 23–24.

Stuckey, Sterling (1994). *Going through the Storm: The Influence of African American Art in History*. New York: Oxford University Press.

Thurman, Howard (1967). "The Meaning of the Spirituals." In Lindsay Patterson (ed.), *The Negro in Music and Art*, 3–8. New York: Publishers Company.

Walker, Sheila (2001). *African Roots/American Cultures: Africa in the Creation of the Americas*. Lanham, MD: Rowman & Littlefield.

Walker-Alexander, Margaret (1942). *For My People*. New Haven, CT: Yale University Press.

Ward, Andrew (2001). *Dark Midnight When I Rise: The Story of the Fisk Jubilee Singers*. New York: Amistad.

White, Sarah D. (1982). "Robert Nathaniel Dett and the Black Spiritual." Unpublished MA thesis. Oberlin College.

Williams, Regennia (2007). "Sing a Good Song When I'm Gone: The Place of Homegoing Spirituals, Hymns, and Gospels in the History of African American Sacred Music." In Regennia Williams (ed.), *Homegoings, Crossings, and Passings: Life and Death in the African Diaspora*. Northridge, CA: New World African Press [forthcoming].

Work, John W. (1923). "Negro Folk Song," *Opportunity*: 292–294.

Manuscript Collections

DPH: R. Nathaniel Dett Papers. Hampton University Library, Hampton, Virginia.

DPNF: The R. Nathaniel Collection. Local History Division, New York Public Library, Niagara Falls, New York.

DPO: R. Nathaniel Dett Papers. Oberlin College Conservatory Library, Oberlin, Ohio.

Chapter 5

Slain in the Spirit: Sexuality and Afro-Caribbean Religious Expression in Nella Larsen's *Quicksand*

Merinda Simmons

Introduction

This chapter uses Zora Neale Hurston's depiction of Afro-Caribbean Vodou in *Tell My Horse: Voodoo Life in Haiti and Jamaica* to examine the struggle between spirituality and sexuality within Nella Larsen's *Quicksand* (1928).[1] Hurston's emphasis on Vodou's intertwining of the physical and spiritual is shared by Larsen, in whose text a mixed-race protagonist refuses to tether herself to absolutes regarding God, the body, sexuality, and maternity. Neither perpetuating the myth of hypersexualized black female bodies, nor resigning themselves to necessarily oppressive versions of spirituality, both Larsen and Hurston tell an unconventional story about black female autonomy, sexuality, and maternity. In contradistinction to this unconventionality, much of the existing criticism on *Quicksand* insists on confining the novel to a Western context that sees maternity and spirituality as necessary evils opposing the endeavor of cultivating an autonomous identity. Keeping their foci on protagonist Helga Crane's sexuality only in terms of her race, Larsen's critics unintentionally fall into the essentialist trap that they attempt to dismantle. Specifically, critical analyses of the novel have confined Helga's sexual tragedy to the framework of feminine ideals in the Christian South. When read in the light of Hurston's analysis of Vodou, however, the novel makes clear that maternity and spirituality are not essentially oppressive forces. Larsen's critics do the text a disservice by avoiding an analysis of the significantly corporeal religious expression in the novel, a kind of spiritual physicality prevalent in systems of faith within the African diaspora.

After surveying the critical field, and then moving into a discussion of Hurston's *Tell My Horse* and its presentation of the complexities within Caribbean ideas of womanhood, I offer a reading of *Quicksand* that engages with both the critical and anthropological contexts. In so doing, I argue that a reading of the novel in light of Afro-Caribbean religious myths and tropes illuminates Larsen's text as a critique not of maternity and spirituality themselves, but of their constructions within a Westernized context.

The Critical Quest for Autonomy

Many readings of *Quicksand* focus on Helga's search for, and ultimate lack of, autonomy. While the criticism surrounding the novel is useful in its emphases on the construction of Helga's maternity and exoticized sexuality, much of it ignores the significance of religion in regards to that construction. For too many critics, spirituality contributes to Helga's tragic end but not to a potentially positive sense of physicality. The real tragedy for Helga is that neither the novel nor its critics value her racial ambiguity and its attendant sexual and spiritual possibilities. In an attempt to pin down the source(s) of Helga's marginalization, too much analysis of *Quicksand* focuses on one of the following three supposed misfortunes: maternity, exoticism, and Helga's own missteps. Dealing with the potential dangers of isolating these usual suspects, I will argue that critics curiously take part in the very sort of polarized thinking that they attempt to dispel by concentrating on the binary of oppression/liberation.

Despite any discrepancies within specific textual analyses, Larsen critics all agree on the following reading of Larsen's protagonist: Helga wants to find sexual autonomy, but her status as a mulatta figures symbolically as her perpetual in between-ness that keeps her ricocheting between the walls of geography and objectification.[2] Thus, much criticism of the novel sees maternity as a huge component of Helga's tragic end and as a necessary evil that she is forced to endure. Patricia Felisa Barbeito, for example, suggests that the novel (along with Hurston's *Their Eyes Were Watching God*) views motherhood as "a critical problem" in the negotiation between self-actualization and sexual expression (1998: 370). In her article on exoticism in *Quicksand*, Debra B. Silverman makes a similar claim by stating that childbirth is something to which Larsen "sacrific[es]" Helga (1993: 612). Jacqueline de Weever deals with this vision of maternity on a more general level in *Mythmaking and Metaphor in Black Women's Fiction*, arguing, "Motherhood is thus not an ideal condition; it does not offer possibilities for personal growth or personal happiness" (1992: 157). The critical dismissal of maternity perpetuates the essentialism in the novel under which Helga suffers, forcing an impossible choice between two versions of physicality: a maternal one that kills or a sexual one that objectifies.

When not reading Helga's body as monstrously maternal, many Larsen critics see her as an exoticized object of the white gaze. In fact, Amelia Defalco, Jeffrey Gray, Ann Rayson, and Debra B. Silverman all mention Josephine Baker in their discussions of Helga's corporeal objectification. Helga thus falls under a critical gaze as well and is, implicitly, a failed Baker, unable to achieve a positive sense of sexual expression. Emblematic of this critical vein is Defalco's compelling essay, "Jungle Creatures and Dancing Apes: Modern Primitivism and Nella Larsen's *Quicksand*." In it, Defalco suggests that "Helga's repeated fleeing functions as a symptom of her eagerness to separate herself from the static stereotypes assigned to the black female body by popular white culture in modernism" (2005: 20).[3] So, too, does she now have to flee the "static stereotypes" of critics who impose similar limitations on the components of her agency. Defalco, along with others such as Debra Silverman and Pamela Barnett, discuss Helga's problematic sense of "primitivism" that turns her into a sexual object for the satisfaction of white hegemony. Though she is seen as an object of patriarchal desire, she still receives blame by some who argue that her drives and desires are what lead her to tragedy.

Many of the critics who discuss Helga's sexuality place emphasis on her psychology, focusing on the ways in which she contributes to her own seeming demise. However, in their well-intentioned attempts to assert Helga's autonomy, they ultimately blame her for her tragedy. The work of Kimberly Monda is especially noteworthy here. In her article, "Self-Delusion and Self-Sacrifice in Nella Larsen's *Quicksand*," Monda claims that the jazz scenes in the novel serve merely to drive Helga away from the stereotypes that she internalizes. She argues that Helga's sexual repression is a result of her failure to connect her desire for men to her desire to reconnect with her absent mother. Thus, her focus remains on "Helga's own contribution to this oppression" (1997: 24). In what I suggest to be a short-sighted, if not unfair, assessment of Helga's culpability, Monda never fully investigates the ways in which other factors, especially Helga's religious experience, develop her sexuality. This critical absence reduces spirituality as diametrically opposed to physicality, keeping the problematic binary in place and ignoring religious expressions of the African diaspora in which the binary does not exist.

Larsen critics have extensively, and often uniformly, discussed *Quicksand* in terms of the complicated ties between Helga Crane's sexuality and race, blaming her maternity and position as, like Ann Rayson says, "yet another tragic mulatta" for her sad end (1998: 92). In the process, they have glossed over the role that spirituality plays in shaping Helga's sexuality. Opening a door for Hurston's discussion of a more fluid form of subjectivity within religious expression allows *Quicksand* conversations more possibilities in regards to Helga's fate. No longer must she be confined to hard and fast definitions of maternal doom and sexual objectification. Rather, delving into the spirituality that is at work in the text, critics can begin to read the novel in the vein of African American women's metaphysical writing that complicates the binary between body and spirit. A reading that deals with the potential relationship between physicality and faith also allows for a more extensive discussion of the ways in which *Quicksand* is not so much a story about the quest for autonomy as it is a critique of the hegemonic systems and institutions that take it away. Reading the novel alongside Hurston's *Tell My Horse*, I suggest that Larsen also critiques the binary opposition between body and soul by exposing the tragedy that results when physicality is boxed within a Western configuration of spirituality.

Hurston's Teleological Topography: Physical Spirituality in the Caribbean

Published only a decade after *Quicksand*, Hurston's examination of Afro-Caribbean Vodou culture is an interesting companion to a reading of Helga's religious experience and the ensuing demands on her life in a Christian social community. Because Afro-Caribbean spiritual expression greatly informs the Black Church in America, Hurston's text provides an important framework with which to read the role of religion in Larsen's novel. In his foreword to Hurston's book, Ishmael Reed identifies the blending of religious styles that has prompted the saying in the Caribbean that "the people are ninety-five per cent Catholic and one hundred per cent Voodoo" (1938: xii). This amalgamated religious identification provides a way of reading Helga's otherwise confusing spirituality, induced by an "orgy" of a conversion experience and then maintained in a confining society with strict expectations regarding a woman's duty. Hurston delineates both the role of the body in spiritual expression and the importance of duty in her examination of Vodou rituals, concentrating on the demands that the *loa*, or Haitian gods, make of those who serve them. Hurston's discussion of one *loa* in particular, Erzulie Freida, shows the complexity of desire, obligation, and sexual freedom in Caribbean ideas of womanhood. One of the most popular goddesses in Haiti, Erzulie is the pagan goddess of love. She exists as a sort of Platonic ideal of womanhood for men, "so perfect that all other women are a distortion as compared to her" (Hurston 1990: 121). As "the perfect female," she must be adored and just as intensely obeyed (121). Among other attributes, like inordinate beauty and intense powers of seduction, Hurston strongly emphasizes the goddess's jealous and possessive nature. Erzulie's male followers will not let themselves receive any sort of affection from mortal women; and even married men, once "called" by Erzulie, are forbidden to maintain a sexual relationship with their wives. Hurston is quick to point out that she is not a passive maternal vessel like Mary in the Catholic tradition even though she is sometimes "identified as the Blessed Virgin" (121). Rather than be exalted for her virginal purity, Erzulie exhibits her perfection through her relationships with mortal men. Hurston describes the goddess as an exotic mulatta, adorned with elaborate jewelry and clothing. Worshipped by both men and women, she occupies very different respective positions for them. To men, she is the incarnation of perfection itself. To women, she is a cruel filcher of their sexual fulfillment. A seductive Mary, a popular goddess even as she "thrusts herself between [a] woman and her happiness," Erzulie thus embodies contradictions and ambiguities. This complicated status, however, helps illuminate Helga's difficult positionality in *Quicksand*. Neither black nor white, American nor European, domestic nor exotic, Helga struggles with the binaries that would label her.

In his *Workings of the Spirit: The Poetics of Afro-American Women's Writing*, Houston A. Baker, Jr. provides a brief discussion of *Tell My Horse* that investigates the liberating potential as Hurston identifies it in Afro-Caribbean religious expression. Through his reading of Hurston's study, Baker rightly claims that Vodou has a "strikingly womanist power." Baker cites Hurston's significant anecdote that discusses the Vodou ceremonial answer to the question, "What is the truth?" (1991: 81). In a chronicle of her encounter with this seemingly unanswerable query, Hurston depicts a ceremony in which a "richly dressed" Mambo, or priestess, is asked the question through rituals and, as a reply, throws back her veil to reveal her "sex organs" (1990: 113). Hurston notes, "The ceremony means that this is the infinite, the ultimate truth. There is no mystery beyond the mysterious sources of life" (113). Ceremonies like this one, along with other anecdotes throughout *Tell My Horse*, reveal the complexities of desire, obligation, sexual freedom, and so forth, in Caribbean ideas of womanhood. Sexuality resides at the center of universe, holding the secrets to "truth" and origin. In fact, as Hurston points out, the Vodou belief is that "in the beginning God and His woman went into the bedroom together to commence creation" (113). Thus, sexuality is central even to the very creation of the world. Its key role in Afro-Caribbean religious belief complicates simplistic and reductive notions about women, especially in regards to duty and desire. Removing stereotypes of the black body as hyperphysical and oversexed from Western contexts, Hurston is able to arrive at different and liberating visions of black female sexuality in her texts. Nella Larsen, however, keeps Helga firmly entrenched within traditional notions of feminine duty and desire in order to critique the systems that destroy her.

Quicksand's Crisis of Faith

Following Helga's journey, physical and spiritual, shows the problems facing a black woman trying to follow a path that is both coherent and authentic. For Larsen's mulatta protagonist who travels from the New South to Harlem to Europe, floundering between black exoticism and white middle-class social mores, religion is a catalyst not only for her final geographical move but also for a new construction of her womanhood. This new identity is problematized, however, because of its forced entry into a maternity freighted with a severe sense of duty. Thus the spiritual conflation of body and soul that has so much potential to "save" Helga with a fluid sense of embodied subjectivity instead requires that she be placed in a misogynistic version of motherhood. In her new role, she is unable to access the agency that the religious community should allow her with its embrace of both the physical and the spiritual. Rather, her body becomes a site upon which the religious community imposes its constricting rules of womanhood. Both the spirit and the body invariably influence the constructions of womanhood in the novel, with the self-sacrificial Madonna figures of Miss Magooden, Sary Jones, and Anne Grey alongside the sexually liberated Audrey Denney and Karen Nilssen. Hovering between these two configurations, Helga Crane seeks a more fluid kind of sexuality in the sphere of the spirit. However, she is unable to find this because the two are caught in an obstinate binary that Larsen exposes through the sad consequences that Helga finds upon conversion.

Physically, Larsen depicts Helga Crane in much the same terms as Hurston describes the lusty Vodou love goddess Erzulie. Helga is a restless mulatta, always moving from place to place in search of self-actualization and contentment. Also, she dresses the part of an exotic seductress in

Copenhagen and receives antagonism even at the beginning of the novel at Naxos for her rich tastes. We see her initially surrounded by silk curtains and a blue Chinese carpet, and she is described as having "sensuous lips" and wearing a "vivid green and gold negligee and glistening brocaded mules, deep sunk in the big high-backed chair" (1986: 2).[4] Men, and in one case the husband of her best friend, are drawn to her, lured by her magnetic and exotic beauty. The correlation between Helga and Erzulie becomes even more striking when Helga moves to Copenhagen. In the Danish city, Helga's aunt finds as many ways as she can to decorate and exhibit her, much to the delight and curiosity of the all-white society: "[Helga] was incited to make an impression, a voluptuous impression... to inflame attention and admiration... to the fascinating business of being seen, gaped at, desired" (74). She becomes the passionate artist Axel Olsen's object, a study in artistic foreignness, and she sits for frequent portraits. He relates her charm to her otherness, telling her: "You have the warm impulsive nature of the women of Africa, but, my lovely, you have, I fear, the soul of a prostitute" (87). Well on her way to seeming like the perfect image of desirability, Helga's fate takes a drastically sharp turn downward upon being rejected by a married man whom she has "called." Robert Anderson's refusal sends her searching once again, but it pushes her into a strict religious community that forces a separation between her body and her sexuality.

Larsen emphasizes the spirit/sexuality relationship by framing the depictions of inauthentic, but socially acceptable, forms of womanhood in *Quicksand* with spiritual characteristics. Most of the women—Miss MacGooden, Sary Jones, and Anne Grey, among others—are pristine figures of either sexual chastity or the sexual "purity" that comes with sacrificial maternity. At Naxos, Miss MacGooden never marries because of the "things in the matrimonial state that were of necessity entirely too repulsive for a lady of delicate and sensitive nature to submit to" (12). Thus, the chaste Miss MacGooden is a kind of virginal holy woman, a priestess of ladylike social mores. Sary Jones is the very portrait of selfless maternal martyrdom. She represents the emphasis in African American Christianity on reward in the afterlife, on long-suffering in this world for recompense in the next.[5] Anne Grey is another saintly woman, "almost too good to be true" with "the face of a golden Madonna, grave and calm and sweet" (45). Significantly, Anne "hate[s] white people with a deep and burning hatred" (48). Her racial heritage, then, becomes something that isolates her into a very safe space of specific identity.

For characters like Audrey Denney, the appearance of racial ambiguity becomes a mark of stigmatized sexuality. Audrey is perhaps the only truly sexually liberated woman in the novel, but she has light skin, "almost like an alabaster," and is looked down upon by "upstanding" members of

society (60). Helga, however, immediately admires her, calling her "lovely"
to Anne. Anne returns the comment with a caustic character analysis,
calling her a "disgusting creature" because she "goes about with white people…and they know she's colored" (60). Race certainly plays an important
part in the construction of sexual identity, as only those who are distinctly
black or white (even in their sexual lives) are granted full respect in their
communities. Larsen portrays Audrey with a kind of visceral sexuality
when she dances, which emotes a desire in Helga that moves beyond the
body and into the spirit: "[Audrey]…swung by that *wild* music from the
heart of the jungle…[Helga] felt a more *primitive* emotion…She felt her
heart throbbing.…She saw only two figures, closely clinging" (62, emphases added). After watching the two dance, Helga is "panting" and "confused" and feels "cold, unhappy, misunderstood, and forlorn" (62). The
significantly sexualized experience leaves Helga exhausted but unfulfilled,
still longing for a different avenue of sexuality that would erase the perim-
eters of race, gender, and class that border her desires and physicality. On
her quest to explore different possibilities in her sexual identity, she must
also try to reconcile her own unsuccessful maternity with her absent
mother.

Certainly Larsen's construction of Karen Nilssen is important to Helga's
construction of identity. Frau Dahl offers her own diagnosis of her sister to
Helga: "…your mother was a fool…[s]elfish" (78). She goes on to credit
her father for any intelligence granted to Helga. This hasty dismissal of the
mother is a mistake made not only by Helga's aunt but also by Larsen
critics.[6] Kimberly Monda, for example, suggests that Helga's identification
with her father "frees Helga from her self-destructive need for recognition
from her distant mother, allowing her to gain temporary access to a sense
of agency and therefore to her repressed sexuality" (1997: 33). To ignore
the mother is to exonerate the father, and this problematizes Helga's sexuality even more. Her autonomy in this sense is a direct result of a man,
necessarily binding her to the father. This is the same unfortunate circum-
stance that she falls into with Pleasant Green, feeling like she owes him the
life that he "redeems." In a Southern black religious community, Helga is
forced into a communal notion of Africanized maternity that she cannot
satisfy. Unable to cultivate a singular racial identity because of her marginalized mulatta status, Helga finds conforming to a specifically racialized
form of maternity an impossible task.

Nonetheless, she opts for a spiritual path in a church whose
hyperphysical congregation accepts her as a "lost Jezebel"; the faithful keep
their hands all over her until she repents in a climax indicated by her own
physical release. In the moment of her conversion, she is "maddened,"
"yell[ing] like one insane" with "torrents of tears stream[ing] down her

face" (Larsen 1986: 113). Rather than the laying on of hands to initiate a healing experience, the congregation figuratively pushes her into the religious box of feminine duty, and her physicality must reside within maternal objectification for the duration of the novel. It is the Western religious construction of the duty attached to this perpetual and exhausting maternity, I suggest, that prevents her from keeping some sort of sexual autonomy. Rather than maintaining a sense of individual embodiment, her body becomes the religious community's object of desire, the women assuring Helga that bearing children is simply what one must do in order to please God and husband. Without a real concept of maternity in her own life, she dwells in a space that is never either wholly daughter or wholly mother. Her sexuality, then, must hover in a gray area informed by religious conviction and obligation where maternity is sacrosanct and corporeal pleasure is scorned.

The relationship between female sexuality and religion in the book is a prominent one, braiding Helga's tripartite search for fulfillment as a woman, a wife, and a new Christian. Larsen depicts religious fervor as markedly sensual, emphasizing the body and its reactions to a run-in with the divine. The dance routine in Denmark to which Helga sneaks repeated visits even though she feels "shamed" by it strikingly resembles the inside of the church during her religious conversion; this again emphasizes the link between an African notion of physicality and spiritual expression. In the Copenhagen show, "the singers danced, pounding their thighs, slapping their hands together, twisting their legs, waving their abnormally long arms, throwing their bodies about with a loose ease" (ibid. 82–83). Likewise, when Helga has her religious experience, "Men and women were swaying and clapping their hands, shouting and stamping their feet to the frankly irreverent melody of the song" (ibid. 112). The conflation of body and soul in the novel allows for a space in which Hurston's examination of physical and spiritual practice can speak.

Hurston's study of Vodou is readily applicable to a reading of the religious expression in *Quicksand*, as the latter is more significantly grounded in African and African diasporic spiritual traditions than it is in Western configurations of Christianity. The storefront church that Larsen depicts in the conversion scene does not closely correspond with the traditional Anglo, Westernized conceptions of Christianity. Rather, it more intimately aligns itself with Joseph M. Murphy's discussion of the Black Church in *Working the Spirit*. Murphy examines the "kinetic expression" of African American churches, paying very special attention to the physicality of religious worship. He notes that the religious experience within the Black Church differs greatly from that of the traditional white Protestant, especially during the moment of conversion (Murphy 1994:

148–149). The storefront church in *Quicksand* certainly hearkens back to the sort of "kinetic expression" that Murphy describes and takes the congregation's "zealous shoutings and groanings" to hyper-sensual levels (Larsen 1986: 113).

During the conversion scene, Helga is fascinated by the physicality, especially "the writhings and weepings of the feminine portion, which seemed to predominate" (113). Larsen describes the congregation growing in intensity: "Behind her, before her, beside her, frenzied women gesticulated, screamed, wept, and tottered to the praying of the preacher, which had gradually become a cadenced chant" (ibid.). Helga notes that the scene harbors something foreign and ceremonial that is not merely the proper praises of an Anglicized god. She stands by watching the others until "there cre[eps] upon her an indistinct horror of an unknown world" and she begins to feel that she is "in the presence of a nameless people, observing rites of a remote obscure origin" (ibid.). This "nameless people," I suggest, refers to the African diaspora and their immediate religious and physical marginalization upon arriving in America. Helga's middle-class mores leave her feeling "horrified" and confused at the scene in the storefront church, but her overpowering longing for a sense of authentic racial heritage leads her to what is initially a sincere conversion. Joseph Murphy's investigation of the ways in which African American spirituality notably differs from white forms of Christianity allows for an even stronger link between the religious practices that Hurston identifies in the Caribbean and that which Larsen presents in *Quicksand*.

Murphy relays a scene from a black church in the South recorded by an abolitionist in 1862 that strikingly resembles Larsen's storefront scene: "The foot is hardly taken from the floor, and the progression is mainly due to a jerking, hitching motion, which agitates the entire shouter, and soon brings out streams of perspiration" (148). Murphy notes the roots of such physical expression in religious worship. He observes, "The connections between initiation and spirit manifestation suggest parallels throughout the African diaspora" (150). In this sense, "[t]he more subtle strain informing the Black Church comes from its more distant roots in the spirituality of ancestors brought over from Africa" (146). Ecstatic movement and clamorous music are informed by African culture, again separating the Black Church from Anglicized versions of worship so that "What might seem to outsiders to be mere 'motor behaviours' remembered from Africa are actually expressions of a dynamic, incarnated spirituality which is found throughout the diaspora" (ibid.).

And so, the fanatical physicality seen in the novel during the conversion scene receives a sociohistorical association with the Afro-Caribbean Vodou rituals that Hurston describes in *Tell My Horse*.[7] Harryette Mullen's essay,

"African Signs and Spirit Writing," usefully relates this African religious history to modern Black Churches and creative texts. She argues

> If…aspects of African religious practice…survive in contemporary worship in many black churches, then it may not be…a stretch to suppose that similar spiritual values, including even a "miniaturization" of spirit possession, might also survive in a…tradition of visionary writing. (1996: 634)

To understand the ways in which the religion rooted in Vodou specifically shapes the "visionary writing" of Helga's sexuality, one must first get a sense of the general notions of womanhood as Larsen constructs them in the novel. After Helga Crane's conversion experience, she almost immediately finds herself in a new role as wife to a minister in rural Alabama. Her newfound faith brings with it a pleasant "anesthetic satisfaction" while simultaneously imposing a socially useful sexuality that produces five children. Upon her conversion, she determines that finally "she had not clutched a shadow and missed the actuality" (Larsen 1986: 118). The assumption of "actual" selfhood, however, guides her into a kind of socio-political quagmire more disappointing than both her Harlem and Copenhagen experiments. It is her final attempt at subjectivity that pushes her into the role of Southern preacher's wife and that ultimately forces her into the shadows as she attempts to negotiate what McDowell calls her "divided psych[e] between a desire for sexual fulfillment and a longing for social respectability" (1986: xvii). Thus Larsen presents the moment of Helga's conversion as an ambiguous one, stating that "she was lost—or saved" (Larsen 1986: 113). If we are indeed to read the novel as McDowell suggests, "through the prism of black female sexuality," the sexual focus receives a significant clarity when filtered through a religious screen that explains part of the feminine sense of obligation to a higher power, whether it be God or man (1986: xii).

As soon as Helga embarks on her religious path, her womanhood comes into a glaring foreground as she marries the Reverend Pleasant Green. Newly converted, Helga finds her sexuality morphing into nothing more than a tedious means to a procreative end. She remains the picture of self-less maternity, but she can never fully be a sacred Mary figure, much like the Vodou goddess Erzulie. However, while Erzulie is praised for her sensuality, Helga is only partially able to enjoy the admiration she receives in Copenhagen. Like her race, her sexual identity is forced into flux, and she remains caught in the binary of sanctity and solicitation. In this way, Larsen presents her as resting squarely within the framework of stereotyped womanhood that Jacquelyn Grant describes in her article "Black

Women and the Church." She is "in the 'background'" and is "merely [a] support worker," a position that Grant suggests the Church uses to "keep women 'in their place' in the denomination" (1982: 141). Her rejection of the objectifying lens through which Copenhagen sees her is thus not enough to signify autonomy. Rather, it simply makes more tragic her final attempt at a valid and fulfilling sense of womanhood.

Larsen's Critique: Implications of Plurality in Text and Theory

Trapped somewhere between the bawdy objectification of the sensual African Venus and the immaculate conception of a maternal black Virgin Mary, Helga Crane ends tragically as the love goddess who almost was. Searching throughout the novel for a place that will allow her to be a self-actualized mulatta with sexual sovereignty, Helga's body ultimately becomes a blank slate on which her spirituality inscribes a stronger sense of her feminine duty. Though the onset of her religious conversion initially allows Helga to feel as though she has found her "promised land," she continues to dwell in the nondescript borderlands of identity. A facile reading of the novel sees Helga's demise merely as an example of her "failed" quest for autonomy, amounting to her being trapped within the "oppressive" frameworks of maternity and spiritual duty that do not allow for any sense of real pleasure. However, I suggest that Larsen is not ultimately concerned with an ideal but with actual conundrums experienced by women placed within intersections of racial, religious, and cultural divisions. The novel serves to complicate, if not disrupt, the hegemonic applications of these divisions that impose fixity onto notions of racial and sexual duty within religious communities.

Hurston's *Tell My Horse* articulates the possibilities of racial, sexual, and spiritual expression when they do not follow linear, hierarchal patterns. Hurston's presentation of Vodou incorporates particular expectations regarding duty and piety. However, in Vodou duty is transformed into something of a loving and powerful relationship—certainly not the corporeal slavery that Helga Crane encounters within the religious strictures that attempt to duplicate white patriarchal constructs of sexual and spiritual obligation. In her depiction of Guedé, the "deification of the common people of Haiti," Hurston illustrates the power of social critique, the very tool that Larsen uses in regards to the black middle class in America and its stringent rules of womanhood, racial loyalty, and religious piety (1938: 219). Guedé is a god whose manifestation "comes as near a social criticism of the classes by the masses as anything in all Haiti" (ibid.). Larsen, too, embarks upon a critique of a Western commitment to singularity, emphasizing hybrid tensions of race, class, gender, sexuality, and religious duty. Guedé uses harsh sarcasm to deride elitist classes of society. Hurston describes the way in which he appears to believers:

> He manifests himself by "mounting" a subject as a rider mounts a horse, then he speaks and acts through his mount. The person mounted does nothing of his own accord. He is the horse of the loa until the spirit departs... "*Parlay Cheval Ou*" (Tell My Horse), the loa begins to dictate through the lips of his mount.... Sometimes Guedé dictates the most caustic and belittling statements concerning some pompous person who is present. (220–221)

In a similar sense, Larsen uses Helga as a vessel of caustic social critique. Helga, like her critics, blames herself for her miserable end, agonizing over "this thing that she had done to herself" (Larsen 1986: 130). She feels "only an astonished anger at the quagmire in which *she had engulfed herself*" and thinks only of how she "had ruined her life" (133; emphasis added). The folly of personal blame in this case, perpetuated by critics and Helga alike, is an understandable one, but is folly nonetheless. In this focus on self-identification and/or actualization, Larsen's critique of oppressive Western religious configurations of duty (especially maternal and marital), race, and the body is too often overlooked.

In *Reconstructing Womanhood*, Hazel Carby points out the problems with psychoanalytic readings of the novel that focus too much on Helga's choices. She notes that the alienation that Helga suffers at the hands of patriarchal culture is "often represented as a state of consciousness, a frame of mind" (1999: 169). As Carby rightly argues, however: "Implied in this definition is the assumption that alienation can be eliminated or replaced by another state of consciousness, a purely individual transformation unrelated to necessary social or historical change" (ibid.). While Helga regrets what Larsen calls her "ruined... life," there is more at stake than just her own poor decisions. Larsen uses her outcome as a way to rethink social orders and systems that cage her. Helga does not make "bad" choices so much as she looks for options in a world that provides her with none. Thus, Hazel Carby makes the convincing argument that Helga's societal alienation "was not just in her head but was produced by existing forms of social relations and therefore subject to elimination only by a change in those social relations" (ibid.). Larsen is at the center of this critique of "social relations." The political importance of Larsen's vision of marginalization as social consequence rather than personal failure has far-reaching critical significance. Perhaps most notably, criticism can begin to deflect its attention from Helga's autonomy to the ways in which religion serves as an emblematic symbol of the Western ideologies that Larsen condemns for their myopic views toward sexuality and womanhood.

In her introduction to *Quicksand* and *Passing*, Deborah McDowell offers some insight into how, when reading the novel in terms of its presentations of sexuality, we might better read Larsen's role as author. She claims that the traumatic textual endings that pervade Larsen's novels actually serve to "illuminate the peculiar pressures on Larsen as a woman writer during the male-dominated Harlem Renaissance" (1986: xii). Thus, as Larsen forges text from out of conflicting spheres of sexual and racial allegiances, McDowell argues, the seemingly conventional roles of marriage and motherhood become politically charged. For Larsen, they are, McDowell suggests, "radical and original efforts to acknowledge a female sexual experience" (ibid.). In addition to her earlier treatment of Nella Larsen's class critiques in *Quicksand*, Hazel Carby discusses Larsen's critical project in terms of sexuality in *Cultures in Babylon: Black Britain and African America*. She states, "...Larsen...reproduces in her novel the dilemma of a black woman who tries to counter the dominant white cultural definitions of her sexuality: ideologies that define black female sexuality as primitive and exotic" (1999: 10). Though she deals with the commonly read issues of primitivism and exoticism, what I want to emphasize is Carby's notion that Larsen is moving against "dominant white *cultural definitions*" and "*ideologies*" (emphasis added). These should be at the center of readings of the novel that deal with sexuality. Once at the center, a vital critical door is open to the "cultural definitions" and "ideologies" present in other applicable religious contexts, especially those of the African diaspora, and Larsen's general critique can include not only constructs of class and sexuality but also those of institutionalized Western religious configurations.

From the very beginning, Larsen presents Christianity in a Western, Anglicized context as "banal," "patronizing," and "insulting" (1986: 2). Piety comes in the form of a "holy white man of God" who, promoting lofty notions of duty, praises the black community at Naxos for having the "good taste" to "stay in their places" (2, 3). Something of an anti-prophet, Larsen proclaims the "truth" by warning society of its dangerously marginalizing allegiances. Like Guedé, whose "mission [is] to expose and reveal" and whose "revelations are often most startlingly accurate and very cruel," Larsen considers no social ill sacred (Hurston 1938: 223). By staring at the source of religious dogmas that confine expressions of sexuality into harsh configurations of consistent maternity or lusty exoticism, Larsen unflinchingly confronts hegemonic systems with their own staggering privilege. The result is the broken figure of Helga, who is not just another tragic mulatta as critics like Rayson suggest. This faulty assumption implies a kind of inevitability to her fate. We should, I suggest, see her outcome as contingent, not tragic.

Helga is emblematic of the kind of figure in black women's writings that Mae Gwendolyn Henderson theorizes in "Speaking in Tongues: Dialogics, Dialectics, and the Black Woman Writer's Literary Tradition." In her visionary essay, Henderson sees as a trademark of black women's texts the "internal dialogue with the plural aspects of self that constitute the matrix of black female subjectivity" (2000: 349). She calls this discursive plurality "speaking in tongues" and argues that its textual practice "neither repress[es] difference nor, for that matter, privileg[es] identity, but rather express[es] engagement with the social aspects of self" (363). While Hurston emphasizes plurality in much the same way—as a liberating source of power—Larsen shines a critical light on the societal forces that keep heterogeneity at bay. Thus, for Helga, her multiplicity becomes her misery. Attempting to reconcile her multiple voices of race, sexuality, corporeality, and spirituality, Helga Crane hears cacophony rather than harmony, as each society she encounters always trumps one vision of identity over another. She is forced into a series of either/ors: she is *either* a Jezebel *or* a lady; she is *either* a sacrificial lamb of motherhood *or* a raging lion of seduction. She tries to escape the New South, only to discover that the middle-class mores of Harlem and the white fetishization of Denmark offer different types of marginalization but still just as much of it. These sad findings lead her right back to the South, this time an older and more fatal one.

Larsen critics thus do Larsen's critique of hegemony a disservice in presuming that Helga simply should have "stayed put" or that she could have been happy if only she had changed one aspect of her attitude or another. By reading *Quicksand* alongside Zora Neale Hurston's *Tell My Horse*, the religious community of the novel can more effectively be examined as the center of a tight web of female conformity—sexual, racial, and maternal—spun by oppressive social discourses. Hurston's study of Afro-Caribbean spirituality provides a useful look at significant roots of the Black Church in America, allowing a broader critical scope that encompasses discussions of the positive potential of deconstructing the binary between religious and physical expression. This wider horizon of critical possibility reveals significant paths not only for literary criticism dealing with the Harlem Renaissance but also for conversations about the role of the "spirit" within Black and Transnational feminist theory. Because Larsen uses such a dialogue in *Quicksand* to critique systems of power, readings of her novel alongside the "spirit-filled" works of her contemporaries like Hurston are revelatory. Such readings, I suggest, disrupt the binary between body and soul and offer characters like Helga other possibilities.

This act of upset provides a notion of "spirit" that does not need to slay Helga in order to affect social productivity. Her sexuality can, in this sense, be an actual source of power. She need not be Josephine Baker to "succeed." Rather, she must simply receive the opportunity to let her spirit and sexuality stop fighting each other.

Notes

1. While Hurston and others use the term "Voodoo," I use the Haitian spelling "Vodou," as Voodoo often denotes Americanized connotations of the actual religion Vodou.
2. See especially Jeffrey Gray's "Essence and the Mulatto Traveler: Europe as Embodiment in Nella Larsen's *Quicksand*" (1994), in which Gray discusses the psychological effects of the traveling mulatto and the white inscriptions/objectifications of black bodies.
3. Defalco usefully chronicles Larsen criticism, highlighting Deborah E. McDowell, Ann Rayson, Debra Silverman, Kimberly Monda, and Pamela Barnett, all of whom discuss at length the sexual objectification that Helga suffers under the gaze of hegemonic culture. See Defalco (2005: 21–22).
4. *Quicksand* was originally published by Knopf in 1928. This and all following quotations are from Larsen (1986).
5. When Helga asks her how she is able to manage having so many children without complaining, she says, "Tain't nothin '...Jes' remembah et's natu'al fo' a 'oman to hab chilluns an' don' fret so...Jus' remembah...we all gits ouah res' by an' by. In de nex' worl' we's all recompense.' Jes' put yo' trus' in de Sabioah" (Larsen 1986: 125).
6. Walker (1998) persuasively traces the traditional rejection of the abject maternal body. She goes on to consider the importance of the maternal body and one's maternal subjectivity for an active construction of an autonomous performative self.
7. For other useful studies of Caribbean Vodou, see Métraux (1982) and Laguerre (1980).

Bibliography

Baker, Houston A., Jr. (1991). *Workings of the Spirit: The Poetics of Afro-American Women's Writing.* Chicago: University of Chicago Press.
Barbeito, Patricia Felisa (1998). "'Making Generations' in Jacobs, Larsen, and Hurston: A Genealogy of Black Women's Writing," *American Literature* 70/2 (June): 365–395.

Carby, Hazel (1989). *Reconstructing Womanhood: The Emergence of the Afro-American Woman Novelist.* New York: Oxford.

—— (1999). *Cultures in Babylon: Black Britain and African America.* New York: Verso.

De Weever, Jacqueline (1992). *Mythmaking and Metaphor in Black Women's Fiction.* New York: St. Martin's Press.

Defalco, Amelia (2005). "Jungle Creatures and Dancing Apes: Modern Primitivism and Nella Larsen's *Quicksand*," *Mosaic: A Journal for the Interdisciplinary Study of Literature* 38/2 (June): 19–35.

Grant, Jacquelyn (1982). "Black Women and the Church." In Gloria T. Hull, Patricia Bell Scott, and Barbara Smith (eds.), *All the Women Are White, All the Blacks Are Men, But Some of Us Are Brave*, 141–152. Old Westbury, NY: The Feminist Press.

Gray, Jeffrey (1994). "Essence and the Mulatto Traveler: Europe as Embodiment in Nella Larsen's *Quicksand*," *Novel: A Forum on Fiction* 27/3 (Spring): 257–270.

Henderson, Mae Gwendolyn (2000). "Speaking in Tongues: Dialogics, Dialectics, and the Black Woman Writer's Literary Tradition." In Winston Napier (ed.), *African American Literary Theory: A Reader*, 348–368. New York: New York University Press.

Hurston, Zora Neale (1990) [1938]. *Tell My Horse: Voodoo and Life in Haiti and Jamaica.* New York: Harper & Row.

—— (2006) [1937]. *Their Eyes Were Watching God.* New York: Harper.

James, Stanlie M. (1993). "Mothering: A Possible Black Feminist Link to Social Transformation?" In Stanlie M. James and Abena P. A. Busia (eds.), *Theorizing Black Feminisms: The Visionary Pragmatism of Black Women*, 44–54. London: Routledge.

Laguerre, Michel S. (1980). *Voodoo Heritage.* Beverly Hills, CA: Sage Publications.

Larsen, Nella (1986) [1928]. *Quicksand and Passing.* New Brunswick, NJ: Rutgers University Press.

McDowell, Deborah E. (1986). "Introduction." In Nella Larsen, *Quicksand and Passing*, ix–xxxvii. New Brunswick: Rutgers University Press.

Métraux, Alfred (1982). *Voodoo in Haiti.* New York: Schocken Books.

Monda, Kimberly (1997). "Self Delusion and Self-Sacrifice in Nella Larsen's *Quicksand*," *African American Review* 31/1 (Spring): 23–39.

Mullen, Harryette (1996). "African Signs and Spirit Writing." In Winston Napier (ed.), *African American Literary Theory: A Reader*, 623–642. New York: New York University Press.

Murphy, Joseph M. (1994). *Working the Spirit: Ceremonies of the African Diaspora.* Boston: Beacon.

Napier, Winston (ed.) (1996). *African American Literary Theory: A Reader.* New York: New York University Press.

Rayson, Ann (1998). "Foreign Exotic or Domestic Drudge?: The African American Woman in *Quicksand* and *Tar Baby*," *MELUS* 23/2 (Summer): 87–100.

Reed, Ishmael (1990) [1938]. "Foreword." In Zora Neale Hurston, *Tell My Horse: Voodoo and Life in Haiti and Jamaica*, xi–xv. New York: Harper & Row.

Silverman, Debra B. (1993). "Nella Larsen's *Quicksand*: Untangling the Webs of Exoticism," *African American Review* 27/4 (Winter): 599–614.

Walker, Michelle Boulous (1998). *Philosophy and the Maternal Body: Reading Silence*. London: Routledge.

Chapter 6

Candomblé, Christianity, and Gnosticism in Toni Morrison's *Paradise*

Maha Marouan

Introduction

Toni Morrison's *Paradise* (1998a) is the third volume in a trilogy with *Beloved* (1987) and *Jazz* (1992) that focuses on the theme of excessive love leading to violence. Morrison explains that while in *Beloved* she examines maternal love, and in *Jazz* she writes about erotic love, *Paradise* is about "the love of God...the passionate, even excessive devotion to God as is manifested in how we construct paradises" (Morrison 1988b). This chapter addresses issues surrounding the representation of religion in Toni Morrison's *Paradise* (1988a). It shows how the novel uses African heritage and diverse religious practices as a way to counteract the notion of paradise in white Christian discourse. Specifically, the novel uses the Afro-Brazilian religion Candomblé and Gnostic mysticism in order to make room for an African American consciousness and a sense of identity that stands in opposition to the exclusionary politics of Christianity. Yet, Morrison's representations of Candomblé and Gnosticism also allow for an interrogation of the extent to which these beliefs can become simplified, exoticized and idealized in Western representation.

Morrison's investigation of religious beliefs takes the form of an examination of two communities: the all-black community of Ruby and the neighboring female community that resides in a home known as "the Convent." Significantly, members of both communities have been brought to their present location by experiences of trauma and rejection. Despite these similar experiences, the two communities are forged around different sets of values and definitions of community: Ruby is a patriarchal and strictly Christian community; the religious beliefs of the Convent women, meanwhile, are unclear on a surface reading, but upon deeper examination, they have their origins in Candomblé and Gnosticism. The men of Ruby accuse the women's community of practicing magic and witchcraft, which they believe exemplifies wickedness and threatens the town's moral values. So, the men of Ruby ride out to the Convent and massacre the Convent's female residents in order to keep the town's Christian morals intact.

My intention here is to consider how the three religious discourses—Christianity, Candomblé, and Gnosticism—interact in the novel. I begin by exploring the way Gnosticism and Candomblé function as alternative belief systems. Morrison uses Gnosticism and Candomblé strategically in order to interrogate historical, cultural, and racial discourses as well as gender politics in direct contrast to the Judeo-Christian tradition. Morrison complicates women's spirituality through Candomblé and Gnosticism, and provides a space for the exploration of female spirituality in its full complexity and humanity. The novel's constant evoking of images of Africa allows Morrison to question the politics of race in America, and to shed light on the historical displacement of African Americans. Morrison's vision of paradise as an "earthly home" where everyone is welcome represents her attempt to deconstruct the traditional Judeo-Christian notion of paradise as an exclusive realm into which only the flawless are admitted.

Gnosticism

"Thunder, Perfect Mind"
For many are the pleasant forms which exist in numerous sins,
And incontinencies, and disgraceful passions and fleeting pleasures, which (men)
embrace until they become sober
And go up to their resting place.
And they will find me there,
and they will live,
and they will not die again.[1]

Morrison's epigraph is extracted from a Gnostic poem found at Nag Hammadi in Egypt in 1947 (MacRay and Parrott 1996: 297). It is delivered in the voice of a female divine power, and represents a vision of paradise, a place where the followers of this divine power "will live, and they will not die again." The poem originates in a religious discourse that contradicts Christianity. The divine power that offers salvation is feminine, and the salvation she suggests does not conform to the Christian concept of salvation, but to the ability to embrace "incontinencies, and disgraceful passions and fleeting pleasures." The poem was found among fifty-two Gnostic manuscripts. These manuscripts range from secret gospels and poems to myths of the origins of the universe and magic formulas. The author, date, and place of composition of this mysterious poem are unknown, but it is generally believed that its cultural milieu is the second- or third-century Alexandria. The text was originally composed in Greek well before 350 CE, the approximate date of the Coptic manuscript. It is written in the first-person and represents the voice of a female divine power. The poem has a riddling nature, cultivating ambiguity and narrative indeterminacy in its extensive use of antithesis and paradoxes. The poem remains difficult to classify as it combines the style of biblical wisdom literature, the paradox of a Greek riddle, as well as the self-proclamation style of the Isis aretalogy inscriptions; and yet, while it "resembles many other ancient texts in various ways, its distinctive combination of features is virtually unmatched in the religious and philosophical literature of antiquity" (McGuire 2000). There have been many speculations about the identity of the female figure of the poem. It has been proposed that she refers to the Sophia figures of Gnostic literature, to the figure of Eve, or to the Jewish Dame Wisdom; but most commentators have agreed that the female figure of the poem represents the Egyptian Goddess Isis. Bentley Layton contends that "the most obvious cross-referent to the persona was Isis—an essentially Egyptian or Egyptianizing feature within Gnostic Sethianism. This feature constitutes a kind of evidence, though certainly inconclusive, that the persona was invented and known in Egypt" (1986: 52).

The poem provides an insight into the textual complexities of the novel, deliberately presented and cultivated by Morrison. The lines, which are delivered in the voice of the female figure, suggest a notion of paradise that calls for the ability to embrace paradox. The poem also alludes to a vision of paradise that stems from ancient Egyptian culture and evokes an Egyptian goddess. Through her use of this poem, Morrison engages with an ancient discourse that combines multiple cultures from both the West and the East; additionally, she calls to mind Afrocentric theories about Egypt. In this way, Morrison reclaims a religious discourse that is in essence African. Furthermore, the intricacy of feminine voice in the epigraph allows Morrison to celebrate the complexity of the feminine power associated with ancient religions. Morrison undercuts the Christian discourse and its suppression of the feminine element. The process of idealizing the virgin mother resulted in the production of the shadow-image of Mary in the figure of the hag. Jeffery B. Russell's study of the symbolism of the feminine element in Christianity explains:

> Christianity traditionally found it difficult to accept the principle of ambivalence in the deity: the Christian God was wholly good and wholly masculine, excluding both the feminine principle and the principle of evil. Repression of the principle of evil from the godhead led to the development of the concept of the Devil. Repression of the feminine principle produced a new ambivalence of idealization and contempt. (1980: 117–118)

Thus, by introducing an ancient female deity and an ancient religion that views the world in terms of multiplicity and ambiguity, the novel ruptures the dualistic oppositions associated with the perception of deity in Christianity. Consolata, the Convent female leader, celebrates the complexity of the feminine element and expresses her opposition to the Christian dualities when she instructs the women in the Convent: "Hear me, listen. Never break them in two. Never put one over the other. Eve is Mary's mother. Mary is the daughter of Eve" (263). Consolata here, like the female figure of "Thunder, Perfect Mind," insists on the merging of the two opposite images of the sinning flesh and the immaculate soul associated with Christian tradition.

Morrison's exploration of paradoxical discourses is also reflected through her contradictory portrayal of the Convent women.[2] The Convent women allow Morrison to engage with feminine power in its ambivalence. While, on the one hand, they are sheltering and spiritual, on the other hand, they are passive and unable to deal with the practical side of life. They are threatening to the patriarchal, Christian, and racially separatist community of Ruby as they form a bond with their natural environment and they do not set boundaries for themselves. When Mavis arrives at the Convent seeking shelter, she is surprised by the isolation of the place. She asks Consolata: " 'You ain't scared to be out here all by yourselves?' Connie laughed: 'Scary things not always outside. Most scary things inside' " (39). This statement stands in opposition to the territorial attitude of Ruby's community to the land and to the community's sense of displacement. In contrast with the racially pure people of Ruby, who are highly conscious and proud of their blackness, the Convent women, who are racially mixed, move beyond fixed racial definition. The Convent women's religious practices are also distinct from those of Ruby and result from a combination of religious beliefs. The women use religious rituals to celebrate their femininity in contrast with Ruby, where religion is used to suppress women's sexuality and confine them to the domestic sphere. Morrison is not explicit about the origin of the Convent women's religious practices; however, I contend that the Convent rituals led by Consolata are a blend of Gnostic mysticism and Afro-Brazilian Candomblé. Through the Convent women, Morrison provides an insight into a concept of paradise different to the one formulated in the orthodox Christian discourse. For the Convent women, religion is liberating rather than restraining. Under the guidance of their spiritual leader, Consolata, they undergo a ritualistic process that enables them to deal with their traumatic experiences and exorcise their pains. Ironically, these women who are criticized for their immorality become the true believers. Through their peaceful ritual they discover the divine within themselves and reach self-knowledge. When one of the Ruby women named Soane visits them she notices the crucial difference:

> [T]he charged air of the house, its foreign feel and a markedly different look at the tenants' eyes—sociable and connecting when they spoke to you, otherwise they were still and appraising... how calmly themselves they seemed. And Connie—how straight-backed and handsome she looked... unlike some people in Ruby, the Convent women were no longer haunted. (266)

The Convent women reach harmony and attain self-knowledge, or what Gnostics call gnosis, which entails a major belief that remains antithetical to the institutional church understanding of a chasm separating God from humanity. Gnostics believe that knowledge comes from within, and that the psyche bears within itself the potential for liberation or destruction.[3] Consolata, for instance, resembles the divine female figure of the Gnostic poem in her complexity. Like the divine power who gives voice to internal contradictions, "I am the honored one and the scorned one I am the whore and the holy one" (Robinson 1996: 297). Consolata also contains contradictions within herself. She is "honored" for her sheltering power, but "scorned" by her ex-lover and the people of Ruby who accuse her of wickedness and witchcraft.

Consolata, who discovers that she is endowed with magical powers, is unable to reconcile her supernatural powers with the devotion to Christian faith instilled in her youth at the convent. She reflects on her situation and wonders why God endows, or rather inflicts, on her such powers: "He was sometimes overgenerous. Like giving satanic gifts to a drunken, ignorant, penniless woman living in darkness unable to rise from a cot to do something useful or die on it and rid the world of her stench" (248). Consolata here is torn between her devotion to Catholicism and her magical powers. Through Consolata's religious dilemma, Morrison interrogates Christian discourse which historically condemned magic. Expressions such as "evil" and "satanic," used here by Consolata, express Christianity's radical denunciation of magic as a non-Christian practice. Morrison instead, celebrates the supernatural powers that enable Consolata to heal others. Specifically, she possesses the ability to raise the dead by "stepping in"—a practice that enables her to reach inside other people. Consolata uses this gift to revive Mary Magna, the mother superior who adopted her, even though Consolata knows that the woman would condemn this non-Christian practice:

> Stepping in to find the pinpoint of light. Manipulating it, widening it, strengthening it. Reviving it, even rising her from time to time. And so intense were the steppings in, Mary Magna glowed like a lamp till her very last breath in Consolata's arms. So she had practiced, and although it was for the benefit of the woman she loved, she knew it was an anathema that Mary Magna would have recoiled in disgust and fury knowing her life was prolonged by evil. (247)

In this way, Morrison rewrites Consolata as a Christ-like female figure who can perform the miracle of resurrection.

Consolata's powers also allow her to resurrect the traumatized Convent women from their hollow existence and lead them to exorcise their pain and reach the salvation that the epigraph refers to as "a place where they will live, and will not die again." In her ability to embrace traumatized women and help them to heal their emotional wounds, Consolata resembles the divine mother in Gnosticism whom Elaine Pagels describes in her much celebrated work, *The Gnostic Gospels*: "Besides being the 'first universal creator' who brings forth all creatures," she also "enlightens human beings and makes them wise" (1990: 141). The character of Consolata as a divine power allows Morrison to emphasize a different aspect of Christianity—one in which women played an important part from the beginning.[4]

Morrison's celebration of female spirituality in its complexity is also expressed through Consolata's ambiguous sexual character. Consolata bears the dyadic nature of the Gnostic God. Some Gnostics adopted the idea that God is masculo-feminine. Pagels claims that "since the Genesis account goes on to say that humanity was created male and female" (1: 27), some concluded that the God in whose image we are made must also be both masculine and feminine—both father and mother" (1990: 72). The novel also seems to suggest that Consolata is masculo-feminine when a mystical male figure appears to her in the Convent. He is her masculine shadow-image, and bears a striking physical resemblance to her, with his tea-colored hair and his distinguished green eyes. Morrison writes

> Not six inches from her face, he removed his tall hat. Fresh, tea-colored hair came tumbling down, cascading over his shoulders and down his back. He took off his glasses then and winked, a slow seductive movement of a lid. His eyes, she saw, were as round and green as new apples.

Consolata asks him who he is and he answers "come on girl you know me" (252). He represents the masculine side of her divine nature. Through him Consolata gets in touch with her other side, and with her dyadic nature, thus embracing the wholeness of her being.

Indeed, it is only after this encounter that Consolata becomes powerful and strong enough to instruct the Convent women, and leads them into a ritual to exorcise the pain of the past. During Consolata's instructions the women find it difficult to recognize the changed Consolata because her features become more masculine, suggesting again her new masculo-feminine identity. She has the "features of dear Connie, but they are sculpted somehow—higher cheekbones, stronger chin. Had her eyebrows always been that thick?" (262). Following Consolata's instructions the Convent women dance all night. Through their dancing they reach an ecstatic state symbolic of their recovery. They attain what the Gnostics call the "Transcendent Kingdom" (Donovan 1990: 3).[5] Consolata, like the divine power in *"Thunder, Perfect Mind,"* becomes powerful and sheltering only when she recognizes her other side and embraces her masculo-feminine nature.

Consolata's encounter with the mysterious man recalls Zechariah's encounter with the walking man (a kind of Moses), who led the black families to their promised land in Ruby. The walking man provides spiritual guidance to the black families in the same way Consolata's double provides guidance for her in her spiritual quest to heal the Convent women. A parallel is established between the black families' spiritual journey and that of the Convent women. Morrison uses biblical imagery in order to create space for women's spiritual experiences and to engage a female quest for spirituality and liberation. Morrison's interrogation of the politics of exclusivity in her novel is also an interrogation of the place of women within the Judeo-Christian tradition and thus, within the African American historical and spiritual struggle. However, a comparison between Ruby's men's religious experience and that of the Convent women seems to suggest that while the Convent women's quest for liberation is spiritual, the holy journey of the black families is territorial. The significance of their journey lies in claiming the land.

Through Gnosticism, Morrison attempts to create a female community
that exemplifies the power of the feminine principle in its fluidity, spirituality, tolerance, and regeneration. In *Rethinking Gnosticism*, Michael Allen
Williams argues that the generalized view of Gnosticism as female-centered is not justified by any ancient self-definition. Gnosticism, according
to Williams, is an umbrella term that has been used in scholarly research
and popular culture to invoke a rather romanticized image of a pre-Christian tradition (1996: 53). While on the surface, this might suggest that
Morrison's novel appeals to an idealized construction of Gnosticism and
elevates Gnostic literature without fully engaging with it, a close reading
shows that Morrison's engagement with Gnosticism is strategic, allowing
her to celebrate female spirituality and rewrite women beyond the moral
dichotomies of Christian discourse. This is highlighted in the way in
which she portrays her female characters:

> Now and then one or another packed a scruffy little bag, said goodbye and
> seemed to disappear for a while—but only a while. They always came back
> to stay on, living like mice in a house no one, not even the tax collector,
> wanted....Consolata looked at them through the bronze or grey or blue of
> her various sunglasses and saw broken girls, frightened girls, weak and
> lying...Not only did they do nothing except the absolutely necessary, they
> had no plans to do anything. Instead of plans they had wishes—foolish
> babygirl wishes. (222)

Morrison here is critical of the Convent women's spirituality and portrays
it as a form of escapism. While associated with openness and spirituality,
they also are women who refuse to engage with the practical side of life.
This inability to engage with reality provides a sharp contrast to the
community of Ruby, which deals with the particularities of daily life and
where social and personal relationships are more complicated. The complexity with which Morrison represents her female characters shows that
Morrison is not committed simply to celebrating Gnostic rituals. More
specifically, Morrison self-consciously constructs Gnosticism as female-
centered religion in order to rewrite women's spirituality and celebrate the
power of the feminine principle in its fluidity, ambiguity, tolerance and
regeneration against male-centered patriarchal religious discourses.

Candomblé

During the 1980s Toni Morrison visited Brazil to learn about the religious
practices of Candomblé. Her trip suggests a link between the rituals

practiced by the Convent women and the Afro-Brazilian religion. While she was in Brazil, Morrison heard a story—which turned out to be untrue—about a group of black nuns who were murdered by a group of men because they were practicing Candomblé. The Convent women in *Paradise* are similarly exterminated by the men of Ruby because they are accused of practicing "strange rituals." They are described by the men of Ruby as "These here sluts out there by themselves never step foot in church and bet you a dollar to a fat nickel they ain't thinking about one either. They don't need men and they don't need God" (276).

The rituals practiced by the Convent women under the leadership of Consolata, who is also Brazilian in origin, stem from Candomblé, the Afro-Brazilian religion practiced by Africans who were brought to Brazil as slave laborers. This religion combines Catholic and African rituals. In *Spirits from the Margin*, Fernando Giobellina Brumana and Elda Gonzales Martinez describe it as a religion that is devoted to

a series of divinities (orixas) whose African names are always connected to those representative of the Catholic pantheon. Each sacred entity is bound to places of the world, human activities, colours, food, etc.; over all of them reigns oxala, equivalent to Jesus. These deities are made present on earth by their mediumist incorporation in their human *filhos*, with clothes, attributes, corporal attitudes, and differential specific dances, in different types of public and private ceremonies, and according to a highly elaborate ritual codification. (1989: 32–33)

Candomblé rituals are both male and female directed. However, women were the first establishers of Candomblé temples in Brazil, and the majority of temples are still led by women. In *Sacred Leaves of Candomblé*, Robert A. Voeks reports that the first houses of Candomblé were established in the early nineteenth century in Bahia, Brazil. They were founded by three freed African Nigerian women, and were dedicated to Yoruba gods and goddesses (1997: 63). Voeks talks about the female directed Candomblé temple where the *mae-de-santo*, or mother-of-saints "represents the principal line of communication between the material world of mortals and the spiritual world of deities" (51).

Morrison's Consolata takes the role of mother-of-saints when she initiates the Convent women. Their initiation is similar to the initiation rites of Candomblé, where the initiates isolate themselves for months to get prepared to meet the orixas. Consolata tells the Convent women "stay here and follow me. Someone could want to meet you" (262), preparing them to meet the orixas. Consolata also recalls from her childhood memories in Brazil "scented Cathedrals made of gold where gods and goddesses sat in the pews with the congregation" (264). The reference to the gods and goddesses here sheds light on the longstanding identification in Candomblé between Catholic saints and African gods and goddesses. The dancing rituals of the Convent women also bear a close affinity with Candomblé dancing ceremony, where the possessed incarnate the deity's energy through dancing.[6] The Convent women are "holy women dancing in hot sweet rain," and when they return to the house after the Candomblé dancing rites they are as "tired from their night dance, but happy" (283–284).

Lone Dupre's remark to Consolata also evokes Candomblé cosmology and the concept of balance that is central to this belief system. She advises Consolata, "You need what we all need: earth, air, water. Don't separate God from His elements. He created it all. You stuck on dividing Him from his works. Don't unbalance His world" (244). This is a reference to the Candomblé worldview that gives a crucial importance to natural elements—water, air, forest, and earth; these are the primary sources from which the orixas gather and impart their universal energy, *axe*, and pass it to their adherents. Any problems in Candomblé communities—physical, spiritual, social, political, or ecological—are seen as a sign of imbalance, and it is this universal energy that redresses and remedies these imbalances (Voeks 1997: 56). The power of *axe* is manifest through possession ceremonies, where the deities bring their transformative power to their devotees. These ceremonies, in which the divine become incarnate in human forms, express the continuous interdependency between the spiritual and material world at the core of Candomblé cosmology. Sheila S. Walker addresses this holistic vision of Candomblé cosmology. In Candomblé, she reports:

> there is no gulf between the natural and the supernatural, between the profane and the sacred. The human and superhuman are not really distinct. They interpenetrate and can become one another. There is no discontinuity between humans and the natural realm that surrounds them because the forces of nature are anthropomorphized. (1990: 125)

Paradise ends with the massacred Convent women who continue to exist again in a parallel universe after their death, which refers to that continuity and dialectic between the spiritual and material world in Candomblé. This parallel plane offers the Convent women the opportunity to address earlier experience of trauma. The Convent women become reconciled with their families. Gigi meets with her father, Pallas with her mother, and Mavis with her daughter. Instead of the broken destroyed women they were, they come out strong and confident. Pallas and Gigi emerge as warriors with

Gigi in army clothes and Pallas carrying a sword. There is a vision of Consolata on the beach with her head on Piedade's lap, just like Jesus in Mary's lap. Morrison describes her as "In ocean hush, a woman black as firewood is singing" (318). Piedade sings of solace while watching ships "heading to port, crew and passengers, lost and saved, atremble, for they have been disconsolate for some time. Now they will rest before shouldering the endless work they were created to do down here in Paradise" (318). Piedade refers to the Egyptian Goddess Isis, but the association with the ocean, the shores and the beach also suggests the connection with the Candomblé goddess of the Sea, Yemanjá, an archetypal symbol of fertility and motherhood, but who is also identified by Candomblé followers with the Virgin Mary (Voeks 1997: 56).

Through Candomblé, Morrison creates an alternative space in *Paradise* to challenge the racial, cultural, and gender politics of white Christian values. The Candomblé belief system has developed as one of the major religious expressions of the African Diaspora and has been recognized as a rich source of African tradition. It has been established in the new world by women, and incorporates elements of both African beliefs and Christianity. *Spirits from the Margin* talks about the harassment that those who practiced Candomblé were exposed to by the Brazilian state, which recalls the extermination of the Convent women by the strictly Christian male community of Ruby. Giobellina and Martinez comment: "Umbanda, together with Candomblé and the other Afro-Brazilian cults, suffered the greatest persecutions at the same time as the Brazilian Left, above all the Communist party, passed through the same experience" (1989: 295). Morrison is giving voice to a belief system that survived the pressure of white dominant culture and succeeded in preserving the link with West African traditions and rituals. Candomblé allows Morrison to establish continuity with the African roots, create a space for women and their spirituality, and provide a model of hybridity between an institutionalized and a non-institutional religion. However, it is not possible to engage with Candomblé without a consideration of the power dynamics involved in the process of syncretism and the way they impinge on the politics of class, race and gender.

Candomblé still remains the religion of the poor and the underprivileged in Brazil. Most Candomblé followers are from the lowest segment of society. David J. Hess who explores the polarities of the religious system in Brazil as marked by race, class, and gender politics writes:

> [a]t the European (white, privileged) end of the spectrum, the Catholic Church hierarchy (priests, bishops, and so forth) is still the province of men. At the African (black, underprivileged) end of the spectrum, women

are usually the only mediums (the mothers-of-the-saints) in the most
orthodox of Yoruba or Nago Condombles. Thus, in the most general sense,
the Brazilian religious system might be pictured as having two poles—a
male, European, elite religion (Catholicism) versus a female, African,
popular religion (Candomblé)—with a variety of other religions in
between. (1994: 144)[7]

Morrison's novel expresses these very same polarities and power dynamics
between the all-black community, which represents the male, white, elite
religion, as opposed to the Convent women who represent an underprivileged female African-based belief system. However, Morrison uses
Candomblé strategically in order to elevate this Afro-Brazilian religion and
intentionally constructs it as a model of racial and cultural hybridity,
religious tolerance, and women's empowerment.

Women's Voices Evoking Africa

The interaction of Gnosticism and Candomblé—two beliefs system that give
voice to women and evoke images of Africa, its culture, and goddesses—
allows Morrison to question the exclusionary politics of white Christian
discourse. The reference to Africa in the novel as a possible utopia allows
Morrison to interrogate white America's racial politics. The Gnostic poem
in the epigraph provides a framework for Morrison's utopian engagement
with Africa. While the Gnostic poem in its multiple religious discourses is
symbolic of the relationship between different cultures, it also alludes to
African culture due to the fact that it arose in Egypt and refers to an
Egyptian divine power. The choice of Candomblé is equally informed by
the connection to Africa. By reclaiming Candomblé in her exploration of
African American cultural and historical identity, Morrison is acknowledging the importance of African roots, as well as evoking the link between
Afro-Brazilian and African American diasporic experiences. The novel
expresses this through Consolata's meeting with the people of Ruby and
with Deacon. When she first visits the town and sees their celebrations, it
reminds her of her childhood home, Brazil:

A memory of just such skin and just such men, dancing with women in the
streets to music beating like an infuriated heart, torsos still, hips making
small circles above legs moving so rapidly it was fruitless to decipher how
such ease was possible. . . . And although they were living here in a hamlet,
not in a loud city full of glittering black people, Consolata knew she knew
them. (226)

Consolata feels the same towards Deacon. She is attracted to him partly because of the familiarity of his dark skin color. She feels that being with him is being "home." She tells Mary Magna "he and I are the same" (241). Here, again, there is another reference to doubling. Deacon becomes Consolata's cultural double, reminding her of her African roots.

Candomblé remains a model of how diasporic religions survived in the New World, with a rich retention of African traditions, rituals and folklore. This process of diffusion is closely intertwined with the history of the transatlantic slave trade. Voeks points out that unlike North America, which had received roughly 5 percent of those reaching the New World, Brazil absorbed "about 40 percent of the total slave population to arrive in the New World over the four centuries of slave trafficking" and was numerically dominated by Africans. This allowed for a continuous diffusion of African traditions, cosmology, and medicine. The survival of African beliefs was also facilitated by the structural similarity of Brazilian Catholicism, which was quite different to the strict Catholicism of Rome. Iberia, Voeks explains, "had preserved a medieval Catholicism of the Counter-Reformation, a folk religion grounded in a hagiology of hands-on, miracle-working saints" (1997: 157). The saint worship corresponded to the worship of orixas, as well as the extravagant Catholic ceremonies that corresponded to African religious rites. Thus, while Catholicism allowed for a basis for identification, North American Protestant churches, according to Voeks, were controlled by Methodists and Calvinists ethics, which differed profoundly from the structure of African religious beliefs and practices (157–158).

It is also important to note that for Afro-Brazilians the connection to Africa is not only symbolic. Rather, it has a real and concrete presence. Melville and Francis Herskovits observed in their 1943 account of Afro-Brazilian religion that to the Afro-Brazilians "Africa is no vague mythical land...It is living reality, whence many of the objects they use in their rituals are imported, where people they know have visited and...where their fathers or grandfathers came from" (Voeks 1997: 150). Voeks further explores how the link between West Africa and Brazil was constant and vibrant through numbers of repatriated Africans who kept the link through the transatlantic trading of goods and items needed by the black population in Bahia, and also through Candomblé as "several of the most important houses of Candomblé were founded by African repatriates who eventually returned to Bahia." Voeks provides examples of Afro-Brazilians who moved to West Africa, learned Yoruba and English, and returned to Brazil to become leaders of Candomblé temples and consultants for Candomblé houses on matters of African rituals. This tangible connection to Africa experienced by Afro-Brazilians and maintained through a vibrant religious diffusion provides a scope for the discussion of Africa and its significance for African Americans (150). Yet, Morrison's invocations of Candomblé entail more than simply a romanticized project of cultural recovery. Through Candomblé, Morrison attempts to undercut the vision of utopia and its association with Africa as some mythical place, and emphasizes a tangible historical and cultural connection to Africa. The link with Africa as maintained through Candomblé provides a sharp contrast with the all-black community of Ruby for whom Africa remains an alien concept—as is the case with Patricia and Soane, for instance. Patricia believes that teaching the kids about Africa is futile as she tells Reverend Misner: "I just don't believe some stupid devotion to a foreign country—and Africa is a foreign country, in fact it's fifty foreign countries—is a solution for these kids" (210). Whereas Soane feels that all the connection she has with Africa is "the seventy-five cents she gave to the missionary society collection. She had the same level of interest in Africans as they had in her: none" (104).

The novel closes with a celebration of black female Goddesses who have been suppressed within the Judeo-Christian tradition. As noted earlier, Consolata is resting on the beach with her head on Piedade's lap, like Jesus in Mary's arms. Meanwhile, on the beach "sea trash gleams. Discarded bottle caps sparkle near a broken sandal. A small dead radio plays the quiet surf" (318). This far-from-idealistic description of the beach expresses Morrison's idea about paradise as an earthly place. Piedade is singing and "the words evoke memories that neither one [Consolata and Piedade] has ever had: of reaching age in the company of the other; of speech shared and divided bread smoking from the fire; the unambivalent bliss of going home to be at home—the ease to come back to love begun" (318). This description of paradise is highly ambiguous and allows for different interpretations. The place that Consolata and Piedade are unfamiliar with, but which brings memories of home to them, is possibly Africa—where the language is recognizable, and where there is no sense of displacement, "the unambivalent bliss of going home to be at home" (318). The paragraph ends with the following images:

> When the ocean heaves sending rhythms of water ashore, Piedade looks to see what has come. Another ship, perhaps, but different, heading to port, crew and passengers, lost and saved, atremble, for they have been disconsolate for some time. Now they will rest before shouldering the endless work they were created to do down here in Paradise. (318)

The association of paradise with the beach and the shore alludes to the transatlantic slave trade that carried slaves from the African shores.

Piedade waits for a ship that is "different." Does that mean that Piedade is awaiting a ship that is different from slave ships? Does Morrison's vision of paradise, then, refer to an Africa that has not been violated by the slave trade? Yet, the description of paradise in this section also deconstructs the concept of paradise as a heavenly place. The beauty of Morrison's paradise is transmitted through its contradictory images; mundane, imperfect images of sea trash, a broken sandal, and bottle caps, as well as through the rhythms of the waves, and peace and solace emerging from Piedade's voice. This earthly paradise is also a place accessible for everyone, "passengers, lost and saved" (318). This description echoes the vision of paradise in the Gnostic poem in the epigraph, in which paradise is a place where all contradictions are embraced. This shows the circular movement of the novel, where the vision of paradise expressed at the beginning of the narrative corresponds with the novel's final vision. *Paradise* ends with a vision of paradise, a place where the Convent women meet again with their spiritual guide, Consolata, and where they meet Piedade who is another goddess-like figure. While casting a skeptical eye towards the notion of utopias, Morrison's paradise is an attempt to celebrate women's spirituality against Judeo-Christian discourses in which the feminine principle remains suppressed.

Notes

1. Morrison uses these lines in her epigraph to *Paradise*. They are from "Thunder, Perfect Mind," a mysterious poem that has been found among the Nag Hammadi transcripts. Most of the information I cite here about the poem is from Hedrick and Hodgson (1986).
2. Morrison's novel becomes extremely complex in the way it portrays the characters especially in relation to the issue of morality and immorality, good and evil, as most characters are a complex combination of both. In her interview with Paul Gray about *Paradise*, Morrison comments that the men of Ruby "are fascinating mixtures of virtues and vices: proud, independent, argumentative, close-minded" (Gray 1998). The Convent women are equally complex. While they exemplify feminine power in its fluidity, spirituality, tolerance, and regeneration, they are at the same time unpractical and weak.
3. For more details about the Gnostic concept of salvation see Elaine Pagels (1990). Pagels writes that "the conviction of whoever explores human experience simultaneously discovers divine reality is one of the elements that marks Gnosticism as a distinctly religious movement" (141).
4. Pagels claims that the early Christian movement showed an openness to women, but this situation was overturned in a remarkably short period of time,

disappearing completely by the second century. She contends that among certain Gnostic groups

> women were considered equal to men; some were revered as prophets; others acted as teachers, travelling evangelists, healers, priests, perhaps even bishops…But from the year 200, we have no evidence for women taking prophetic, priestly, and Episcopal roles among orthodox churches. (81)

5. According to Donovan, the Gnostics believed that they belonged to the realm of good or the transcendent realm, but they existed in an evil world. They felt displaced from their original world, but it was this transcendent part of their beings, or "pneuma," that identified them as beings from another world or "The Transcendent Kingdom." Donovan compares Gnosticism to Existentialism and finds them similar inasmuch as they both view human beings as fundamentally alienated:

> The Gnostics perceived them as thrown into a world controlled by archons; Existentialists saw them as thrown into the alienating clutches of bureaucracy or into a state of tyranny under the mores of what Heidegger called *Das Man*. In each vision humanity has been uprooted from the ground of meaning; each urges that it be re-rooted in a sacred ground. (7)

6. Voeks contends that "the most intimate ritual act is that of being possessed by the spiritual force of the orixa, of making this energy manifest by incarnating it in one's flesh; dancing for and as an orixa" (1997: 124).

7. Hess also looks at the issue of sexuality in both religions and argues that "The fathers of the Catholic priesthood are unmarried (as are gay men), whereas the women of Candomblé s are referred to as 'mothers-of-saints' a term that suggests procreation and therefore heterosexuality" (1991: 145).

Bibliography

Donovan, Josephine (1990). *Gnosticism in Modern Literature: A Study of the Selected Works of Camus, Sartre, Hesse, and Kafka*. London: Garland Publishing.

Giobellina, Fernando Brumana and Elda Gonzales Martinez (eds.) (1989). *Spirits from the Margin: Umbanda in Sao Paulo*. Uppsala, Sweden: Uppsala University Press.

Gray, Paul (1998). "Paradise Found," *Time*, January 19. <http://www.time.com/time/magazine/1998/dom/980119/cover 1.html>. Accessed December 16, 2000.

Hedrick, Charles W. and Robert Hodgson (eds.) (1986). *Nag Hammadi, Gnosticism, and Early Christianity*. Peabody: Hendrickson.

Hess, David (1991). *Samba in the Night: Spiritism in Brazil*. New York: Columbia University Press.

Layton, Bentley (1986). " 'The Riddle of the Thunder' (NHC VI, 2): The Function of Paradox in a Gnostic Text from Nag Hammadi." In Charles W. Hedrick and

Robert Hodgson (eds), *Nag Hammadi, Gnosticism, and Early Christianity*, 37–54. Peabody, MA: Hendrickson.

MacRay, George W. and Douglas M. Parrott (trans.) (1996). "Thunder, Perfect Mind." In James M. Robinson (ed.), *The Nag Hammadi Library in English*: *The Definitive New Translation of the Gnostic Scriptures*, 4th revised edition, 297. Leiden: E. J. Brill.

McGuire, Anne (trans.) (2000). "The Thunder: Perfect Mind (CG VI.2: 13, 121, 32)" <http://www.stoa.org/diotima/anthology/thunder.shtml>. Accessed December 18, 2000.

Morrison, Toni (1987). *Beloved*. New York: Knopf.

—— (1992). *Jazz*. New York: Knopf.

—— (1998a). *Paradise*. New York: Knopf.

—— (1998b). "A Conversation with Toni Morrison," Borders.com <http://go.borders.com/features/mmk98004.xcv>. Accessed December 16, 2000.

Pagels, Elaine (1990) [1979]. *The Gnostic Gospels*. London: Penguin.

Robinson, James M. (ed.) (1996). *The Nag Hammadi Library in English*: *The Definitive New Translation of the Gnostic Scriptures*, 4th revised edition. Leiden, Holland: E. J. Brill.

Russell, Jeffrey B. (1980). *A History of Witchcraft: Sorcerers, Heretics, and Pagans*. London: Thames and Hudson.

Voeks, Robert A. (1997). *Sacred Leaves of Candomblé: African Magic, Medicine, and Religion in Brazil*. Austin: University of Texas Press.

Walker, Sheila S. (1990). "Everyday and Esoteric Reality in the Afro-Brazilian Candomblé," *History of Religions*, 30: 103–128.

Williams, Michael Allen (1996). *Rethinking "Gnosticism": An Argument for Dismantling a Dubious Category*. Princeton: Princeton University Press.

Part 3

Diaspora in Latin America and the
Caribbean

Chapter 7

The African Diaspora in Mexico: Santería, Tourism, and Representations of the State

Angela N. Castañeda

Introduction

This chapter addresses the need to revisit and reinvigorate academic research on the African diaspora in Mexico. Using examples from ongoing ethnographic fieldwork in Veracruz, this research illustrates how performances involving representations of the African diaspora and the Afro-Cuban religion of Santería in particular are shaped and informed by both local and national government funding, and as a result, directly linked to multiple agendas.[1] This research deconstructs the use of an African-derived religious tradition in conjunction with a reinterpretation of the *mestizaje*, or race-mixing, concept so integral in the Americas. The importance of religion is highlighted as a cultural tradition commercialized via festivals into foreign symbols of local identity.

Veracruz City and State

Extending approximately 500 miles along the Gulf of Mexico, the state of Veracruz is historically home to such rich civilizations as the Huastec,

Totonac, and Olmec, while the port city of Veracruz was witness to the Spanish invasion and shortly thereafter the arrival of approximately 250,000 African slaves.[2] The eleventh largest state in the Republic, Veracruz covers an area of more than 45,000 square miles and approximately 3.7 percent of Mexico's national territory (INEGI 2002: 33). Its history is overflowing with bouts of foreign intrusion led by the Spanish (1825), the French (1839), and the United States (1847 and 1914). Each of these invasions sparked further strength and independence in the local people while simultaneously exposing them to new cultures, peoples, and ideas that would later shape their own way of seeing the world. Today, Veracruz is still strongly tied to the land as many of its nearly 7 million residents continue the cultivation of tobacco, coffee, sugar, and cattle ranches; but by far this state's main source of income flows from the sea and the earth from fishing and oil respectively.

El Puerto de Veracruz, more commonly known as just El Puerto or simply Veracruz, is one of the oldest port cities in the Americas. It is located approximately 7 hours or 261 miles due east of Mexico City, the nation's capital, and only 2 hours or 65 miles southeast of the state capital of Xalapa. Unfortunately, the strategic location of this port city served to welcome foreign intervention, and on April 21, 1519, Hernan Cortés, accompanied by his Spanish fleet, landed on the coast of Veracruz at a point facing the *Isla de Sacrificios* or Sacrifice Island. The Spanish named their settlement *La Villa Rica de la Vera Cruz* or The Rich Village of the True Cross. The original city was actually situated about fifty miles north of its present location, and in 1525, the Spanish moved their base to La Antigua, between present day Veracruz and Zempoala, before they finally established their colony at the present site of Veracruz in 1598 (Ramos 1992: 44). Its history is bursting with bloody battles, as after Cortés's arrival the city was immersed in a stormy era dominated by the Spanish, pirates, and the slave trade. Veracruz remained the only port allowed to handle trade with Spain until the year 1760. Despite the rich trading possibilities linked to the city's location and the monopoly over incoming Spanish products, Veracruz did not flourish as one of the largest cities in Mexico mainly owing to the numerous pirate attacks and rampant tropical diseases such as malaria and yellow fever. Damaged by disease, Veracruz has struggled against misfortune since the time of its founding. Despite Mexico's victory of independence as a nation in 1820, the Spanish continued to attack Veracruz for twenty-six months—from September of 1823 to November of 1825. Later, in 1838, Veracruz again had to withstand foreign invasion, this time from the French, who occupied the city and demanded reparation for damages suffered after the War of Independence. In 1847 American troops occupied the city and again in 1914 as marines halted a shipment of arms to

Mexican dictator Victoriano Huerta. The city has even christened itself *Cuatro Veces Heróica* or Four Times Heroic because of these four military invasions that it has suffered.

As noted above, African slaves came to Veracruz shortly after the arrival of Cortés. Within the state, two regions in particular attracted great numbers of African slaves—El Puerto de Veracruz and Los Tuxtlas. The Veracruz port became the main entry point for slaves and Los Tuxtlas provided the fertile lands that would require the hard labor of African slaves in the production of both sugar and tobacco. The first slaves to arrive in Veracruz are believed to have come from Angola and the Congo, but over time the practice of bringing slaves directly from Africa decreased. The majority of slaves to arrive later in Veracruz were known as *negros criollos* because they were the first generation of slaves born in the Americas and came principally from the Caribbean (Naveda 2001: 32).

Research on African influences in Mexico has centered on historical perspectives with particular emphasis on the colonial period (Bennett 2002; Palmer 1976; Richmond 2001; Twillie 1995). During this time period a comparison between the number of people of African descent to that of Spaniards in Mexico is of importance. Bennett's research (2002) points to the abundance of African descent people, which in the sixteenth and seventeenth centuries outnumbered the Spanish.

The exact number of Africans brought into Mexico remain unclear. After factoring in the unreliability involved in the documentation of the actual arrival of slave ships and the amount of undocumented slaves via pirate ships and other routes, it becomes quite clear that to arrive at an exact number of slaves in any given port in the Americas is nearly impossible. However, we can estimate, and in so doing it becomes obvious that the numbers recorded in different sources reflect the theoretical and political views held by the authors. According to research conducted in the book *Africa in Latin America*, Manuel Moreno Fraginals estimates a minimum of 9.5 million slaves were brought to the Americas. This is contrasted with the book *No Longer Invisible*, where Minority Rights Group cites between 10 and 50 million with the largest numbers arriving in Brazil, Cuba, the Caribbean, and the United States.

Focusing specifically on the case of Mexico, we also find a fairly large margin of difference in actual numbers of slaves brought into the country. Gonzalo Aguirre Beltrán notes in his work *Cuijla: Esbozo etnográfico de un pueblo negro*, "Blacks in Mexico were a minority group; they represented from 0.1 to 2% of the colonial population; the numbers introduced were not more than 250,000 individuals during the course of three centuries" (1958: 8).[3] Adriana Naveda's work further emphasizes the lack of accuracy associated with the slave trade in Veracruz, noting that "The real numbers might never be understood because there weren't any complete registries of the slaves brought legally through the Port of Veracruz, not to mention the evidence that suggests the extended presence of an illegal commercial operation" (2001: 32).[4]

Besides the actual slave trade, Naveda points to other more recent migrations of people of African descent to Veracruz. She notes that many soldiers who fought with the U.S. and France included people of African descent who ultimately stayed in Veracruz after their service. Alongside military influences, there are economic reasons that led to an increased African presence in Veracruz. During the *Porfiriato*[5] many workers from the Caribbean, mainly Jamaica, were brought to work on the construction of railroads in this state (Naveda 2001: 41).

Historically, the port of Veracruz has continued to be used as a major destination for both people and products from all over the world. Its presence as a bustling port city, with materials arriving in the port daily, cultivates communities that are more likely to mix with other cultures. While these characteristics of this port city are often times interpreted as further diluting any links between African influences on Veracruz culture, this work demonstrates that indeed African-derived influences can be found in Veracruz today and are representative of a more recent Afro-Caribbean influence.

Reconstructing Local Identity

While Veracruz is physically separated from other Caribbean nations, the desire to become functionally integrated, via festival performance, as part of the Caribbean community also means facing the challenge to recognize the African presence inherent in both its past and present. When addressing issues of blackness in Mexico, some scholars opt for a very narrow historical lens (Naveda 2001; Martínez Montiel 1995; Thompson 1983), attempting to find a continuous link connecting the past with the present and discovering pure identifiers of African elements. In contrast to this unilateral approach, other scholars note the multiplicity of black identities that are "defined and redefined, imagined and reimagined, performed and performed again within the flux of history and within specific, changing, spatially determined societal structures" (Rahier 1999: xxiv). In order to assess the "presence of blackness" in Mexico today, it is imperative to recognize this difficulty in identifying "pure" African elements. It is also important to frame notions of blackness within this study to the separate levels on which this concept is interpreted: national, state, and local, each with a different set of political, cultural, and contextual influencers. Indeed, the African diaspora in Mexico exists in various forms in accordance with different levels of state and national agendas. Official notions of a national identity created by elites in Mexico, as well as in other Latin American countries, revolve around the process of *mestizaje* or race-mixing. This process involves the whitening both racially and culturally of all other groups—highlighting indigenous contributions while negating African influences. Renowned Mexican anthropologist Gonzalo Aguirre Beltrán attributes this lack of interest in Mexico's African diaspora to a fascination with its indigenous roots. He writes, "We only had eyes for what was indigenous and we closed our minds to anything else that represented something other than our romantic understandings of the indigenous" (1958: 11). This lack of recognition of all three cultures was also noted by one young man in Veracruz who stated, "People here don't have any understanding of this African root. The fact that we have mixed the three together has made us forget some or to have preference towards others. In fact, we have lost that vision that we came from three" (Interview with F. T. L.). Despite attempts to paint Mexico as a homogenous society, cultural variation does exist within its borders as evident in the Veracruz case.

In an effort to illustrate the complexity inherent in the racial discourse surrounding *mestizaje* in the Americas, colonial governments used the images in paintings, which attempted to neatly categorize each racial type or *casta*. In opposition to the classification imposed by *casta* paintings, José Vasconcelos, in his book *The Cosmic Race* (1997 [1925]), argued for a more pan-mestizo identity that was a spiritual as opposed to biological understanding of the *mestizaje* concept. In effect, "The reference to race as 'cosmic' shifted the semantic weight from the material to the spiritual" (Miller 2004: 29) thus leaning toward a more unifying interpretation of this concept at the national level.

Indeed, most historical scholarship has looked at *mestizaje* as a nation-building ideology. Though this definition of *mestizaje* appears seemingly inclusive in nature, over the years scholars have readdressed this concept with a critical eye toward the everyday implications it has on people throughout the Americas. In particular, the apparent inclusivity of the term was famously critiqued by Ronald Stutzman (1981) who redefined *mestizaje* as an "all-inclusive ideology of exclusion," appropriately making note of the term's exclusion of blacks and indigenous peoples.

Recent scholarship is challenging this ideological interpretation of "*mestizaje*ness." A focus on the embodied and performative notion of the lived experience has been introduced as an alternative understanding of this concept. In particular, Peter Wade's work on Afro-Colombian communities (2005) addresses this ideology and adds that *mestizaje* should also be looked at as a lived process, focusing on how people themselves deal with this racial-cultural mixture on a daily basis. Ultimately, Wade proposes an image of *mestizaje* to include a mosaic

> made up of different elements and processes, which can be manifest within the body and the family, as well as the nation. Seen in this way, *mestizaje* has spaces for many different possible elements, including black and indigenous ones, which are more than merely possible candidates for future mixture. (Wade 2005: 254)

In conjunction with Wade's approach, the work by Diana Taylor offers a particular performative interpretation of culture where performance is seen "a way of knowing, not simply an object of analysis" (2003: 16). Thus, performance then has the ability to "transmit memories, make political claims, and manifest a group's sense of identity" (17). By incorporating a performative interpretation to the *mestizaje* concept, we are able to identify other types of "knowledge" that includes "a shift from written to embodied culture" (16). Indeed, Taylor notes that from its very conception, *mestizaje* dealt more with the body than with the text since "the primary site of *mestizaje* is the body, linked as it is to the mestizo/a, the child born of European and indigenous parents" (94). Taylor also argues that even the casta paintings revolved around issues of performance, noting that "both the indigenous groups and the Spaniards had a highly codified system of identification grounded in visible social markers" (87). By highlighting the use of religious symbols in festival performances, the power behind a performative and embodied interpretation of the African diaspora in Mexico is illustrated.

Festival History and Politics

Festivals in general serve as occasions for a community to reflect on and define themselves. In particular, this research focuses on the annual International Afro-Caribbean festival created in 1994 and sponsored by the Veracruz Institute of Culture or IVEC.[6] The IVEC itself is a state-funded cultural institute whose director is appointed by the governor. In addition to state funding, the IVEC also receives support and grants from the federal cultural institute known as CONACULTA or the Consejo Nacional para la Cultura y las Artes.

The original goals of this state-sponsored festival sought to revalorize, research, and share the rich history and culture of Afro-Caribbean communities. Specifically, IVEC leaders proposed to "go further than just a mere celebration in itself or a simple event, to a singular act of justice for a culture up until now marginalized" (Arias Hernández 1997: 12). The festival format was originally organized into three main parts: artistic, academic, and religious. The artistic portion of the festival consisted of live performances of music, dance, and theater, while the academic component included the presentation of books, videos, and roundtable discussions bringing together academics and diplomats from around the Caribbean. Last, the section of the festival dedicated to religion enabled both local and visiting Caribbean communities to publicly share elements of their religious beliefs in the form of altars, rituals, and consultations. It is within this context that local healers and practitioners of the Afro-Cuban derived religion of Santería could be found.

Santería is an Afro-Cuban religion with its roots in West African belief systems. It was brought to Cuba by slaves, many of whom were of Yoruban descent, and mixed with a version of Roman Catholicism practiced by the Spanish colonizers. This process of syncretism brought together Catholic saints and African deities. Santería relies heavily on a structured hierarchy and rituals that include song, dance, spirit possession, and animal sacrifices.

Figure 7.1   Santería ritual at 1996 IVEC festival
Source: Photograph by Salvador Flores Gastambide

Unfortunately, over the years the public space for religious expression fostered by this Veracruz festival has slowly diminished. In fact, changes in IVEC leadership have altered fundamental initiatives on which the festival was originally founded. Most recently, we find a festival with dwindling community ties yet increased commercial connections. These festival changes began in 1998 when, after public protests over religious ritual performances, IVEC administrators eliminated the religious portion of the festival. Up until this point, the local presence of Santería was readily apparent in festival activities that included public altars, performances of sacred music, and ritual sacrifices.

The removal of this portion of the festival marked an obvious denial of the very important religious roots that permeate daily life in Veracruz and other Afro-Caribbean communities. Ultimately, the IVEC as an institution succumbed to the protests by staunch Catholic-affiliated religious groups and animal rights organizations. These protests revolved around the sacrifice of animals for religious rituals, which some determined to be inhumane and "satanic." Locals recalled that demonstrations were organized at key tourist spaces such as the Aquarium and the boardwalk where protestors handed out flyers opposing any attendance at festival activities. Ultimately, the success of these protests, although small in number, resulted from their ability to target key tourist zones. Because the majority of festival events take place in public spaces such as downtown, on IVEC grounds, and at local beaches, the physical location of festival activities reinforces the interaction between the two main faces of this city—locals and tourists.

Despite acknowledgment from both locals and IVEC employees that the religious portion of the festival was by far the most popular in both attendance and participation (yet another sign of the importance that religion has for the local community and in particular the presence of Santería practitioners in Veracruz), it was ultimately cancelled the following year in 1999. This modification in festival organization was also met with criticism from some locals who asked, "How are you going to deny a young person the Afro-Caribbean culture from which we come? Hiding what they do in the Caribbean is not a way to teach others about our culture" (Interview with L.F.C.). Indeed, locals questioned how the IVEC could boast its goal of sharing their Afro-Caribbean culture if they then decided to choose which parts of that culture were worthy enough to share. Excluding certain parts of a culture, such as the religious aspects of Santería, seemed to negate the original goals of the festival.

In addition to the format change excluding Afro-Caribbean religions, 1999 also marked a temporary name change in the festival. The "Afro" portion of the title was omitted and the festival was simply called the International Caribbean Festival. The name change was also reportedly a consequence of

Figure 7.2   Santería sacrificial offering in 1996 IVEC festival
Source: Photograph by Salvador Flores Gastambide

Figure 7.3   Public altar for Santería worship in 1996 IVEC festival
Source: Photograph by Salvador Flores Gastambide

the previously mentioned protests against African-influenced religious practices. An additional change in 1999 was the introduction of overarching festival themes that included sugar, tobacco, and coffee. By highlighting products directly linked to Veracruz local and state economy, the IVEC further solidified its concern with utilizing the festival as a tool for marketing local products to visiting tourists and increasing trade with neighboring Caribbean communities.[7]

While the festival was apparently "whitened" via its exclusion of an Afro-Caribbean presence in 1999, the 2002 festival activities were marked by the reincorporation of select symbols representative of Afro-Caribbean religion and culture. In particular, publicity for this year's festival activities was marked by the depiction of a shirtless man with strong African phenotypes wearing necklaces or *collares,* which directly symbolize participation in Santería. As individuals begin their journey into the religious faith of Santería, they learn about each deity and make ritual offerings to them in exchange for spiritual blessings and energy known as *ashe.* With gradual initiations into the religion, people earn their *collares* or necklaces, each one symbolic in bead color of a particular deity.

Ultimately, by highlighting an exotic Afro-Caribbean identity in Veracruz via posters and other festival publicity, the IVEC was able to

Figure 7.4 Poster for 2002 IVEC festival
Source: Photograph by author

market their festival to a wider audience and distinguish it from festivals found in other Mexican states. In this way, festival organizers reframed the connection with an African past for their own means—with particular attention on how this correlation might increase the tourist-based economy. In addition, the IVEC attempted to capitalize on its historical links to construct new relationships with other Caribbean communities. This Afro-Caribbean link was reimagined and re-created to serve the needs of those in power. In effect, Veracruz was transformed into a "cultural battlefield" where popular cultural forms were threatened by appropriation and commodification by a state government in need of unifying symbols (Hall 1981: 237). The removal of Afro-Caribbean religious elements from the festival only later to be reinscribed without any contextual support from the local community illustrates the imbalance of power behind representation in the IVEC festival.

Santería in Veracruz

Blurring transnational boundaries from its very beginning as it moved from West Africa to Cuba, the flow of Santería into Mexico continues to move in two directions. One is to Veracruz and the other is to Mexico City where many Cubans reside. In Veracruz, there is a constant exchange with Cuba, bringing people back and forth between the sister cities of Havana and the port of Veracruz. This movement of people sparked cultural exchanges in dance, music, food, and religion. Today this port city of over a half-a-million people continues to serve as an open window to the Caribbean with the continual coming and going of material goods and cultural influences swept in and out of the port by the never-ending tides.

Similar to the difficulty obtaining precise records on the number of slaves brought through the port, the number of people practicing Santería in Veracruz also remains elusive. As a result of years of persecution and discrimination against Santería practitioners in Cuba and abroad, this religious tradition was practiced in underground communities. Not until recent changes in globalization and a push toward tourism and commercialization did Santería begin a more public practice (Hagedorn 2001).

Within Veracruz the number of Santería centers varies between three and ten depending upon levels of establishment. These centers are places where people offer consultations usually in the form of divination with coconut shells. They are not necessarily places where an extended religious family lives or engages in ceremonies. This fact suggests that one of the key differences in the development of Santería in Veracruz is its lack of structure. In many religions of the African diaspora such as Vodou and Candomblé, one of the main functions of the religion is to serve as a religious family for its practitioners. They constitute mutual aid societies, highly structured, and grounded in tradition. In Veracruz, unlike in Cuba, Santería does not foster the creation of a religious family; instead, people are brought together to fulfill a ritual and often never see each other again afterwards.

Many times Cuban practitioners of Santería, or *santeros*, are brought to Veracruz in package deals that include their airfare, lodging, and participation in religious rituals. It becomes more economical to bring one priest or *babalao* to Veracruz than to travel to Cuba with all the objects necessary for the rituals. These visits are described as nonstop ceremonies followed by quick goodbyes. The need to fulfill ritual obligations fuels this practice while at the same time negating the creation of a strong religious community in Mexico. Although links to Cuban santeros are maintained via mail and phone, the political nature inherent in this transnational relationship does not allow for a tangible community necessary to produce positive and long-lasting religious communities in Mexico. Thus, the creation of a religious family is nonexistent. This lack of a strong community also contributes to the underground nature of the religion in this space. Though there may be people who consult or mix religious practices, there is no definite community. The community can thus be defined as transitory.

In contrast to other areas in the Americas where the African presence is much larger and accepted, such as the case of Salvador de Bahia in Brazil, there are no known registered houses of worship for Santería in Veracruz. Consequently, there are only pockets of initiates who work individually with locals on consultations ranging from financial, marital, health, and romantic problems. People seeking solutions to their troubles do not necessarily cultivate strong allegiances with the santeros they consult, and thus this fosters a competitive atmosphere among practicing santeros, which makes the links with Cuba all the more valuable in terms of "authentic" religious background experiences.

Thus, another characteristic of Santería practice in Veracruz is the degree of prestige linked with rituals done either by Cubans or in Cuba, which are sharply contrasted with those ceremonies performed by Mexicans or in Mexico. In the eyes of many Mexicans, Cuba takes the place of Africa and thus is viewed as more real, powerful, and closer to the roots of the religion. When a person who was brought into the religion via Mexican santeros decides to make the next step to initiate in Cuba as opposed to in Mexico, a break in the lineage and relationships occurs causing a great deal of conflict and friction. This jealousy also stems from a person's access to additional knowledge whether via books or through practical experience in Cuba. As one person continues to evolve in the religion, this creates fear and jealousy among other santeros within the community because it translates into stronger competition as opposed to a more unified community. As knowledge equals power, there is the constant battle on an economic level over access to information and the subsequent monopoly over clients.

Rosa's Story[8]

This friction is most aptly illustrated in the story of one woman, Rosa, who for numerous reasons is symbolic of the Santería community in Veracruz. Her story illustrates the lack of religious family and the prestige associated with rituals completed in Cuba. It also exhibits the rivalry among Santería practitioners and highlights the point that economic needs, rather than the formation of a mutual aid society, fuels participation in the religion.

Rosa began her journey into the world of Santería as an academic. Once employed by a major cultural agency in Veracruz, Rosa worked to research Caribbean religious traditions for educational programs and publications. In fact, her investigation into local Santería practice was integral in the founding of the religion and ritual portion of the Veracruz festival. Her initial interest was later followed by a more personal calling when she became more familiar with local practitioners. In 2000, her participation gradually increased from researcher to participant as she slowly began the multiple levels of initiation into the religion. Her experience is typical of other locals as her first two initiations were conducted by Mexican santeros with help from Cubans who made temporary visits to complete the necessary rituals. As Rosa's interest in the religion expanded, she began to contemplate the idea of traveling to Cuba to take the last step of full initiation into the religion. This idea was not welcomed by the Mexican santeros who had up until this point directed her religious training.

Ultimately, Rosa found this lack of support stifling and decided to travel in 2004 to Havana on her own to become fully initiated in the religion. The cost of her initiation, which included transportation, food, lodging, and ritual materials, including necessary participants, was approximately US$2,500. Upon her return to Veracruz, Rosa was met with unsupportive responses from local santeros. In their eyes, her decision to become initiated in Cuba created more competition and enabled her access to a more "authentic" Santería experience.

Since her initiation, Rosa's desire to use her Santería training has progressed from working only on her own issues to helping others for free; now she has started to contemplate the idea of dedicating her career to Santería consultations. Having felt the economic decline after losing one of her jobs to budget cuts, Rosa now views Santería as an alternative source of income.

Festival Impact on Santería

Given the characteristics of Santería in Veracruz, it is important to note the impact of the IVEC festival on the formation and subsequent development of this religious tradition. Though Santería was practiced before the initial 1994 IVEC festival, it was not until the promotion of religion and rituals within the festival that locals became more comfortable practicing their religion in public. Not only did the festival change the attitude of practitioners, but it also brought attention to this religious tradition in a celebratory manner, via IVEC sponsored events such as altars, ceremonies, and consultations, which sparked further interest in new initiates. After the religious portion of the festival was cancelled, Santería returned to a more underground status—having, in the process, cultivated more followers.

One example of this influence can be found in a local restaurant bar where this visible shift in Santería's presence in Veracruz is readily apparent. At the entrance to this local establishment is an alcove that holds a small shrine for the Holy Child of Atocha or Santo Niño de Atocha. This image of Jesus as a child is well revered in the Catholic Church throughout Mexico. He protects travelers and rescues people in danger and is also noted as the patron saint of those unjustly imprisoned.

Figure 7.5   Before and after picture of Santo Niño de Atocha or Elegua
Source: Photograph by author

Within Santería, this saintly image has a dual persona translated into an association with the deity Elegua who himself can be childlike in nature. He is known to be a trickster, who, like a child, likes to play games and eat candy. Elegua is also associated with travelers because his domain is the crossroads. In addition, both Santo Niño de Atocha and Elegua share healing powers. Elegua cured another diety, Olofi, the creator of the universe, and, thus, Olofi awarded Elegua by naming him owner of the crossroads to whom all others must first pay homage before any other deity can be consulted. This same healing power is also found in Santo Nino de Atocha who is noted for his ability to cure the sick, particularly children and prisoners.

After several years of the IVEC sponsored festival, the transformation of this religious shrine began to take shape, and in 2004 the alcove was transformed into the colors of Elegua—red and black. Without this change in colors locals could have continued their syncretistic worship of Elegua; however, the fact that they felt less insecure about their participation and worship of this African deity is a direct result of the apparent public embrace of Santería practice fostered by the festival. The transformation of this altar symbolizes one example of how locals reacted to the mixture of religion and performance in festival by crafting a sense of pride in their beliefs.

In addition to the publicity created by the festivals, Santería has also increased in popularity due to economic reasons. With recent cuts in local and state budgets, unemployment has been on the rise in Veracruz. This atmosphere where people have more problems creates the need for alternative solutions, and Santería is able to fill that gap. Not only do people look to Santería for help, but they also see it as a viable means of living. Many people offer consultations as a way to make money, and since many claim their patients only feel cured when they are charged, this becomes an alternative source of income. A newspaper advertisement that appeared in the service section of the classifieds exemplifies this phenomenon. Sandwiched between two announcements for antistress massages, the ad claimed that a consultation with this Yoruban priestess could solve the most impossible problems; but she would only be available for a few days in Veracruz. As it turned out, the Yoruban priestess in the ad was originally from Veracruz. She now resided in Miami, where she was initiated into Santería. She had come back to Veracruz for a few days of vacation and wanted to test the waters for giving spiritual advice. Working with coconut shells, she charged 250 pesos or approximately US$25 for a consultation—a cost slightly higher than other locals who charge 200 pesos or US$20. Ultimately, this newspaper advertisement reveals the economic, transitory and transnational nature of Santería practice.

Conclusion

In Veracruz, the presence of Santería has undergone a process from being ignored, included, excluded, and finally reintroduced, but with new restrictions that reflect an increased economic dependence on tourism. This process illustrates the more recent shift from neglecting the African presence in Mexico to reconstructing its image on a more local scale.

While both the national and state levels of cultural performance invoke the *mestizaje* concept, they do so with different intentions. On the one hand, national institutions circulate imagery that denies any African heritage while promoting national unification with the "*todos somos iguales*" or "we are all equal" ideology. At the same time, a provincial institution such as the IVEC reenvisions its own localized version of national culture to include a strong African element. Ultimately while the national level seeks to blend any cultural or ethnic differences into one new and united population, the Veracruz state embraces this *mestizaje* ideology by concentrating on the African component used to distinguish this state from others, thereby creating a new and exotic image to coincide with its bid for increased tourism. Peter Wade addresses this confrontation between racial and national identities in his work on communities of African descent in Colombia (2001). Wade notes, "we need to understand the tensions that exist between sameness and difference and to grasp how difference is a positive as well as a negative resource for representations of nationhood and processes of constructing identities" (2001: 856).

Ultimately, this Veracruz model shows several representational strategies at work. Festival performances represent the region by performing Mexican national, state, and local identity. In conjunction with the multiple identities inherent in performance, festival activities are also defined as state-subsidized performances. This external control on local identity presents the African diaspora and Santería as sometimes embraced and exoticized or sometimes resisted and denied, but always influenced by changing political, social, and economic conditions.

The current trend to reimagine links to African elements in Veracruz can be viewed as a "process of the active construction of otherness by national elites" (Wade 2001: 855). In this case, elites craft state-sponsored festivals that translate Veracruz culture through political, rather than local, notions of identity. This is illustrated by the exclusion of certain sectors of the local culture, specifically Santería, from IVEC festivals. Indeed, this disconnection in dialogue between festival creators and locals in Veracruz is the cause for misrepresentation and misinterpretation found in these festivals. And since representation itself implies a kind of power to both describe and define, the festivals sponsored and organized by state institutions exhibit their power over the performances and the people they seek to represent.

What is needed now is a new mode of cultural production that includes local voices in dialogue with state agencies. This approach would recognize that "the means of cultural production are not exclusively 'owned' by elites; one that does not locate productive power always and only on one side of a two-sided 'state/society' equation; one that accommodates the interplay and exchange of ideas and practices among all" (Askew 2002: 288). Katherine Hagedorn's work in Cuba (2001) illustrates an alternative blend that crafts Santería religious performance on both local and state levels. During the special economic period facing Cuba in the early 1990s, the Castro regime chose to selectively support some of Cuba's African-based religious traditions. This support led to the legalization of certain religious practices linked to tourism called *santurismo*, thus representing Santería's increase in social and economic power. Both the Cuban and Veracruz cases illustrate, as Hagedorn notes, "a historicized process in which an inward directed, noncommodified religious tradition becomes outward-directed, commodified, staged, and secularized" (2001: 9). Unfortunately, the Veracruz case illustrates an even more unequal balance whereby local practitioners and followers of Santería are not included in the festival process. Despite this exclusion from formal festival decision making, locals in Veracruz are continuing to exhibit their devotion to Santería.

In the Santería religion, there are no journeys that can begin without first recognizing Elegua, keeper and opener of all doors. And just as Elegua stands at the crossroads, so too does the future of Santería development in Veracruz. While external factors—political and economic—influence Santería practice, the multiple paths to worshipping within this religion are evident in the complexity of identity formation highlighted in this research. Indeed, Santería in Veracruz aptly demonstrates the performative, flexible, and multivocal nature of this religion: key characteristics that foster its survival on an ever-increasing global scale.

Notes

1. The port city of Veracruz is commonly referred to as simply Veracruz, not to be mistaken for the state by the same name.
2. This is based on Gonzalo Aguirre Beltran's research (1958). The number also corresponds to three centuries of history.
3. Los negros fueron en México un grupo minoritario; representaron del 0.1 al 2.0% de su población colonial; el número de los introducidos no fue mayor a 250,000 individuos en el curso de tres siglos. Unless otherwise noted, all translations in text are by the author.
4. Las cifras reales tal vez nunca se conozcan en virtud de que no existen registros completos de los esclavos introducidos legalmente por el Puerto de Veracruz, además de que hay evidencia de la extendia presencia de un comercio clandestine.
5. The presidential term of Porfirio Díaz from 1876 to 1911 is associated with the rise of capitalism in Mexico.

6. El Instituto Veracruzano de Cultura or Veracruz Institute of Culture is referred to as the IVEC.

7. With such an emphasis on tourism to the success of the local economy, the overlapping of festival dates with summer months like August, when more than 80 percent of hotel rooms are occupied, further solidified the importance of tourism to the IVEC's agenda. Indeed, according to the 2000 census, the tourism and hotel sector is the fourth largest employer in the port city of Veracruz.

8. A fictitious name was used to protect the identity of my consultant.

Bibliography

Published Works

Aguirre Beltrán, Gonzalo (1958). *Cuijla: Esbozo etnográfico de un pueblo negro.* Mexico: FCE/SEP.

Andrews, George Reid (2004). *Afro-Latin America, 1800–2000.* Oxford: Oxford University Press.

Arias Hernández, Rafael (1997). *Festival Internacional Afro-Caribeño.* Xalapa, Veracruz: Instituto Veracruzano de Cultura.

Askew, Kelly (2002). *Performing the Nation : Swahili Music and Cultural Politics in Tanzania.* Chicago: University of Chicago Press.

Bennett, Herman L. (2002). *Africans in Colonial Mexico: Absolutism, Christianity, and Afro-Creole Consciousness, 1570–1640.* Bloomington: Indiana University Press.

Hagedorn, Katherine J. (2001). *Divine Utterances: The Performance of Afro-Cuban Santería.* Washington, DC: Smithsonian Institution Press.

Hall, Stuart (1981). "Notes on Deconstructing 'the Popular.'" In Raphael Samuel (ed.), *People's History and Socialist Theory,* 227–249. Amsterdam, Holland: Van Gennep.

INEGI (2002). *Cuaderno Estadístico Municipal.* Aguascalientes, México: Instituto Nacional de Estadística, Geografía e Información (INEGI).

Martínez Montiel, Luz María (1995). *Presencia Africana en México.* Mexico City: Consejo Nacional Para la Cultura y las Artes.

Miller, Marilyn Grace (2004). *Rise and Fall of the Cosmic Race: The Cult of the Mestizaje in Latin America.* Austin: University of Texas Press.

Naveda Chávez-Hita, Adriana (2001). *Pardos, mulattos y libertos: Sexto encuentro de afromexicanistas.* Xalapa, Mexico: Universidad Veracruzana.

Palmer, Colin A (1976). *Slaves of the White God: Blacks in Mexico 1570–1650.* Cambridge, MA: Harvard University Press.

Rahier, Jean Muteba (1999). "Presence of Blackness and Representations of Jewishness in the Afro-Esmeraldian Celebrations of the Semana Santa

(Ecuador)." In Jean Muteba Rahier (ed.), *Representations of Blackness and the Performance of Identities*, 19–47. Westport, CT: Bergin & Garvey.

Ramos, Alejandro (1992). "Veracruz: variaciones de la entidad estatal." In Ida Rodríguez (ed.), *Horizante*, 31–34. Veracruz: IVEC.

Richmond, Douglas (2001). "The Legacy of African Slavery in Colonial Mexico, 1519–1810," *Journal of Popular Culture* 35/2: 1–16.

Shay, Anthony (2001). *Choreographic Politics: State Folk Dance Companies, Representation, and Power.* Middletown, CT: Wesleyan University Press.

Stutzman, Ronald (1981). "El Mestizaje: An All-Inclusive Ideology of Exclusion." In Normal E. Whitten (ed.), *Cultural Transformation and Ethnicity in Modern Ecuador*, 45–94. Urbana: University of Illinois Press.

Taylor, Diana (2003). *The Archive and the Repertoire: Performing Cultural Memory in the Americas.* Durham, NC: Duke University Press.

Thompson, Robert Farris (1983). *Flash of the Spirit: African & Afro-American Art & Philosophy.* New York: Vintage Books.

Twillie, Gendolyn B. (1995). "The Contributions of Enslaved Africans and Their Descendants to the Growth and Development of the Americas," *Journal of Black Studies* 25/ 4: 419–430.

Vasconcelos, José (1997) [1925]. *The Cosmic Race.* Baltimore, MD: Johns Hopkins University Press.

Wade, Peter (2001). "Racial Identity and Nationalism: A Theoretical View from Latin America," *Ethnic and Racial Studies* 24/5 (September): 845–865.

———— (2005). "Rethinking *Mestizaje*: Ideology and Lived Experience," *Journal of Latin American Studies* 37: 239–257.

Recorded Interviews

F. T. L. (2002). Interview by author. Tape recording. El Puerto de Veracruz, Veracruz, September 25. (F. T. L. refers to the abbreviation system used when conducting interviews as per the approval of the human subjects committee to protect the identity o s.)

L. F. C. (2002). Interview by author. Tape recording. El Puerto de Veracruz, Veracruz, October 10. (L. F. C. refers to the abbreviation system used when conducting interviews as per the approval of the human subjects committee to protect the identity of consultants.)

Chapter 8

Writing Out Africa? Racial Politics and the Cuban *regla de ocha*

Christine Ayorinde

It is the aspects of Negro life customarily deemed least
desirable that are held to be African and are thus regarded
as vestiges of a savage past.

—Melville Herskovits

Introduction

Today, the number of people who worship the orishas or Yoruba gods and goddesses outstrips several of the "world religions" including Judaism (McKenzie 1997: viii; Cañizares 1993: 121–126). A religious practice that originated in West Africa has many millions of followers in the Americas and elsewhere. In Cuba the local form of orisha worship, Santería, also called the *regla de ocha*, is being hailed by many as the national religion. What makes this particularly remarkable it that it has occurred in the midst of a socialist revolution that until recently promoted scientific atheism.

The gradual emergence of African-derived religions from a position of marginality is a diaspora-wide phenomenon. Throughout much of their history, these religious practices formed part of the national discourse only insofar as the ruling classes struggled to eradicate them. For Africans and their descendants, however, the practices were vehicles for cultural and religious expression and also the foci for concrete forms of resistance. Yet these religions also functioned as an alternative set of cultural practices for Cubans of all colors. This explains why Santería has developed into the symbol of a mestizo (mixed) nation and of *cubanía* (Cuban-ness).

For many Afro-Cubans, the spread of their religion and its inclusiveness confirms the value and strength of their culture. Nevertheless, the recent emergence from marginality and greater contact with orisha worshippers elsewhere has also inspired a move by some practitioners to identify the religion more closely with its African roots. The "Yorubization" or re-Africanization tendency within the Cuban *regla de ocha* is an attempt to recover a religious orthodoxy that is perceived as having been lost over time and space.

Africa in Cuba

A number of factors account for the presence in Cuba of religious and cultural forms that can be traced to specific African cultures. In contrast to North America and the English-speaking Caribbean, the Cuban slave trade continued well into the 1870s. New influxes of Africans from the continent were therefore able to renew and revive traditions that had become established on the island. Significantly, during the colonial period, the government encouraged Africans to congregate in associations called *cabildos de nación*.[1] These provided members with a niche within which they could preserve and recreate their specific cultural traditions. The Spanish colonial government supported the maintenance of ethnic differences as part of a divide-and-rule policy which aimed to preempt pan-African rebellion against the state. This policy contrasted with the British colonizers' blanket suppression of manifestations of black culture in North America and the Caribbean. Spanish pragmatism not only permitted, but encouraged, practices that did not affect the exploitation of slave labor. Furthermore, Cuban society was characterized by a religious laxity that meant catechization of the black population rarely went beyond perfunctory baptism.

With the abolition of slavery and moves toward independence from Spain in the latter half of the nineteenth century, the policy of cultural fragmentation changed to one of assimilation. Whereas constructions of

Cuban nationality had hitherto excluded Africans and their descendants, now the black and white *mambises* or troops in the Liberation Army struggled against a common enemy. This forged a vision of patriotism based on ethnic fraternity and a supra-racial Cuban-ness that dismissed racial categories. The Cuban patriot José Martí (1962: 298–299) eloquently articulated this in his statement, "Cuban is more than white, more than mulatto, more than black" (in the original Spanish: *"Cubano es más que blanco, más que mulato, más que negro"*).

Although the Creole elite were attempting to fuse national and racial identities, fears of the Africanization of Cuba did not recede.[2] With the coming of the Republic in 1902, the modernization of the Cuban state was seen to be threatened by cultural and biological legacies of its slavery past. The influence of European scientific racism and positivistic social thought cast into question the ability of Latin American nations with racially mixed populations to meet international standards of progress. The U. S. domination of the island also led some white Cubans to fear they would be viewed as inferior. Civilization and modernity became the defining tenets of Cuban nationality in formation and markers of Africanity had therefore to be repudiated (Pérez 1999).

A liberal constitution promised equality for all citizens. Black Cubans were to be prepared for citizenship. Nevertheless, they remained largely excluded from economic and political power. At the same time, the integrationist discourse sustained the notion that what held Afro-Cubans back was not their race but their lack of education and culture. Some among the Afro-Cuban elite also subscribed to the fallacy that minimizing cultural differences would help lessen discrimination against black Cubans. In their pursuit of assimilation, they dissociated themselves from their African-born forebears and strove to bring the masses up to their own level. African-derived religious practices were linked with illiteracy and both had to be combated by a modernizing nation.

The white Cuban lawyer and ethnographer Fernando Ortiz was the first scholar to acknowledge the African influence on national traits at a time when this was obscured by the white elite and the Afro-Cuban intelligentsia. The turn toward Africa was enabled and mediated by the Africanist literature of the time, which Ortiz cites in his 1906 book, *Los negros brujos* [*The Black Witchdoctors*]. But the pioneer of research into Afro-Cuban cultural and religious traditions had an agenda: to show how they differed from national culture. By examining barriers to assimilation, his work underpinned assumptions of white moral and cultural superiority. Influenced by the current pseudoscientific theories, he and his contemporaries were compelled to "construe hitherto fairly vague conceptions of cultural Africanity into a social pathogen, the extirpation of which would form a precondition for the achievement of Cuban modernity" (Palmié 2002: 30).

Ortiz drew on the work of Italian criminologist Cesare Lombroso, whose theory of atavism assumed that criminals in a "civilized" society display primitive biological characteristics. While his contemporary Israel Castellanos, a criminologist, studied jailed Afro-Cubans and measured their body parts in a vain attempt to discover distinguishing features, Ortiz sought cultural rather than biological explanations for their alleged backwardness. He believed that the persistence of African atavisms explained the alleged preponderance of Afro-Cubans in the criminal underworld (Ortiz 1995: 17).

The prevailing view was that, as Africans and their descendants advanced within society, manifestations of their culture and religion would gradually disappear. What soon became apparent, however, was that rather than dying out along with the African-born population the religious forms were "infecting" the Creole or Cuban-born black and white populations. Ortiz recommended the suppression of Afro-Cuban religious practices, at the time known as *brujería* [witchcraft], because he felt that African religious atavism represented a threat to the population as a whole (1995: 6).[3] While legislation to criminalize the Afro-Cuban practices never reached the statute books and religious freedom was enshrined in the constitution, systematic campaigns were launched against them at various times in the twentieth century. The press reported alleged cases of the abduction and murder of white children for ritual purposes. Most of the cases were dismissed for lack of evidence. Yet the image of the black *brujo* became embedded in the white psyche and this association of Afro-Cuban religious practices with criminality has proved extremely persistent. The *brujería* scares had the effect of reinforcing apparent cultural distinctions between black and white Cubans and between sections of the Afro-Cuban population, some of whom did not favor the continuance of what they regarded as outdated superstitions.

It was only in the 1920s that, rather than proposing the wholesale elimination of the African cultural heritage, selected elements began to be co-opted in the project of creating a national culture. In the face of growing discontent with American political and economic domination, the bongo drum became an "antidote to Wall Street," as the Cuban writer Alejo Carpentier observed (Kutzinski 1993: 41). The *afrocubanismo* literary and artistic movement aimed to use cultural traditions to further a nationalist agenda. Cuban intellectuals were influenced by international trends such as European *vogue nègre*, inspired by Oswald Spengler's *The Decline of the West* and the work of the German ethnographer Leo Frobenius.[4] However, this attempt to "clean up" and universalize black forms avoided racial questions by focusing on cultural synthesis. As with later attempts to make Afro-Cuban culture respectable, some elements were incorporated into the national ethos while others were rejected. Afro-Cuban mythology, music, and dance tended to be treated as arts independent of the religious practices, responding to the view that such practices were no longer relevant in a modern, scientific, and industrial society.

At around the same time the work of Ortiz also began to move in a new direction. He was influenced by a new set of foreign ideas, this time British and North American anthropological trends such as functionalism and culturalism, which challenged ethnocentric prejudices. His work began to examine the process of cultural syncretism. Ortiz developed his theory of transculturation as a critique of U. S. anthropologist Melville Herskovits' acculturation theory. This he regarded as mechanistic and ethnocentric as it implied the loss or uprooting of a supposedly inferior culture following contact with a superior culture.[5]

Transculturation, on the other hand, referred to the process whereby the Hispanic and African cultures mutually influence each other to create a new culture. The end product would be a synthesis, a *cubanía* [Cubanness] in which purely racial factors would have lost their capacity for divisiveness. Ortiz's cultural model was represented by a Cuban stew, the *ajiaco*. In contrast to the melting pot, each component in the mixture retains its identity. He believed that syncretism represented the same process in religion (Ortiz 1970). Ortiz elaborated on the ideology of a raceless nation formulated by Martí, stating that: "In order to understand the Cuban soul one does not need to study the races but the cultures" (Oritz 1993: 9). Nevertheless, it was generally believed that cultural differences among black and white Cubans could be overcome by education. Few questioned that, as Afro-Cubans progressed within society, their cultural and religious forms would survive only as folklore.

Subculture or National Culture?

After the Cuban Revolution of 1959, the interests of the popular classes became the nation's motivating force and there was a drive to revalue their culture. Accentuating the African presence in Cuba and the island's ties to the mother continent became increasingly important and was also used to create links with the newly independent African states. The Revolution included among its expressed aims the elimination of the bases of institutional racism and attempted to challenge racism as an ideology. However, the leadership also carried over the longstanding discourse of integrationism.

The emphasis on revolutionary consensus not only prevented the open expression of dissent, it also did not recognize diversity. Certain styles of dress, tastes in music, and sexual orientation were seen as potentially counterrevolutionary. This included afro-hairstyles and race-based organizations. The definition of Cuba as an Afro-Latin country precluded giving space to those wishing to proclaim a separate black identity. Whereas previously the integrationist discourse stated that Cuba's racial problem did not exist, now it was claimed that the Revolution had solved it.

In the early years of the Revolution, amid the political experimentation and cultural exuberance, there were attempts to find a place in the national psyche for the previously marginalized Afro-Cuban religions. Although some Christian churches, which were threatened by the new socialist structures, sheltered counterrevolutionary activity, the Afro-Cuban religions benefited from their association with the exploited classes. These had most to gain from the revolutionary social transformations and were believed to be more likely to support it.

From the mid 1960s through the 1980s, however, a commitment to the atheist state meant that longstanding prejudices toward Afro-Cuban religions began to resurface in scholarship and official attitudes. All religions were anachronisms, leftovers from the past. Research into what were termed the "so-called syncretic cults" was carried out in government-sponsored institutions such as the Departmento de Estudios Sociorreligiosos (Department of Socio-Religious Studies, or DESR), set up in 1982. The research took as its starting point Marx's view that religion was of interest only insofar as it presented an obstacle on the path to a just society. It recycled prerevolutionary assumptions about the cultural and sociological role of Santería. These included regarding the practice as a "black problem" associated with a low level of integration into society, manifestations of social pathology, and even criminality. The DESR research also echoed Comte and Tylor in referring to African religions as animism, magic, and fetishism (Argüelles Mederos and Hodge Limonta 1991: 2, 35–36). The Afro-Cuban practices were also termed mongrel forms that had incorporated elements of religions from "superior social stages." They were believed to have no sacred texts, no organized clergy, and no links with national or international bodies that could help to maintain a uniform doctrinal and liturgical system.

At the same time, as part of its bid to revalue aspects of the former subculture, official policies recommended using the aesthetic features of the African-derived religions to create revolutionary art forms. The music, dance, and instruments were to be assimilated, secularized, and transformed into a national folklore. This had precedents in attempts earlier in the twentieth century to alter or "refine" the cultural forms and harness them to a national agenda. It was a policy of *rescate* [rescue], not only of a former subculture, or of the positive elements which could be extracted from the religious practices, but of forms doomed to extinction with the construction of a new society. Items associated with the Afro-Cuban practices were consigned to the past and exhibited in museums.

The problem for revolutionary scientific atheists, however, was that, as the DESR researchers soon discovered, the "unredeemed" forms continued to evade policies aimed at controlling them. In fact, rather than discouraging the practice of Afro-Cuban religious expressions, the Revolution appeared to have stimulated it. This contrasted strongly with the marked decline in the practice of Christianity since the 1950s. They had been dismissed as anachronisms, but the vitality of the Afro-Cuban practices was evident. This prompted a search for explanations as to why the beliefs and practices were flourishing among sectors of the population.

It became clear that the "rescue" of the related cultural forms had unintentionally given a new impulse to the religious practices. Another factor was that believers came predominantly from humble backgrounds and the increased employment opportunities and earning capacity among this sector meant more were able to afford the costs of an initiation ceremony. The researchers also suggested that the increase in initiations and membership of these religious groups indicated that some people felt the "need" to express their beliefs without this necessarily implying a distancing from the revolutionary process. They concluded that the Afro-Cuban practices could not simply be considered leftovers from the past [*rezagos*] but that in fact had "considerable weight in the field of the struggle of ideas" (Argüelles Mederos and Hodge Limonta 1991: 144, 156–157, 216–218).

By the late 1980s, the diminishing economic and ideological support from Eastern Europe compelled the Cuban government to rethink aspects of the revolutionary project. It is generally acknowledged that the adoption of scientific atheism at an earlier period was a mistake. In an atmosphere of greater tolerance, African-derived religions are emerging for the first time from a position of marginality. The existence of Afro-Cuban religious institutions with official recognition such as the Yoruba Cultural Association, a nongovernmental organization (NGO) that promotes Yoruba religion and culture, is indicative of the degree to which these religions have gained in prestige. The Eighth World Orisha Conference was held in July 2003 at the International Convention Center in Havana and sponsored by the Cuban government.[6] Seminars on religious themes were presided over by Cuban practitioners and scholars but also by the same party functionaries who had once predicted the disappearance of the religion. Of course, apart from official explanations for the growing acceptance of religious practice, Cuba is now heavily dependent on tourism and if seen to be discriminating against believers this would obviously not be good for business.

Cubanization or Africanization?

The redefinition of the religious practices within the national context makes the presentation of Santería, its practices and historical narratives, important. Nowadays the official term for what was formerly called *brujería* and later "so-called syncretic cults" is "Cuban religions of African origin." What was viewed in the early twentieth century as a threat to the population as a whole is now hailed as a marker of national distinctiveness. This has prompted a debate among those inside and outside of the religion as to what extent it is a black, African, or national religion. Of course, since the late nineteenth century, when ethnically heterogeneous cult groups replaced the cabildos de nación, Creole blacks, mulattos and whites have been able to assume a Lucumí "ethnicity" through religious initiation.[7] Many white Cubans head *casas de santo*. Most of the practitioners that I interviewed insist that Santería is a Cuban religion, while acknowledging its African roots.

Yet, as elsewhere in the diaspora, there is a growing awareness among Cuban practitioners that Santería represents one strand of a transnational religious complex. This was reinforced by the 1987 visit to Cuba of the Yoruba king and religious leader, the Ooni of Ife. Some years later, in 1992, a proposal for the structured *yorubización* [Yorubization] of Santería was mooted at the International Workshop on Yoruba Culture in Cuba.[8] This position advocated an emphasis on African roots, replacing the term Santería by the *regla de ocha* or *culto a los orichas* [cult to the *orichas*], eliminating Roman Catholic elements, and recovering orthodoxy in ritual through a return to the liturgy of the Nigerian *orisha* cults. For many *ocha* practitioners, this Yorubization or re-Africanization is part of a recovery process that aims to complete or deepen and extend ritual knowledge. They believe that religious knowledge was lost either in transmission from Africa or over the centuries in Cuba. Others disagree, arguing that Santería with its Roman Catholic elements is no less orthodox than orisha cults in Africa. This recognizes that the African forms have also not remained static. A concern with exclusiveness and purity is also generally not a feature of orisha worship in Africa, which is flexible and incorporative.[9]

Like scholars, and sometimes in tandem with them, practitioners have elaborated ideologies of cultural legitimacy. According to Stephan Palmié, intellectual reciprocity and feedback resulted in the mutual self-construction of Afro-Cuban religion and Afro-Cuban anthropology (2002: 253). This was the case in Brazil too, where ethnic specificity and purity of preservation became the criteria for the selection of adequate objects of study and academically legitimated versions of Africanity were grafted onto local practices. Candomblé priests and priestesses in Bahia seized on this to confer prestige on their cult groups. On a practical level, scholarly patrons could also ensure protection from official persecution.

Earlier re-Africanization tendencies in Cuba may have been fuelled by visiting anthropologists and scholars. The French photographer and ethnographer Pierre Verger, who visited Cuba for three months in 1957, seems to have been influential in promoting a pan-Yoruba theology in Cuba. In the 1950s, translations of works on the Yoruba by the Africanists that had appeared in Ortiz's works found their way into religious texts.[10]

For religious practitioners, both national pride and economic interests underlie the desire to claim the *regla de ocha/Santería* as a uniquely Cuban form closely related to but no less orthodox than orisha cults in Africa. For most Cuban *santeros* (Santería practitioners) today, being "Yoruba" does not mean being or wanting to be African. Even the re-Africanization of the *regla de ocha* has less to do with skin color and more to do with a search for authenticity. Yet despite the fact that thus far it seems to be a minority tendency, the issue of Yorubization or anti-syncretism has aroused a strong reaction from scholars and officials in Cuba, as well as the Catholic Church, though for different reasons.

Cuban cultural nationalists dismiss suggestions that items from Yoruba culture should be used to develop Cuban liturgy on the grounds that contemporary versions are more important than older forms. They see the workings of the Cuban environment on the cults as having more than compensated for the losses of the Middle Passage. Cultural and religious syncretism is now regarded as not merely a survival strategy but as a process of exchange that has nourished the national identity. This reflects the rethinking of theories of syncretism and acculturation within anthropology and other disciplines in recent years. The new model of culture change is creolization, a term derived from linguistic theory. This defines African American cultures as new synthetic entities. Rather than focusing on loss, this looks at how Africans remade themselves in the New World (Mintz and Price 1976: 26, 44).

One argument used against Yorubization is that a search for orthodoxy perpetuates the erroneous view that what are regarded as heterogeneous cultures are inferior. Clearly, the predominance of such views by state-sponsored researchers until recently may make practitioners feel called upon to respond to them. Another issue raised by Jorge Ramírez Calzadilla of the DESR is that, even though they were mistaken in previously analyzing the products of African culture from the perspective of Western cultural models, to counter this by suggesting a return to the African roots implies more than simply reinterpreting them in their rightful dimension (Ramírez Calzadilla 1995). Lázara Menéndez, a professor at the University of Havana, suggests that the return to a nebulous orthodoxy would imply an immobilization of living practices which interact with their current sociocultural context (Menéndez Vázquez 1995). This ignores the fact that, until quite recently, the cultural policy attempted to confine a living culture within museums and to harness cultural and religious forms to a revolutionary agenda.

Yorubization is also regarded as an example of importing an identity crisis. It is seen as a campaign originating, not so much in Nigeria, but among U. S. practitioners who have visited Africa and whose explorations into the Yoruba roots of Santería create an anxiety about orthodoxy in the minds of some Cuban practitioners.[11] In fact, the United States provides an example of the effect of a more racially polarized society on an inclusive religious practice like Santería. In the 1960s, after Santería reached the United States with exiled Cubans, it became linked with the black cultural nationalist arm of the Civil Rights Movement (Brandon 1993: 115–119). This coincided with a shift in the Movement from a desire for integration to a wish to be different and separate. Although many African American *santeros* in the United States still practice Cuban-style "syncretic" Santería, one group broke away to form the American Yoruba Movement. Moving to North Carolina to establish a "traditional Yoruba" community, the Movement rejected Catholic imagery and its members perform African-style initiations and refuse to initiate whites (Palmié 1995).[12]

This contrasts with Brazil where, by the 1970s, the inclusive nature of the *candomblé nagô* made it symbolic of *mestiçagem* (racial mixing) and linked it to the notion of racial democracy. For the white middle class, *Candomblé* was a universal rather than an ethnic religion and therefore no longer simply an expression of Afro-Brazilian identity. Yet for Afro-Brazilians, it remains a potential source of racial consciousness and mobilization. In the face of ongoing racial discrimination, traditional expressions of black culture (as well as foreign ones from the US and Jamaica) are being used in the affirmation of a black identity within a more radical African diasporic discourse. In *candomblé nagô*, the idea of African purity is used by some, not merely to symbolize the withdrawal into an otherworldly "Africa," but in a political sense. Thus distinct and even competing interpretations can develop around a single ritual space (Agier 1998: 155).

In Cuba, the head of the Catholic Church, Cardinal Ortega, also opposes the re-Africanization of Santería. For him, syncretism is a process in which the religion with the higher degree of conceptualization and more coherent set of ethics, that is, Roman Catholicism, will have the decisive influence (Bolívar Aróstegui and López Cepero 1995: 40–42). Ortega's assertion contradicts both Ortiz's transculturation theory and U.S. anthropologist William Bascom's research on Cuban Santería in the 1950s. This indicated a shift, not toward fusion with Catholic beliefs, but toward a greater emphasis on the distinctive features of the African religion (Bascom 1950). Ortega's reaction reflects the stance of most Christian churches in Cuba that largely refuse to engage with the issue of religious syncretism. The Cuban Catholic Church is orthodox both in its liturgy and pastoral activities. Unlike the rest of Latin America, it rarely incorporates local traditions into worship. With a few exceptions, statements made by clergy over the years seemed to be aimed at rousing animosity rather than promoting ecumenism. Cardinal Ortega himself has stated that Santería is not a religion, describing the Afro-Cuban practices as "primitive rituals."[13]

Ortega's stance reflects the fact that the growing recognition of Afro-Cuban religions by the Cuban leadership has revived old antagonisms between them and the Catholic Church. During his 1998 visit, Pope John Paul II insisted on at least three occasions that the true Cuban tradition is Christian. At the end of his stay, he cautioned against putting the Roman Catholic Church on a par with Santería and other Afro-Cuban religions.[14] This contradicts the view of Cuban officialdom and *santeros* that Roman Catholicism is simply one of the many religions practiced in Cuba.

There are also fears that extrareligious agendas lurk behind moves to re-Africanize. The government is aware that the Afro-Cuban practices could once again become a focus for the disaffected. Despite the rhetoric of *mestizaje* and national homogeneity, the economic crisis of recent years has shattered social equality and prompted a rise in overt racism. This, combined with more contact with the outside world, means that there is a growing movement of race-based identification. In recent years, movements such as Rastafarianism and the Nation of Islam (NOI) have established themselves on the island. In the case of Rastafarianism, an official from the Office of Religious Affairs commented that, "It worries us that forms of behavior that have nothing to do with this society are transplanted to Cuba." According to him, while in other societies where people are marginalized and discriminated against they might feel the need to assume particular oppositional stance, this was not the case in Cuba.[15]

Nevertheless, the origins and past role of the Afro-Cuban practices mean that they can be used to represent an exclusively black identity. They are testimony to the resistance to deculturation by Africans and their descendants and have a long history as escape mechanisms as well as niches within which concrete forms of opposition could be organized.

Conclusion

The 1959 Revolution followed previous regimes in subscribing to an Enlightenment view of modernity. Marxism-Leninism, yet another strand of European intellectual tradition, was to provide the means to implement a more wide-ranging modernizing project than previously possible. Afro-Cuban religious practices were relegated to a "premodern" sphere and viewed by the leadership as anachronisms that would inevitably disappear, though there were attempts to accelerate the process.

As a result, until very recently, there was little written on Afro-Cuban religions that reflected their dynamism and relevance in society. Even though many Cubans visited African countries during the internationalist campaigns and thousands of African students lived in Cuba, African studies programs in academic institutions did not focus on contemporary Africa and its cultures. Unlike Brazil, where Yoruba is taught in some universities, there have been only a few short-lived attempts to run classes in Cuba. Some *santeros* even believe that Yoruba is a dead language.

Today what was viewed in the early twentieth century as a threat to the population as a whole is now hailed as a marker of national distinctiveness. The official term for what was formerly called *brujería* and later "so-called syncretic cults" has become "Cuban religions of African origin." Santería is recognised as a valuable commodity by various sectors, including the revolutionary government. The Afro-Cuban religions are now part of the tourist package and initiations into Santería are a lucrative business—one from which everyone benefits.

Yet the assumption of a more popular *cubanía* alongside the celebration of *mestizaje* and racial synthesis, even if done out of the best motives, is perhaps another example of the essentialization of hybridity in the service of nationalist projects. In Cuba, as elsewhere in Latin America, although racial classifications may be more fluid and negotiable than in North America, the official discourse simultaneously pretends difference does not exist while continuing to privilege whiteness and western or at least *mestizo* elements as opposed to black or African ones (Wade 1995: 18–19). Even the apparent cultural inclusiveness may mean writing out Africa, yet again. As Fernández Robaina observed,

> I believe that the day may come when one can speak of Cuban culture as a whole but we are very far from that because there are still many prejudiced minds who do not value the contributions of the African heritage in the same way they do others.[16]

Although national unity may dictate that Africa is not foregrounded in the interest of racial or religious exclusivity, it remains important for the recovery and the rehabilitation of a cultural past. [17] This is required to counter essentialized views of African "originals," to move beyond the notion of the nebulous African past, and to act as a counterpoint to the nationalization of Africa as a racially unmarked aspect of Braziliannness and Cuban-ness.

Notes

1. The cabildos de nación were mutual aid societies, legally recognized civil institutions whose members were both enslaved and free Africans from the same ethnic group.

2. The example of Haiti where, in 1791, a slave revolt led to the establishment of a black state, induced fears among some whites that this could also happen in Cuba. In the mid-nineteenth century, white Cubans made up only 41.4 percent of the population, while slaves represented 43.4 percent and free blacks 15.2 percent. See the Cuban census figures cited in Knight (1970: 22, 86).

3. *Brujo* became the Spanish translation of *feiticeiro*, from *fetiço*, a term used by the Portuguese to refer to African objects of adoration.

4. Frobenius had visited West Africa where he was so impressed by the Yoruba civilization that he did not believe it could be African in origin. He maintained that it had been introduced by Etruscans who reached Africa via the lost continent of Atlantis.

5. Herskovits developed the theory that Africans and their descendants in the Americas had preserved (if unconsciously) a number of "Africanisms." Where diasporic forms were perceived to diverge from an African original, this was explained by variable degrees of acculturation. These were attributed to the origins of enslaved Africans, the tenacity of their cultural forms, and the levels of contact between bearers of African and European traditions. His theory suggested that the population regarded as less cultured could not withstand contact with Western culture and its benefits. See Herskovits (1967 [1941]).

6. An indication of the changing response of the state to Afro-Cuban practices is that fact that, in 1992, prospective foreign delegates for the International Workshop on Yoruba Culture were refused visas.

7. *Lucumí*, the name formerly given to the Yoruba in Spanish America.

8. The workshop was reported in the weekly newspaper *Granma International*: "The freedom of worship and respect for all religious traditions," June 14, 1992: 4.

9. The notion of a settled African environment for the Yoruba traditional religion is a construction. In Yorubaland, migration and upheaval caused by wars resulted in the diffusion of some orisha cults to new areas. The "traditional" religions were also compelled to accommodate themselves to Christianity and Islam. The incorporative, decentralized, and flexible nature of the orisha cults

made them eminently suitable for transmission and growth that was occurring in Africa as well as in the diaspora. See Barber (1981); Drewal (1992); Matory (1994); and Peel (1997).

10. Ernesto Pichardo, personal communication, Miami, June 1996. On the role of Verger and others, see Díaz Fabelo (1960: 115–116); León (1971: 139–151); and Martínez Furé (1979: 212).

11. In Brazil, as in Cuba, the myth of racial democracy dictates that attempts to assert a collective black identity must be presumed to be external in origin. The Black Soul Movement of the 1970s, when Afro-Brazilians adopted American soul music, was an example of the way in which people of African descent in one national-cultural context adopt forms created by people in another. Gilberto Freyre, the proponent of racial democracy, condemned Black Soul as an example of U.S. imperialism. However, as something independent of white elite definitions of Brazilian-ness, Black Soul acted as a catalyst for black identity creation in Brazil. See Hanchard (1994: 115).

12. Palmié 2005 offers an account of how, despite their wish to break away from "syncretic" Cuban-style practice, the Oyotunji members still depend upon the services of Miami Cuban ritual specialists.

13. Ortega's remarks are recorded in at least two newspaper articles: "Cardenal Ortega pide nueva evangelización," *El País*, January 24, 1998: 3; and Juan Tamayo, "Afro-Cubans say Catholics have Slighted their Religions," *Miami Herald*, January 12, 1998. In the latter article, one Havana priest is quoted as saying: "this [Cuban] government has promoted Santería as a virtual official religion, giving oxygen to friendly *babalawos* to earn tourist dollars while trying to asphyxiate the church."

14. *Associated Press*, "Pope: Afro-Cuban Cults not Religion," January 26, 1998. www.cubanet.org/Cnews/y98/jan98/26e91.htm 16. Accessed September 16, 1999.

15. Carlos Samper, interview with the author, Havana, January 24, 2003.

16. Tomás Fernández Robaina, interview with the author, Havana, January 19, 2003.

17. As Andrew Apter notes, "'Africa' has been ideologically constructed to create imagined communities in the black Americas but such invented identities cannot be totally severed from their cultural analogues if not origins in Africa." See Apter (1991: 235–260).

Bibliography

Agier, Michel (1998). "Between Affliction and Politics: A Case Study of Bahian Candomblé." In H. Kraay (ed.), *Afro-Brazilian Culture and Politics: Bahia, 1790s to 1990s*, 134–157. Armonk, NY: M. E. Sharpe.

Apter, Andrew (1991). "Herskovits' Heritage: Rethinking Syncretism in the African Diaspora," *Diaspora* 1/3: 235–260.

Argüelles Mederos, Aníbal and Ileana Hodge Limonta (1991). *Los llamados cultos sincréticos y el espiritismo: Estudio monográfico sobre su significación social en la sociedad cubana contemporánea*. Havana: Editorial Academia.

Barber, Karin (1981). "How Man Makes God in West Africa: Yoruba Attitudes towards the Òrìsà," *Africa* 51/3: 724–745.

Bascom, William (1950). "The Focus of Cuban Santería," *Southwestern Journal of Anthropology* 6/1: 4–68.

Bolívar Aróstegui, Natalia and Mario López Cepero (1995). *Sincretismo religioso? Santa Barbara/Changó*. Havana, Cuba: Editorial Pablo de la Torriente.

Brandon, George (1993). *Santería from Africa to the New World: The Dead Sell Memories*. Bloomington: Indiana University Press.

Cañizares, Raúl (1993). *Walking with the Night: The Afro-Cuban World of Santería*. Rochester, VT: Destiny Books.

Díaz Fabelo, Teodoro (1960). *Olorun*. Havana: Teatro Nacional.

Drewal, Margaret Thompson (1992). *Yoruba Ritual: Performers, Play, Agency*. Bloomington: Indiana University Press.

Hanchard, Michael (1994). *Orpheus and Power: The Movimiento Negro of Rio de Janeiro and Sao Paulo, Brazil, 1945–1988*. Princeton: Princeton University Press.

Herskovits, Melville J. (1967) [1941]. *The Myth of the Negro Past*. Boston: Beacon.

Knight, Franklin (1970). *Slave Society in Cuba during the Nineteenth Century*. Madison: University of Wisconsin Press.

Kutzinski, Vera (1993). *Sugar's Secrets: Race and the Erotics of Cuban Nationalism*. Charlottesville: University of Virginia Press.

León, Argeliers (1971). "Un caso de tradición oral escrita," *Islas* 39/40: 139–151.

Martí, José (1962). *Obras completas*, vol. II. Havana, Cuba: Editorial Nacional de Cuba.

Martínez Furé, Rogelio (1979). *Diálogos imaginarios*. Havana, Cuba: Editorial Arte y Literatura.

Matory, J. Lorand (1994). *Sex and the Empire That is No More: Gender and the Politics of Metaphor in Oyo Yoruba Religion*. Minneapolis: University of Minnesota Press.

McKenzie, Peter (1997). *Hail Orisha: A Phenomenology of a West African Religion in the Mid-Nineteenth Century*. Leiden: Brill.

Menéndez Vázquez, Lázara (1995). "Un cake para Obatalá?" *Temas* 4: 38–51.

Mintz, Sidney and Richard Price (1976). *An Anthropological Approach to the Afro-American Past*. Philadelphia, PA: ISHI.

Ortiz, Fernando (1970) [1940]. *Cuban Counterpoint*. New York: Vintage.

——— (1993). *Etnia y sociedad*. Havana: Editorial de Ciencias Sociales.

——— (1995) [1906]. *Los negros brujos*. Havana, Cuba: Editorial de Ciencias Sociales.

Palmié, Stephan (1995). "Against Syncretism: 'Africanizing' and 'Cubanizing' Discourses in North American Òrìsà Worship." In R. Fardon (ed.), *Counterworks*, 73–104. London: Routledge.

——— (2002). *Wizards and Scientists: Explorations in Afro-Cuban Modernity and Tradition*. Durham: Duke University Press.

Peel, J. D. Y. (1997). "A Comparative Analysis of Ogun in Precolonial Yorubaland." In Sandra Barnes (ed.), *Africa's Ogun,* 263–289. Bloomington: Indiana University Press.

Pérez, Louis A. (1999). *On Becoming Cuban: Identity, Nationality, and Culture.* Chapel Hill: University of North Carolina Press.

Ramírez Calzadilla, Jorge (1995). "*Los reavivamientos religosos en períodos de crísis: la religiosidad en el Período Especial cubano.*" DESR (Formerly part of the Cuban Academy of Sciences) (mimeo).

Wade, Peter (1995). *Blackness and Race Mixture: The Dynamics of Racial Identity in Colombia.* Baltimore, MD: Johns Hopkins University Press.

Chapter 9

Macumba Has Invaded All Spheres: Africanity, Black Magic, and the Study of Afro-Brazilian Religions

Kelly E. Hayes

New Year's Eve Tribute to Yemanjá

Every New Year's Eve in Rio de Janeiro, hundreds of Cariocas[1] dressed head-to-toe in white converge along miles of city beachfront to honor Yemanjá, the Afro-Brazilian goddess of the sea. From the moment the last rays of the sun dissolve into the horizon until they crest again the following dawn, small, autonomous groups migrate to the beach bearing flowers, candles, food, and drink. They come to praise and petition the sea goddess, into whose warm and salty embrace they will launch offerings of flowers and other small gifts. It is one of Rio's most enchanting customs, attracting believers and nonbelievers alike—the latter of whom are drawn to the proceedings, as the journalist Alma Guillermoprieto observed, "for the same reasons that agnostics elsewhere celebrate Christmas: because it is a lovely and meaningful part of their tradition" (1991:152).

Come dawn the beach is choked with the remnants of these offerings, seaside altars of bedraggled gladiolas and still-flickering candle stubs, as the municipal cleaners, armed with rakes and plows, begin their daily rite. A significant percentage of the sanitation force's effort involves disposing of the ritual remains of these and other Afro-Brazilian ceremonies. Such offerings may be found not only on New Year's Day but at any season of the year throughout the city: planted at a crossroads, wedged into the base of a tree, or nestled in the underbrush of one of Rio's stately plazas. For practitioners of Afro-Brazilian religions, ritual offerings of food and drink constitute an important means of interchange with the spirit world.

Apart from New Year's seaside homage to Yemanjá, the public evidence of Afro-Brazilian ritualizing is linked with a much more sinister heritage, evoking a *frisson* of dread rather than delight among middle-class Brazilians. Streetside offerings in particular are associated with Macumba: a term used to denominate Afro-Brazilian religious cults, practices, and ritual objects in general, but most especially those thought to involve *feitiçaria*, sorcery or black magic. Macumba is widely considered an occult practice drawing on nefarious powers for nefarious purposes through the use of sacrificial offerings, spells, incantations, and other magico-ritual practices. It is associated particularly with the cultivation of a set of boisterous spirit entities called *exus*, referred to by their devotees as *povo da rua*, people of the streets. In image, story and song, Exu spirits are linked with urban street life and its illicit desires—vice, lust, crime, and sensual indulgence. Deeply intertwined with Rio's history, Macumba and its characteristic spirits represent a side of urban life that many Cariocas are far from embracing.

The discrepancy in public attitudes toward these two manifestations of Afro-Brazilian religious praxis is significant. It points to the deep ambivalence of the Brazilian public toward these religions, once considered degenerate superstition that threatened the progress of the nation. It provokes the question of why certain Afro-Brazilian practices focused on certain deities, such as the annual tribute to Yemanjá, have gained widespread social acceptance, while other practices have retained this stigmatized association with black magic. This question is germane not only for those interested in Afro-Brazilian religions, but for scholars in general because it illustrates some of the far-reaching social and political consequences of the classificatory schemas used to interpret and order data. Although scholarship is not the only medium through which claims to religious legitimacy may be staked, academics often possess the requisite authority, as well as the means, to sway elite opinion. The history of the study of Afro-Brazilian religions is an especially revealing example of this process.

Macumba and Classificatory Schemas

I first became interested in this discrepancy in the course of my fieldwork in Rio de Janeiro with a small community of Macumba practitioners located on the sprawling, working-class periphery of the city. Although I had observed that members freely used the term Macumba among themselves to refer to their distinctive spiritual practices, the group's leader advised me to avoid using this term when speaking to outsiders.

Indeed, in choosing to focus my study on this community I soon found myself on the nether side of a divide that, while obscure to me, seemed glaringly apparent to my middle-class colleagues and friends, who repeatedly advised me that Macumba was, if not utterly nefarious, at the very least the practice of charlatans. I was counseled instead to turn my attentions to Candomblé, particularly the form associated with the traditional houses of Bahia.

My Brazilian interlocutors considered Candomblé an authentic religion, one whose pure African ancestry made it worthy of serious study. This African ancestry was forcefully symbolized by orixás, African deities such as Yemanjá who constitute the focus of Candomblé devotion. By contrast, they argued that Macumba, the Afro-Brazilian tradition associated with Rio, had been corrupted in the cosmopolitan environment of the erstwhile Portuguese Imperial capital, losing the integrity of its African heritage and degenerating into little more than black magic. For many Brazilians like my friends and colleagues, the depravity of Macumba was both symbolized and confirmed by the prominence of the Exu spirits. Uncultured at best and criminal at worst, Exu spirits, like Macumba itself, are associated with the lowest levels of the Cariocan social order.

Searching through the scholarly literature for data on Macumba, I encountered the same set of prejudices, buttressed by similar arguments. The most prominent accounts of Afro-Brazilian religions centered on Candomblé of Bahia, which was presented as the reconstitution of an African tradition fractured by slavery and displacement. Those elements that deviated from a putatively African model were minimized, ignored, or dismissed as aberrant. In much of this literature, the term Macumba was used to refer to an especially syncretistic, impure or degraded variant of the Afro-Brazilian tradition associated with the city of Rio de Janeiro and with black magic.

In a separate (but at times convergent) literature, Macumba was also distinguished from Umbanda, the label given to an eclectic set of beliefs and practices influenced by the theories of the nineteenth-century French spiritist-philosopher Allen Kardec. Umbanda seemed to have emerged in Rio in the early decades of the twentieth century, and by the 1950s its advocates had established a flourishing cottage industry of conferences, federations, and publications dedicated to its promotion and doctrinal codification. In much of the literature on Umbanda, Macumba was characterized as *baixa espiritismo* (low spiritism) whose practitioners cultivated inferior spirits for morally questionable purposes like securing a lover's

fidelity, exacting vengeance, or ensuring personal gain—practices
denigrated as black magic. Integral to Macumba were rituals of blood
sacrifice, drumming, and other vestiges of a "primitive" or "uncivilized"
African past—a past from which many Umbanda practitioners sought to
distance themselves.

The conflicting opinions about what, exactly, constituted Macumba
also found expression in disputes over the term's etymology. Some scholars
linked Macumba to a Bantu language, and a type of percussive musical
instrument. Given the centrality of percussion in African and African-
derived religions, this may account for the scholarly use of the term in
reference to the ritual practices of Bantu-speaking slaves and their descendents, who were especially prominent in Rio from the late eighteenth to
the mid-nineteenth century (e.g., Ramos 2001; Carneiro 1991). Others
associated the term with communities of runaway slaves (Lapassade and
Aurélio Luz 1972: xxiv). Although each side offered suggestive linguistic
parallels as evidence, it remained unclear—as Diana Brown concluded in
her study of Umbanda:

> whether the term macumba was ever closely identified with a specific set of
> practices by those who practiced them; whether...it acquired meaning as a
> generic reference to diverse practices; or whether...it may have also acquired
> its generic usage as well as its pejorative implications at the hands of upper
> sector nonpractitioners. (Brown 1994: 25)

Although there was little agreement in the various literatures about the
meaning of the term, its linguistic origins, or the specific practices it
denoted, Macumba's deviant status was a point of widespread accord. This
was expressed in the close association made between Macumba and the
illegitimate in its various incarnations. Most often this took the form of
accusations of *feitiçaria* or black magic—an allegation that was once
applied to all African-derived religions in Brazil. At other times, Macumba's
illegitimacy was expressed as impurity, corruption, and primitivity, or in
accusations of charlatanism and debauchery. Not surprisingly, those persons whose spiritual practices were labeled Macumba were subject to various forms of social control intended to police, cure, or otherwise control
the deviance that, by close association, so thoroughly invested them.

Rather than search for some original meaning to the term, or treat it as
a distinct and identifiable set of religious practices, we ought to consider
Macumba's indeterminacy: its ability to shift content in accordance with
shifting social and academic concerns. This labile quality not only accounts
for the term's conceptual relevance but provides insight into a larger trajectory that has dominated elite discourse on Afro-Brazilian religions for

much of the past seventy-five years. In this chapter I analyze subtle shifts in the meaning of Macumba since the late nineteenth century, an era of tremendous political and social change in Brazil that saw the legal establishment of religious freedom and the simultaneous prohibition of African-oriented spiritual practices as forms of black magic. This created a situation in which the need to distinguish "legitimate" from "illegitimate" spiritual practices was one that structured, implicitly or explicitly, much of the scholarship on Afro-Brazilian traditions. Here I focus in particular on the works of three influential scholars of Afro-Brazilian religions: Nina Rodrigues (1862–1906), Arthur Ramos (1903–1949), and Roger Bastide (1898–1974).

On the basis of my analysis of these authors, I argue that from obscure origins the term Macumba came to designate that set of spirits, practices, and religious goals classified as illegitimate by a diverse set of actors in the struggle to assert the legitimacy of their own set of spirits, practices, and religious goals. In an environment in which Christianity served as the unquestioned model for what constituted "religion," this struggle was articulated within a shifting set of alliances and conflicts between masters and slaves, blacks and whites, politicians and priests, government and church officials, scholars and cult leaders.[2] Over time, an array of groups that in some way confused the categories employed to delineate "legitimate" forms of Afro-Brazilian religiosity came to be loosely classified under the rubric of Macumba. Understood from this perspective, the term Macumba straddles an uneasy—and shifting—fault line between competing classificatory strategies as several generations of Brazilians wrestled with the relationship of religion to magic, magic to Africanity, and Africanity to the nation.

It is important to remember that throughout the nineteenth and well into the twentieth century, Afro-Brazilian religions were not generally considered religions at all, but superstitions borne of ignorance, illegitimate forms of magic, or offenses against public morality and the social order. Practitioners were subject to persecution by civil authorities and their ritual objects periodically confiscated in police raids. Throughout this period, lurid news accounts portrayed these religions as depraved and their adherents as prone to the most obscene acts of violence, immorality, and criminality—characteristics that still typify the portrayal of Macumba in the popular press today. A deeply rooted sense among elites of the primitivity of Brazil's black populations and their cultural forms contributed to a climate of official illegitimacy that varied from periods of relative tolerance to outbreaks of virulent repression.

Against this backdrop, advocates for Afro-Brazilian modalities like Candomblé and Umbanda argued for the legitimacy of their chosen variant by distancing it from the negative stigma once associated with all Afro-Brazilian religions. The formulations of elite patrons and scholar-advocates like Ramos and Bastide were disseminated in a variety of media including newspaper articles and radio spots, conference proceedings and position papers, literary and academic tomes. These scholarly accounts helped confer legitimacy on particular modalities of Afro-Brazilian religious praxis not only by granting them the elite imprimatur of science, but by systematizing them to accord with various criteria of legitimacy. While these criteria changed over time, legitimacy was always articulated in opposition to illegitimacy. This meant that categories like black magic constituted important foils against which claims to legitimacy could be established.

Candomblé and Umbanda thus are better understood as ideal types: models that are "historically determined and linked to processes of legitimation by the cults and their spokespeople" (Capone 1999: 27; see also Dantas 1988; Harding 2000). Central to these processes, I argue, was the category of Macumba that came to represent the illicit, the abject, the deviant, against which—and by virtue of which—legitimate forms of religion could be identified. In this way, two distinct models of orthodoxy were forged from an eclectic and ever-changing religious field, granting social and political benefits to the practitioners of some forms of Afro-Brazilian praxis while denying them to others. One result of this process today is that certain Afro-Brazilian practices, such as the annual seaside offering to Yemanjá, have been embraced by the public as part of a legitimate and much beloved tradition, while others are considered Macumba, that is: an illegitimate form of black magic.

Religion and Magic: Categories of the Legitimate and the Illegitimate

The palpable concern to differentiate legitimate from illegitimate religious practices took definitive shape in the context of the legal, social and political changes in Brazil that culminated in the final abolition of slavery (1888), the overthrow of the monarchy (1889), and the establishment of the first Republic (1891). These transformations raised profound questions about how to regulate the relations between former slaves and their former masters; the future of the Brazilian nation; and the relation of race to social progress (Johnson 2002; Skidmore 1993). Influenced by contemporary European theories of race, Brazilian elites of the late nineteenth century were preoccupied with the social consequences of African degeneracy for the nation, particularly for its ability to modernize. Especially perturbing to these elites were the spiritual practices of the blacks and lower classes, felt to reflect their primitive mental state and credulity, but also the potential—in the form of black magic or *feitiçaria*—to wreak social havoc. A typical newspaper report of this period denounced the debauchery and immorality perpetuated by "clever Africans," who attracted

> married women seeking remedies to ensure that their husbands remain sexually attracted to them, slaves requesting ingredients [for a potion] to lessen the wrath of their owners, women seeking advice on the ways to attain happiness, and even businessmen desiring success in their endeavors! (Graden 1998: 63)

By threatening established social hierarchies—of, for example, husband to wife and master to slave—the activities of Afro-Brazilian sorcerers were a source of concern for landowners, church officials, civil authorities, and other elites. Not only were these sorcerers beguiling the public with charms and potions, but they represented a folk expertise that competed with the emerging disciplines of medicine and psychiatry that had begun to be established in Bahia and Rio de Janeiro in the latter half of the nineteenth century. In 1890, lawmakers emended three provisions to the Penal Code explicitly prohibiting the practice of medicine, dentistry, pharmacology, and homeopathy without legal certification, as well as the activities of *curandeiros* (popular healers), *feiticeiros* (sorcerers), fortune tellers, diviners, card readers, and spirit mediums.[3]

This established a legal framework within which various popular spiritual practices were declared *illegitimate* offenses against public health and made subject to the official apparatus of punishment and extirpation.[4] Because the Constitution of 1890 established the separation of church and state, those practices classified as *legitimate* forms of religious expression were protected from official interference. Although in practice this meant activities centered on or sanctioned by the Catholic Church or civil authorities, the constitution did not define exactly what constituted a legitimate form of religious expression. Further legislation adopted in 1893 recognized as legitimate only those religious associations that registered with civil authorities and did not promote "illicit or immoral" ends (Maggie 1992: 43–44). Here again, what constituted illicit or immoral ends was left unspecified.

The net result was the creation of a complex legal, bureaucratic, and regulatory apparatus by which the activities of individuals accused of violating the Penal Code could be judged to be legitimately religious or not, and punished accordingly. Knowledge was central to this system: knowledge about various spiritual techniques; knowledge about a diverse array of ritual practices and their intent; knowledge about the ritual use of confiscated objects; in short, an intimate, yet objective knowledge such as could be produced by a dispassionate, learned specialist. In the course of the late nineteenth and early twentieth centuries, a range of disciplinary specialists contributed to the production of knowledge about Afro-Brazilian spiritual practices, including medical doctors, psychiatrists, forensic scientists, police detectives, judges, criminologists, and anthropologists.

Nina Rodrigues: Hierarchies of Race and Religion

It was in such an environment that the first scholarly study of Afro-Brazilian religions was produced by the forensic psychiatrist, (Raymundo) Nina Rodrigues (1862–1906). Rodrigues held the popular view of his day that Afro-Brazilians were less evolved than their white neighbors, more prone to superstition, psychologically immature, and incapable of "civilized behavior." In order to accurately assess this population's mental and cultural state, Rodrigues embarked upon the first scientific study of Afro-Brazilian religious beliefs and practices, which he arrayed along an evolutionary continuum. Of the Africans brought to Brazil, Rodrigues claimed that the "Sudanese," particularly the Nagô (Yoruba), were the most advanced because of their complex mythology and organizational structure of their religion, which he referred to as Candomblé.[5] Inferior to the Nagô were a variety of "less advanced" tribal groups whose religions lacked a developed pantheon and a graded structure of authority (Rodrigues 1977: 215). But the most inferior religions of all in Rodrigues's schema were those of the creoles and *mestiços*, which, like those groups themselves, had lost any original integrity by becoming hopelessly intermixed with elements of other belief systems.

In Rodrigues's classificatory schema we see a hierarchal contrast between the Nagô tradition of Candomblé and more mixed cults that begins to be correlated with the opposition between religion and *feitiçaria* or magic, a process that was developed more fully by his successors. Within the evolutionary continuum that Rodrigues established, Nagô Candomblé was seen as the most elevated and pure form of African religion and therefore closer to the pole of true religion; while non-Nagô forms such as Bantu were less developed, inferior, and prone to eclecticism, thus constituting degradations closer to the pole of magic. In the generations after Rodrigues, Macumba came to be the term that was applied to those especially syncretistic forms of Afro-Brazilian religious praxis associated with a Bantu heritage and found particularly in Rio de Janeiro, as distinct from the more "pure" Nagô Candomblés of Bahia. This framework was developed most fully in the work of Arthur Ramos (1903–1949), a self-professed disciple of Rodrigues who published a series of influential essays drawing on Rodrigues's material, and who was responsible for editing and reissuing much of Rodrigues's work in the 1930s.

Arthur Ramos: "Macumba Has Invaded All Spheres"

A medical doctor who specialized in forensic medicine and psychiatry, Ramos wrote extensively on various aspects of Afro-Brazilian culture in Brazil and his work continues to be a reference for students of Afro-Brazilian religions. Influenced by a growing nationalist sentiment that had taken hold in Brazil in the first few decades of the twentieth century, Ramos was part of a vanguard of scholars, writers and artists of the period who had begun to reexamine the question of race and its relationship to the nation.[6] As these elites turned away from the European-derived evolutionary theories that had so preoccupied their predecessors, they developed a radically different understanding of Brazil's multiracial and multicultural heritage, one that explicitly valorized certain African contributions to Brazilian culture.

This reassessment both coincided with and enriched a larger movement taking shape throughout the Americas and the Caribbean that focused on the African contributions to New World cultures. Its intellectual coherence was established by anthropologists like Franz Boas and Melville Herskovits. Indeed, Herskovits visited Brazil as part of his efforts to document the African heritage of the New World, writing several articles about Afro-Brazilian religions and maintaining a friendly correspondence with Ramos (see Herskovits 1937; 1943; 1956). From the late 1930s onward, the academic literature on Afro-Brazilian religions began to reflect Herskovits's emphasis on African "survivals" or "retentions," a perspective that eventually supplanted the late-nineteenth-century understanding of these traditions as primitive fetishism or *feitiçaria*.

In many ways Arthur Ramos, one of the most prominent intellectuals of the 1930s and 1940s, bridged these two different understandings of

Afro-Brazilian religions. Although dedicating much of his intellectual life to the study of Brazil's African heritage, Ramos, like his turn-of-the-century predecessors, was preoccupied with the problem Brazil's black populations posed for national development. Unlike them, Ramos did not see Afro-Brazilians as racially inferior, but as a *classe atrasada* (backward class) possessed of a "pre-logical mentality" (2001: 30–32). Drawing on Lévy-Bruhl, Ramos argued that this mentality was not a sign of racial inferiority, but rather a primitive psychological state characterized by "magical thinking." Such a state occurred in all races under a variety of conditions, manifesting itself in "the poor, children, and neurotics, as well as in dreams, art and determined conditions of psychic regression" (2001: 31). But it was most evident in the syncretistic religions that predominated among the least advanced segments of the population: blacks, mestiços and lower class whites. For Ramos, the problem hampering Brazil's advancement was not its African blood per se, but the "magical thinking" of the lower classes. He saw his work as part of a larger educational intervention through which this mentality could be raised to "higher stages" (32).

According to Ramos, just as Brazilian society embodied a spectrum that ranged from the "more advanced" classes to the "less advanced," so too Brazilian religions ranged from the more advanced—for example, Catholicism—to the less advanced. Of the religions of the "backwards classes," he identified Nagô Candomblé of Bahia as the most advanced. By contrast, Macumba of Rio de Janeiro, a religious modality that Ramos identified with an original Bantu heritage that had become adulterated, represented the least advanced. Compared to Nagô Candomblé, Ramos wrote, Macumba was of little interest to the scholar, "such is the level of its dilution, its rapid transformation with the civilization of the *litoral* [coast]" (1971: 104). While Candomblé had preserved a high level of African purity and thus an integrated, collective system of belief and ritual, Macumba had disintegrated into magic:

> Macumba today is a generic term in all of Brazil that has come to designate not only religions of the Negro, but various magical practices—*despachos* [hexes], diverse rituals—that at times only remotely retain a connection with the primitive religious forms transplanted from Africa. Today there are macumbas for any purpose. The work of syncretism knows no limits. Macumba has invaded all spheres. It is at the root of popular forms of magic, which inherited much from the Negro but also has strong roots in the magical corpus of European origin... (Ramos 2001: 144)

Ramos argued that although religion and magic were fused in Africa, in Brazil under the destructive impact of slavery and white domination they had become separated: the magical function had been disengaged from the sacerdotal. Macumba resulted from a process of degradation of the African heritage that emerged at the point at which religious leaders "exceeded their sacerdotal functions and became counselors, fortune tellers, card readers, etc."—that is, attended to the romantic, economic and practical realities of their devotees (135). Drawing on theories elaborated by Émile Durkheim, Marcel Mauss, and Henri Hubert, Ramos distinguished between religion as "the belief in extra-human entities, implying an attitude [of submission] in the face of these divinities," and magic as "a social phenomenon, comprised of acts that seek the subjection of these forces (135; Mauss 1972; Durkheim 1965). He reasoned that Candomblé, organized around the veneration of African deities called orixás and the ritual reenactment of their complex mythologies, constituted a true religion— although one inferior to Christianity. Heterogeneous Afro-Brazilian forms like Macumba, whose "connection with the primitive religious forms transplanted from Africa" was compromised through syncretism, had degenerated into magic (154).

Within Ramos's analytical framework, religious legitimacy was framed not only in terms of purity of African origins—an approach that was successful not only in Brazil, but other national contexts as well— but also in terms of collective acts of submission to transcendent gods. From this perspective, Macumba was illegitimate not only because it had absorbed outside influences and become impure, but because in the process it became oriented around the satisfaction of individual desires. Macumba, in short, represented the inverse of Candomblé (see figure below).

Candomblé	Macumba
purity (preservation of African tradition)	impurity (degradation of African tradition)
collective acts of submission	individual acts of manipulation
religion	magic

Ramos's model is a cogent example of how an intellectual paradigm that privileged African survivals and contemporaneous theories of religion and magic converged to structure the scholarly discourse on Afro-Brazilian religions in ways that opposed collective tradition and individual desires, purity and impurity, Candomblé and Macumba. It was in the hands of Roger Bastide, however, that this model was articulated in its most powerful—and enduring—formulation (Fry 1986; Morães von Simson 1986; Negrão 1986; Brown 1994; Capone 1999).

Roger Bastide: "Macumba Results from Social Parasitism"

Although he was certainly not alone in extolling the African purity of Nagô Candomblé, the French scholar Roger Bastide attracted an international audience, a factor that makes his writings particularly important. Still considered a classic, Bastide's *The African Religions of Brazil* is required reading in a number of fields including sociology, anthropology and religious studies. One of the most distinguished and prolific contributors to the scholarship on Afro-Brazilian religions, Bastide's work was wide-ranging and encyclopedic; indeed, few aspects of his adopted culture escaped his analytical gaze. But it was his extensive studies of Candomblé that constituted the heart of his vast oeuvre. Over the course of this work, Bastide established and refined a series of categorical oppositions between Candomblé and Macumba that approached the status of an ontological dichotomy. And it is this particular vision of the field of Afro-Brazilian religions that continues to influence both popular and intellectual accounts of Afro-Brazilian religions.[7]

In *Le Candomblé de Bahia (Rite Nagô)*, published in France in 1958, Bastide argued that Candomblé represented "a piece of Africa" in the New World, a "harmonious and coherent system of collective representations and ritual gestures" that transplanted to Brazilian soil the ancestral world of Africa and restored to the slave the dignity lost to him under slavery (2001 [1958]: 73, 23–24). In claiming Africanity as the source of Candomblé's religious legitimacy, Bastide equated Africanity with a collective tradition best exemplified by the "obvious" purity of the Nagô cults of Bahia. Like others before him, Bastide distinguished the purity of these Nagô cults from the more syncretistic Bantu cults. Following Arthur Ramos, Bastide felt that Bantu religion had a less developed organizational and mythical structure and therefore had absorbed a great deal of outside influence, in the process admitting errors and deviations. But the admixture had not stopped there. Elements of popular Catholic and Amerindian practices, as well as European spiritism, had also been absorbed over time, giving rise in Bastide's analysis to the Macumba characteristic of Rio de Janeiro:

> In Rio de Janeiro, the African nations merged with one another, allowing themselves to be profoundly penetrated by external influences—Amerindian, Catholic, Spiritist—giving birth to an essentially syncretistic religion, macumba. (30)

In this way, Bastide described Macumba as an especially syncretistic, Bantu-derived agglomeration of disparate elements typical of the Afro-Brazilian cults of Rio de Janeiro and the Southeast, a gloss that he would use in later writings as well (1973).

In a subsequent work entitled *Les Religions Africaines au Brésil: Vers une Sociologie des Interpénétrations de Civilisations*, published in 1960, Bastide further refined this distinction between Macumba and Candomblé. Here he argued that Candomblé fused sexual, economic, and religious behavior into a comprehensive system regulated by the mythical prototypes of the African deities called orixás—a system in which the principle of reciprocity, or the rule of prestation and counter-prestation, served as the organizing principle. By contrast, Macumba was the net result of the disintegration of African traditions under the hegemonic impact of capitalism. This was a process that reached its culmination in the years following the Second World War in the industrialized cities of Rio de Janeiro and Sao Paulo (Hess 1992).

The thrust of Bastide's argument was that Bahian Candomblé, through its "subjacent metaphysics," preserved pre-capitalistic modes of exchange and a communitarian ethos; while Macumba was a product of the newly emerging capitalist economy that produced "social parasitism," class exploitation, and the loosening of moral boundaries:

> Candomblé was and is a means of social control, an instrument of solidarity and communion; macumba results from social parasitism, from the shameless exploitation of the credulity of the lower classes, or from the triumph of immoral tendencies, ranging from rape to—all too frequently—murder.
> (1960: 414)

Here, in the course of a single paragraph, Bastide linked Macumba not only with the degradation of more "authentic" forms of Afro-Brazilian practice, but with a range of "immoral tendencies" that, in this logic, inevitably culminates in rape and murder.

Although Bastide was, on the whole, an extremely sophisticated thinker whose views developed over the course of his long career, his depiction of Macumba as a debased form of Candomblé populated by profligate charlatans in which immorality, criminality, and vice were given full reign, effectively equating Macumba with moral, social, and economic degradation. Candomblé, on the other hand, was presented as a communal utopia of reciprocity and regulated desires rooted in pre-modern Africa. Here fidelity to African tradition promoted sociocultural cohesion, while the lack of fidelity to these traditions resulted in depravity.

Umbanda and Quimbanda

Bastide's work also serves as a useful point of entry into a second scholarly literature in which Macumba has played a role comparable to the one it has played in discussions of Candomblé. This is the literature describing an Afro-Brazilian religion that seems to have consolidated itself in Rio de Janeiro some time in the 1920s: Umbanda. Like Candomblé, the history of Umbanda is one that is intimately tied to a series of efforts on the part of practitioners and elites to legitimate it as an authentic religion. Unlike the case of Candomblé however, claims for the authenticity of Umbanda were framed not in terms of Africanity, but in terms of whiteness.

Bastide was one of the first scholars to take Umbanda seriously as a new phenomenon, a product of the new social arrangements spawned by the urbanization and industrial development of the Southeast that, although sharing a certain heritage with Macumba, was significantly different. Bastide posited that Umbanda emerged from a process that was the direct converse of that which had produced Macumba: a process of cultural and social *reintegration* among the lower classes in which "what remained of the African religions" was "restructured" to accord with the values of dominant, white society (1960: 303). This "restructuring" took place through Kardec-influenced spiritism, in which the African gods were recast as inhabitants of a Kardecist, hierarchical universe. As Bastide put it, Umbanda

> answered the needs of the new mentality of the more highly developed black, socially on the rise, who realized that macumba lowered him in the eyes of the whites but who was nevertheless reluctant to abandon his African tradition altogether. (319)[8]

Or, to put it another way, Umbanda reflected the ambivalence of a rising mulatto and black working class towards their African heritage.

Despite the heterogeneity of Umbanda beliefs and practices, Bastide thought he recognized a common thread in the strategic efforts of practitioners to whiten Umbanda and distance it from Africanity. These efforts ranged from the rejection of African practices of blood sacrifice and "orgiastic dancing"; to claims that Umbanda was an ancient religion derived from Hindu, Egyptian, or "ancient Lemurian" civilizations; to the reinterpretation of African gods as moral principles, astral fluids, elemental forces, and so forth (319–334). These ideas were promoted in a series of conferences organized by Umbanda leaders beginning in the 1940s, and by the formation of several federations whose specific aim was to codify beliefs and practices so that Umbanda would be recognized as a legitimate religion not only by the State but by Brazilian society at large.

Bastide argued that it was largely through such conferences and federations, as well as a variety of popular publications, that Umbanda advocates attempted to "purify" their possession practices of the "primitivity" that they associated with African religions (especially practices such as animal sacrifice). Against accusations of "low spiritism," Umbanda practitioners claimed that they cultivated only the more "evolved" spirits. These more evolved spirits included deceased European philosophers, but also spirits associated with the Brazilian past: *caboclos* (the spirits of Brazil's native inhabitants) and *pretos velhos* (the spirits of African slaves). At the same time that they sought to purge Afro-Brazilian religious practices of what they saw as their primitive elements—drumming, animal sacrifice, and spirits deemed "without light" (*sem luz*) (labeling these as deviant or demonic)—Umbanda's founders asserted that they were practicing Brazil's *true* religion. This was symbolized most cogently by Umbanda's mixture of European, caboclo, and preto velho spirits: the mythical three races that Gilberto Freyre famously claimed had come together harmoniously to form the Brazilian nation.[9]

According to Bastide, these efforts at whitening, although they eventually would prove successful in legitimating Umbanda as a uniquely Brazilian religion to a larger public,[10] had also resulted in the bifurcation of Macumba into

> Umbanda spiritism, which retained only the civilized elements, and Quimbanda magic, which was associated with demonic powers. This split made it possible to upgrade the ancestral traditions by purging it of anything disgusting to modern-day man. (322)

The whitened aspect of Macumba thus became known as Umbanda. And, according to Bastide, because Umbanda practitioners themselves accepted the conventional notion of Macumba as primitive black magic, that which had been purged from their own practices became known by the oppobrious term "Quimbanda," the opposite of Umbanda.

In this Bastidian analysis we have a two-stage operation that is correlated to larger processes of social dissolution and reintegration. In the first stage, Macumba was the product of the social transformations wrought by urbanization and industrialization: the rupture of ethnic ties in a market economy, the dissolution of the African collective memory, and the fragmentation of African traditions under conditions of urban alienation. In a second stage, driven by the consolidation of a class-based society, the Afro-Brazilian tradition was reinterpreted to accord with the values of modern society, producing Umbanda. And while Umbanda retained only the socially acceptable aspects of Macumba, Quimbanda represented that which was rejected in the process of whitening; the residue of Africanity that could not be assimilated: the Macumba of Macumba.

In the work of Bastide we may distinguish several distinct valences to the term Macumba. Like earlier scholars, Bastide used the term to denote: (1) a syncretistic cult of Bantu origin; and (2) a fragmented form of the Afro-Brazilian heritage closely linked to black magic and charlatanism. But he also identified it as: (3) the unassimilated residue of Africanity that could not be reinterpreted within the context of Umbanda; that is: Quimbanda. For Bastide, Macumba was thus both prior to Umbanda, and, in the guise of Quimbanda, its converse. What distinguished Macumba/Quimbanda above all, not only for Bastide but for later disciples like Renato Ortiz, was the cultivation of a category of trickster spirits known collectively as exus (Oritz 1978).

Exu Spirits

In Bastide's work, one of the characteristics that differentiated Candomblé from Macumba and Umbanda from Quimbanda was the role of the Yoruba-derived deity called Exu. In the pure, Nagô forms of Candomblé, according to Bastide, Exu was the orixá of divination and the crossroads, the intermediary between the world of the gods and that of humans. A classic trickster figure—lawless, unpredictable, and capricious—Exu was always honored before any of the other orixás and then dispatched so that they could be invoked without his troublesome presence. Bastide asserted that in these communities, Exu was reserved a special niche outside of the *terreiro* (religious center) proper, and although highly respected, was not cultivated in the same manner as the other orixás. Unlike these, he had no *filhos* ("children," or initiates); that is, he was not cultivated through possession but through regular sacrifices that served to keep him satisfied—and at bay. In fact, wrote Bastide, so chaotic and unruly was Exu that possession by this orixá signaled pathology.[11]

By contrast, in Umbanda and Quimbanda, under the influence of spiritism, the Yoruba trickster Exu had been transformed into a phalanx of demon-like figures inhabiting the lowest levels of the spirit hierarchy. As "spirits of the shadows," exus formed a category of marginal spirits especially associated with the illicit: lawlessness, delinquency, immorality, and the unrestrained reign of the passions. As we have seen, Bastide linked Quimbanda or Macumba with the satisfaction of individual desires, symbolized by the cultivation of these lower-level Exu spirits. By contrast, he described Candomblé as oriented toward a collective morality rooted in the preservation of an African tradition, a morality linked with the absence of possession by the unpredictable Exu.

Yet there is evidence in the literature that contradicts Bastide's careful distinctions. Ruth Landes, for example, reported that among the Nagô Candomblés that she studied in Bahia, Exu the orixá had proliferated into various kinds of exus, often described as the "slaves" of the orixás. As she wrote: "Every god appears to have one or more Eshu [Exu]-lackeys doing dirty work for him; the warrior goddess Yansan has a 'gang' of at least seven of the 'wildest' and they are all female." However, "[n]o Eshu can be represented within the temple with the gods" (1940: 261–270). Landes went on to say that whereas the other orixás were employed in socially approved ways such as ensuring a healthy childbirth:

> Eshu is employed secretly to arrange a rendezvous, to force a seduction, to disrupt or even mend a marriage. "Mothers" of the renowned fetish temples deny employing Eshu, indicating that they consider themselves above petty interests, but they all know what formulas to use with him and they undoubtedly resort to him privately. (263–264)

Landes's findings indicated that the proliferation of Exu into a variety of lawless Exu spirits—a process that Bastide associated with Umbanda/Quimbanda—had occurred in some of the most "orthodox" houses of Bahian Candomblé by the late 1930s and probably much earlier.[12] But perhaps more significantly, her observations suggested that Exu was intimately involved with rituals of a sort Roger Bastide surely would have identified as black magic: arranging rendezvous, forcing seductions, and disrupting marriages. As we have seen, for Bastide such rituals had no place in Candomblé, which was oriented towards communal tradition and collective morality, not the petty satisfaction of individual desires.

Conclusion

Did Bastide simply ignore evidence that would have compromised his attempt to portray Candomblé in ways that accorded with a scholarly model of religious legitimacy? I think he was too careful and principled a scholar for that. Rather, the example of Exu highlights several aspects of the scholarly project. First, there are blind spots within any classificatory schema—those dimensions of social life that are rendered invisible because they do not conform to a theoretical model, or because such a model shifts analytic attention elsewhere.

Second, there are sociopolitical dimensions to any scholarly analysis: the ways that theory-making intersects with the social commitments of scholars and their informants. As I have tried to show, Bastide's analysis was part of a much larger process through which certain Afro-Brazilian traditions, long disparaged as black magic or primitive superstition, gained social legitimacy through the constant displacement of characteristics associated with illegitimacy. This process developed over the course of several generations out of the mutually reinforcing discourses of various actors, including scholars, religious leaders, and informants, whose interests overlapped at certain points. Significantly, both Bastide and Ramos derived their data from a small circle of Candomblé communities, including the house that Nina Rodrigues first studied at the end of the nineteenth century, and a variety of its satellites—that is, houses that had been established by members of the initiatic lineage it represented.

Third, theory-making not only explains human behavior, but creates knowledge and apportions power in ways that carry real-world consequences. For example, because of the status of text as a privileged medium of communication, the scholarship on Afro-Brazilian religions has shaped contemporary ritual practice as communities look to and model themselves after the "authentic" traditions described in anthropological texts. Leaders and practitioners alike proudly display these works on their shelves and consult them on matters of practice. In this way, the works of scholars like Arthur Ramos, Roger Bastide, and others have influenced not only the ways that scholars understand these religions, but how they are practiced "on the ground."

In an environment of competition for religious legitimacy, advocates for certain Afro-Brazilian religions such as Candomblé and Umbanda were successful in establishing these traditions as socially legitimate—largely through a process of differentiating them from those practices they denigrated as illegitimate. Although the terms of denigration changed over time, the net result has been the stigmatization of a certain set of religious practices, spirits, and goals that is grouped under the rubric of Macumba. Because of their association—in terms of imagery and comportment—with the devil, Exu spirits in particular have become metonymic of Macumba, and the evil that it is widely thought to cultivate.

Drawing on the traditions and testimony of a relatively small circle of informants, scholars like Roger Bastide and Arthur Ramos presented Candomblé in ways that: (1) conformed to an academic model of religion and (2) distanced it from the many characteristics associated with the illegitimate category of *feitiçaria* or black magic. While advocates for Candomblé typically described Macumba as impure because it had lost the integrity of its African roots and degenerated into black magic, advocates for Umbanda argued the opposite: Macumba, from their perspective, was too African. Their legitimizing strategy focused not on Africanity but on "whitening": emphasizing the European origins, spirits, or values of Umbanda and distancing it from anything they considered primitive. Although they differed on what constituted Macumba, both camps were in agreement on its illegitimate status as black magic.

As I have tried to show, the opposition between religion and magic is discursive not practical: the result of a continuous process of identity formation in which "magic" is progressively displaced onto another. What separates the two is the degree to which those groups who claim to practice religion have achieved a measure of social legitimacy by distancing their own practices from accusations of magic. Just as scholars have designated "magic" as the illegitimate underside of that set of practices labeled "religion," so the category of Macumba has represented that stigmatized domain in contrast to which particular forms of Afro-Brazilian religious praxis like Candomblé have established their legitimacy and claimed a place as praiseworthy constituents of a distinctive national culture. Because scholars and scholarship are part of a much larger system of knowledge production that has real life consequences for both the knower and the known, the academic quest to define, order, and categorize can reinforce other classificatory processes that apportion power and prestige in determinate ways. In the New Year's homage to Yemanjá in Rio de Janeiro we see a tangible example of this process.

Notes

An earlier version of this chapter was published as "Black Magic and the Academy: Macumba and the Construction of Afro-Brazilian Religious Orthodoxies," in *History of Religions* (Hayes 2007). Permission to republish portions of this text is gratefully acknowledged.

1. The local term for inhabitants of the city of Rio de Janeiro.
2. To paraphrase Peter Fry's elegant summation in his "Introduction" to Dantas (1988: 15).
3. Article 156 prohibited "the practice of any medicine, dentistry or pharmacology, homeopathy, hypnotism or animal magnetism without necessary legal certification." Article 157 prohibited "the practice of spiritism, magic and its

sorceries, the use of talismans and cartomancy to arouse sentiments of love or hate, the promise to remedy curable or incurable illnesses; in sum to fascinate and subjugate public credulity." Article 158 prohibited "administering or prescribing any natural or prepared substance as a curative for internal or external use, thus performing or exercising the office denominated as *curandeiro*" (religious healer). See Maggie (1992: 21–22).

4. For a more extensive discussion of this period, see Johnson (2002: 81–83).

5. The term Nagô is used in Brazil to refer to Yoruba-speaking peoples. It was used by slave traders to refer to slave cargo that departed for the New World from the Bight of Benin on the West coast of Africa. It appears to be derived from *anago*, a Fon (Dahomey) term for Yoruba speakers. For this derivation see Verger (1981: 14); Omari (1994: 137).

6. Several authors have examined the intellectual developments of this period with regard to the topic of Afro-Brazilians in greater detail than is possible here. I have found the following to be particularly useful: Dantas (1988); Skidmore (1993); Corrêa (1999); and Costa Lima (1987).

7. There have been some notable attempts in the scholarship of Afro-Brazilian religions to rethink this dichotomy, although they have had little impact on popular conceptions of Macumba. Perhaps the earliest was *O Segredo da Macumba* (*The Secret of Macumba*) coauthored by Georges Lapassade and Marcos Aurélio Luz in 1972. Against the Bastidian view, Lapassade and Luz argued that Macumba ought to be understood as a form of resistance to white domination sublimated to the symbolic realm. Macumba represents the "return of the repressed"; an expression of social and sexual liberation. As such, the spirits of Macumba are "heroes of liberty" who express the dreams of the oppressed. Beatriz Goís Dantas (1988) was one of the first to analyze the trope of Nagô purity in studies of Candomblé; her work has been influential for a generation of Brazilian scholars concerned with how scholarly schemas have privileged certain ritual communities within a complex and heterogeneous religious field. Patrícia Birman (1995), David Hess (1992), and Stefania Capone (1999), among others, have incorporated Dantas's insights into their own analyses of Afro-Brazilian religions in different ways. Nonetheless, that set of practices termed Macumba has not received serious scholarly attention (although it has been addressed in the popular press) and most scholarship continues to be oriented toward Candomblé, on the one hand, or Umbanda on the other.

8. Later interpreters such as Diana Brown (1995) have seen this as a process strongly shaped by middle sector whites who sought to reconfigure Afro-Brazilian religions in accord with their own values.

9. In his 1933 masterpiece, *Casa Grande e Senzala*, translated into English as *The Masters and the Slaves* (1956), Freyre argued that Brazil's multiracial and multicultural blending was its greatest resource, and that Brazil constituted a racial democracy.

10. Brown reported that when she began her field studies in 1966, Umbanda, despite growing popularity, was still considered an inferior cousin of Candomblé, and was often disparaged as Macumba in the social science

literature. This negative opinion was shared by educated Brazilians, who dismissed Umbanda as "ignorance." Yet by 1970, Umbanda had won significant public and academic attention and was widely acclaimed as Brazil's true, autochthonous religion. See Brown's Preface to the Morningside edition of *Umbanda* (Brown 1995).

11. On the rare occasions when Exu did possess a devotee, this possession "was different from that of other orixás by its frenzy, its abnormal, pathological character, its destructive violence…if Exu attacks a member of the candomblé it is necessary to dispatch him, to send him away immediately" (Bastide 2001: 37–38).

12. Landes's fieldwork was conducted in 1938.

Bibliography

Bastide, Roger (2001) [1958]. *O Candomblé da Bahia: Rito Nagô*, trans. Maria Isaura Pereira de Queiroz. Sao Paulo: Companhia das Letras.

——— (1960). *Les Religions Africaines au Brésil: Vers une Sociologie des Interpénétrations de Civilisations*. Paris: Presses Universitaires de France.

——— (1973). *Estudos Afro-Brasileiros*. Sao Paulo: Editora Perspectiva.

Birman, Patrícia (1995). *Fazer Estilo Criando Gêneros*. Rio de Janeiro: Relume Dumará.

Brown, Diana (1995) [1986]. *Umbanda: Religion and Politics in Urban Brazil*, Morningside ed. New York: Columbia University Press.

Capone, Stefania (1999). *La Quête de l'Afrique dans le Candomblé: Pouvoir et Tradition au Brésil*. Paris: Éditions Karthala.

Carneiro, Edison (1991) [1948]. *Candomblés da Bahia*, 8th ed. Rio de Janeiro: Civilização Brasiliera.

Corrêa, Mariza (1999). "Peles Brancas/Máscaras Negras? Raça e Gênero na Antropologia." Unpublished paper presented at the symposium "A Desafio da Diferença: Articulando Gênero, Raça e Classe." Salvador da Bahia, April 9–12.

Costa Lima, Vivaldo da (1987). "O Candomblé da Bahia na Década de Trinta." In Waldir Freitas Oliveira and Vivaldo da Costa Lima (eds.), *Cartas de Édison Carneiro a Artur Ramos: De 4 de Janeiro de 1936 a 6 de Dezembro de 1938*, 39–73. Sao Paulo: Corrupio.

Dantas, Beatriz Góis (1988). *Vovó Nagô e Papai Branco: Usos e Abusos da África no Brasil*. Rio de Janeiro: Graal.

Durkheim, Émile (1965) [1912]. *The Elementary Forms of the Religious Life*, trans. Joseph Ward Swain. New York: Free Press.

Freyre, Gilberto (1956). *The Masters and the Slaves*. New York: Knopf.

Fry, Peter (1986). "Gallus Africanus Est, Ou, Como Roger Bastide Se Tornou Africano no Brasil." In Olga R. de Morães von Simson (ed.), *Revisitando a Terra de Contrastes: A Atualidade da Obra de Roger Bastide*, 31–45. Sao Paulo: USP.

Graden, Dale (1998). " 'So Much Superstition among These People!' Candomblé and the Dilemmas of Afro-Bahian Intellectuals, 1864–1871." In Hendrik

Kraay (ed.), *Afro-Brazilian Culture and Politics. Bahia, 1790s to 1990s*, 57–73. Armonk, NY: M. E. Sharpe.

Guillermoprieto, Alma (1991). *The Heart That Bleeds: Latin America Now*. New York: Knopf.

Harding, Rachel (2000). *A Refuge in Thunder: Candomblé and Alternative Spaces of Blackness*. Bloomington: Indiana University Press.

Hayes, Kelly (2007). "Black Magic and the Academy: Macumba and the Construction of Afro-Brazilian Religious Orthodoxies," *History of Religions* 46/4 (May 2007): 283–315.

Herskovits, Melville (1937). "African Gods and Catholic Saints in New World Negro Belief," *American Anthropologist* 39/4, Part 1 (October–December): 635–643.

———— (1943). "The Southernmost Outpost of New World Africanisms," *American Anthropologist* 45/4, Part 1 (October–December): 495–510.

———— (1956). "The Social Organization of the Afrobrazilian Candomblé," *Phylon* 17/2: 147–166.

Hess, David (1992). "Umbanda and Quimbanda Magic in Brazil: Rethinking Aspects of Bastide's Work," *Archives des Sciences Sociales des Religions* 79: 135–153.

Johnson, Paul C. (2002). *Secrets, Gossip, and Gods: The Transformation of Brazilian Candomblé*. Oxford: Oxford University Press.

Landes, Ruth (1940). "Fetish Worship in Brazil," *Journal of American Folklore* 53/210 (October–December): 261–270.

Lapassade, Georges and Marcos Aurélio Luz (1972). *O Segredo da Macumba*. Rio de Janeiro: Paz e Terra.

Maggie, Yvonne (1992). *Medo de Feitiço: Relações entre Magia e Poder no Brasil*. Rio de Janeiro: Arquivo Nacional.

Mauss, Marcel (1972). *A General Theory of Magic*, trans. Robert Brain. London: Routledge, Kegan and Paul.

Morães von Simson, Olga R. de (ed.) (1986). *Revisitando a Terra de Contrastes: A Atualidade da Obra de Roger Bastide*. Sao Paulo: USP.

Negrão, Lísias Nogueira (1986). "Roger Bastide: Do Candomblé à Umbanda." In Olga R. de Morães von Simson (ed.), *Revisitando a Terra de Contrastes: A Atualidade da Obra de Roger Bastide*, 47–63. Sao Paulo: USP.

Oliveira, Waldir Freitas and Vivaldo da Costa Lima (eds.) (1987). *Cartas de Édison Carneiro a Artur Ramos: De 4 de Janeiro de 1936 a 6 de Dezembro de 1938*. Sao Paulo: Corrupio.

Omari, Mikelle Smith (1994). "Candomblé: A Socio-Political Examination of African Religion and Art in Brazil." In Thomas D. Blakely, Walter E. A. van Beek, and Dennis L. Thompson (eds.), *Religion in Africa*, 135–159. Portsmouth, NH: Heinemann.

Ortiz, Renato (1978). *A Morte Branca do Feiticeiro Negro: Umbanda e Sociedade Brasileira*. Petrópolis: Editora Vozes.

Ramos, Arthur (1971) [1939]. *O Negro na Civilização Brasileira*. Rio de Janeiro: Casa do Estudante do Brasil.

———— (2001). *O Negro Brasileiro*, 5th ed. Rio de Janeiro: Graphia.

Rodrigues, Nina (1977) [1906]. *Os Africanos no Brasil*, 5th ed., with a Preface by Homero Pires. Sao Paulo: Campanhia Editora Nacional.

Skidmore, Thomas (1993). *Black into White: Race and Nationality in Brazilian Thought*. Durham, NC: Duke University Press.

Verger, Pierre (1981). *Orixás: Deuses Iorubás na África e no Novo Mundo*. Sao Paulo: Editora Corrupio.

Part 4

Diaspora in Theory

Chapter 10

Early American Pentecostalism: Race, Religion, and the Politics of Anticipation

Matthew Waggoner

Introduction

In its formative years during the early 1900s, American Pentecostalism was, according to many historians, audaciously interracial. Largely because it did not appear to have begun as an exclusively black phenomenon, its inclusion among African diasporic religions has not been universally recognized. Nevertheless, comparative study of the performative elements of early American Pentecostalism confirms the rationale for placing it squarely within the lineage of African-derived expressive traditions (Murphey 1994; Raboteau 1978; Tinney 1978; Lovett 1975; Hurston 1981). In addition to the complexity of its origins, Pentecostalism achieved near ubiquity within Western culture and, during the last thirty years, globally; indeed, it claims about 150 million adherents worldwide. To understand how an African-derived religion contributed so significantly to the shaping of the late modern world we must expand the meaning and analytic value of diaspora. That, in brief, is the work I propose to do in this chapter.

Zora Neale Hurston's *The Sanctified Church*

There is no more insightful place to begin this examination than with the Zora Neale Hurston's overlooked text, *The Sanctified Church* (1981). Written in the late 1930s, the essays in *The Sanctified Church* compile ethnographic and reflective studies of Southern folklore, language, and expressive habits, with a focus on the religious cultures of the black South. The most important contribution Hurston makes in these essays is to challenge what is meant by "originality." Hurston argues that if mimicry seems a pervasive element of black expression, mimesis is not a derivative quality; it does not, in other words, passively copy already established forms of expression. Mimicry instead indicates the action-oriented centrality of drama and performativity to black expressive idioms. Of "the Negro" she writes, "His very words are action words...one act described in terms of another...hence the rich metaphor and simile" (49). After an initial analysis of how black culture has "done wonders to" (51) the English language by transforming it, she disabuses readers of the belief that black culture freezes authentic expressions of an original African experience, insisting: "Negro culture is not a thing of the past. It is still in the making" (56). In short, Hurston contests the view that black culture lacks originality, a view predicated on a narrow appreciation of mimesis.

Reappraising the concepts underpinning traditional models of diaspora by doubting access to origins and by recovering another connotation of originality as *creativity*, Hurston suggests that origins elude us and that we understand cultures best not as the preservation of original forms but as ongoing processes of invention:

> It is obvious that to get back to original sources is much too difficult for any group to claim very much as a certainty. What we really mean by originality is the modification of ideas....So if we look at it squarely the Negro is a very original being. While he lives and moves in the midst of a white civilization, everything that he touches is reinterpreted for his own use. He has modified the language, mode of food preparation, practice of medicine, and most certainly the religion of his new country. (58)

By the same token, host cultures throughout the Atlantic world are equally shaped by cultural exchanges created by the intimacies and proximities of colonial, imperial and slave subjugations and the trans-Atlantic movements they produce. Hurston had already resisted what emerged decades later as the trendy but naïve tendency to view *Pentecostalism* as a "syncretistic" religion while treating *Western culture* as a bounded and relatively fixed body of ideas, attitudes, and behaviors. As African expressive idioms mingled with American idioms, both African and American cultures altered, and they altered in dialogue. Whatever might be posited as "American culture" is as much the product of the "modification of ideas" as black culture. Moreover, it is the product of modification *in interaction with* black culture, that is, it has been modified *by* black culture. American culture has not simply imposed itself ready-made onto the cultures it subjugates, necessitating in them a syncretistic process which it is apparently immune to; it is also undone and remade by subjected others. Like jazz, Pentecostalism typifies the way Western culture formed vis-à-vis the contributions of the peoples and cultures of the Atlantic world system. Hurston comments at one point in *The Sanctified Church* that while everyone is familiar with black culture's modification of white musical instruments, it is equally true that "black interpretation has been adopted by the white man himself and then reinterpreted…Thus has arisen," she concludes in the book's bravest claim, "a new art in the civilized world, and thus has our so-called civilization come. The exchange and re-exchange of ideas between groups" (59).

Hurston's essays preceded most Pentecostal history-writing; and yet, they continue to provide a corrective model for comprehending the movement's identity and implications. They insist that Pentecostalism did not simply appear spontaneously in the early 1900s as the result of a "revival," the onset of tongues-speaking, or the culmination of theological ideas (as is suggested by the characterization of Pentecostalism as a "restoration" movement). It was instead the culmination of a trajectory of black expressive culture in the realm of religion, and its idioms could be traced to well-known features of African religion brought to America by the slave trade. "The rise of various groups of 'saints' in America in the last twenty years," Hurston concludes, "is not the appearance of a new religion as has been reported. It is in fact the older forms of Negro religious expression asserting themselves against the new" (103).

Nonetheless, the blackness of Pentecostalism has been susceptible to a process of eradication not only in the white Pentecostal imagination but in fashionable portrayals of the movement during the last decade and a half. Just as the first wave of Pentecostal historians portrayed the movement as something entirely new and without cultural precedent, the recent resurgence in Pentecostal Studies tends to ignore or minimize the movement's African contributions. This all-but-disavowal of Pentecostalism's African aesthetic, in conjunction with the tropes through which it is described and analyzed, popularize and perpetuate patterns of representation that unwittingly repeat well-rehearsed styles of Western racism. By suppressing

Pentecostalism's blackness, scholars "fetishize" the movement in ways consistent with old habits of imagining Africa.

"Whenever I think of That Little Church I Think of Lois": The Sexual Titillations of Black Religion

Historians frequently suppress the cultural ancestry of the Pentecostal movement in African dispersion and portray Pentecostals as "primitive" and "erotic"—often with little insight into the racial encodings of their discourse. Grant Wacker, for instance, innocuously put forward the thesis that Pentecostalism combines "pragmatic" and "primitive" elements (1995: 437–458) without considering the familiarity of that distinction, that is, how it is reminiscent of nineteenth-century characterizations of "the West" and "Africa" according to distinctions like rational/magical, scientific/ superstitious, intellectual/sexual, and so forth. Wacker's argument and its acceptance within Pentecostal studies illustrates the way Africa persists as an uncanny presence within the Western psyche (cf. Nandy 1989). Scholars find themselves strangely attracted to the wildness and eroticism of primal Pentecostalism without considering that their own desire recapitulates and restages histories of colonial interaction and intimacy with the peoples and cultures of the "dark continent" (Khanna 2003).

This was nowhere more explicit than in Harvey Cox's acclaimed *Fire From Heaven* (1995). Cox begins by reflecting, interestingly enough, on the uncanny feeling that upon entering the steamy world of Pentecostalism (as ethnographer-theologian) he harbored some deep-seated but barely understood connection, if not attraction, to the movement. His effort to draw parallels between Pentecostalism and his own Quakerism is of less interest than the confession that in his youth he had encountered a Pentecostal service in the context of his infatuation with a girl named Lois. Cox leaves Lois's racial identity ambiguous (consistent with his anxious avoidance of race matters in all but superficial ways) but describes her, in any case, as an "exotic" girl with "wide brown eyes," "creamy skin and beautiful straight black hair" (Cox 1995:9).

With sultry language, Cox recalls this event in an effort to dramatize his encounter with a religion in which "the erotic and the spiritual" commingle, in which there was something "frankly physical" (10) about the entire experience. He describes himself as a suburban youth with an uneventful boyhood who knew two titillations growing up: Lois and her "little church," and the big city. "Both exuded the allure of the forbidden," Cox writes; "both could scare you; both also gave off a slightly seductive, mildly wanton scent. Both conveyed an unmistakable impression of a just-barely-controlled chaos" (11). In these moments Cox's book reads like a colonial travelogue, eroticizing and exoticizing the gendered native other with the usual cocktail of horror and seduction. In the fourteen pages of the introduction Cox reiterates how "fascinated" and "curious" he was made by Pentecostalism's alluring mix of bodies and chaos; he was "aroused," "scared," "exhilarated," "seduced," "drawn"; he found it "alluring," "wanton," "gratifying," "primal," and multiple times "fascinating" (9–17).

As with Wacker, Cox's eroticized language and its parallels with the rhetoric of colonial discourse is permissible only after minimizing what would, were it explicit, turn all of his rhetoric into an embarrassing *faux pas*. Indeed, diminishing the significance of its diasporic genealogy, as Cox and Wacker do, is the mechanism that enables Pentecostalism to become and remain an unwittingly fetishized, sexualized, uncanny object of fascination.

Unlike others who have intervened in the narrow accounts offered by Pentecostal historiography by identifying the movement with racial subjection, terror, and antiracist struggle, the contemporary trend is to render Pentecostalism a congenial interlocutor in the nation's struggling egalitarian civil society. A key strategy in this myopic representation of the movement is to treat 1906 or 1901 as a magical year in which Pentecostalism spontaneously burgeoned, and then to note with sentimentality the mingling of races and ethnicities present at the first Pentecostal meetings. "They started out," Cox writes, as "rebellious antagonists of the status quo," "a radically inclusive spiritual fellowship in which race and gender discrimination virtually disappeared" (17). Within the climate of pop multiculturalism this may be a fashionable way to portray Pentecostals. But by locating their "starting point" at the beginning of the twentieth century, Cox silences important pre-histories of Pentecostalism that would otherwise shed more complicated light on the textures and disparities of those inter-racial contact zones, and on the significance of the movement beyond the fascination and titillation that its "primitivism" provides for uneventful suburban boyhoods.

Race and Racism in Early American Pentecostalism

It is significant that scholars dispute whether the movement began in 1901 or 1906. Charles Fox Parham first began teaching the doctrine of tongues-speaking in Topeka, Kansas, and later in Houston, Texas, where William Seymour encountered him. But it was William Seymour whose mission in Los Angeles, a few years later, saw the first collective practice of tongues-speaking. We know that Parham, a white person, segregated his participants; indeed, according to some reports he prevented Seymour from attending his lectures because Seymour was black. According to Vinson Synan, this may have encouraged Seymour's departure for Los Angeles, where he began the Azusa mission and practiced nonsegregation. Eventually Parham went west to visit the Azusa mission. Synan recounts that Parham disapproved of what was taking place in the meetings because of their (in Parham's own words) "disgusting similarity to Southern darkey camp meetings" (Synan 1971: 180). This remark coupled with Parham's intention to de-Africanize the movement (Lovett 1975) illustrates how the disavowal of Pentecostalism's blackness was present already in the nascent period of its history. Synan also reports that Parham later became a supporter of the Ku Klux Klan.

Tensions with Parham and tensions with another early white leader, William H. Durham, may account for the fact that after the golden years of the Azusa Revival, Seymour drafted an independent church constitution that instituted and defended the exclusion of whites from positions of leadership within his congregation. In *The Doctrines and Discipline of the Azusa Street Apostolic Faith Mission of Los Angeles, Cal.*, written in 1915, Seymour expressed exasperation with the failed dream of multi-racial spiritual collaboration after experiencing the persistence of racism within the leadership of the early movement. This text is replete with all the ambivalences and contradictions that were most characteristic of the early movement. On the one hand, Seymour reacted to Parham's racism by saying "if some of our brethren have prejudices and discriminations, we can't do it" (Seymour 1915: 2). On the other hand, while Seymour's newly founded post–Azusa Street community would remain desegregated, he lamented what he regarded as the necessity to avoid further manipulations by restricting leadership positions to black members only.

These are some of the "family secrets" of Pentecostal scholars committed to the nostalgic version of racism's disappearance in early American Pentecostalism. They are reinforced by the quite obvious racial segregation that followed those early years, leading to the establishments of the Church of God in Christ as an almost exclusively black Pentecostal denomination and the Assemblies of God as a predominantly white Pentecostal denomination (particularly in its leadership). The racial politics of the early movement is, of course, not really a secret; rather, like most family secrets, the politics are known by all, but they are kept out of the discussion. Indeed, in this case, they are systematically excluded from any substantive account of the complex racial dynamics of the early movement—complexities that risk disrupting the blissful picture marketed by conservative multiculturalism. Apart from Synan, the few scholars to give serious attention to these matters have been black historians claiming the African origins of the movement. The common contention among those who look to Africa for the origin of Pentecostalism is that "whites came to an already black Azusa Street revival" and that the problem with interracial theories is that they "fail to make the clear-cut critical distinction between the early interracial stages of the movement and [its] actual founding" (Lovett 1975: 136). While this view relies on an origins claims much stronger and ultimately incompatible, I think, with what Hurston observed in her essays, they not only signal an attempt to preserve for memory the racial identity of the movement but also serve as a reminder that the movement was forged in the crucible of white racism and a painful black experience. Lovett articulates the point succinctly: "black Pentecostalism emerged out of the context of the brokenness of black existence" (138).

This context is poignantly documented by Douglas Nelson. As part of his doctoral dissertation at the University of Birmingham, England, where Synan taught, Nelson introduced his topic of early American Pentecostalism by including images of lynched and burning black bodies, surrounded by proud white mothers and fathers and their children (Nelson 1981: 30, 41b). One of the most interesting aspects of this struggle over the identity and origins of the early movement is that it in many ways coalesced around efforts to claim possession, interpretively, of certain images—that is, photographs—that might provide insight into the race dynamics of Pentecostalism.

Nelson's incorporation of images of black suffering is just one example. Another can be seen in the work of visual translation undertaken by James S. Tinney in his article "William J. Seymour: Father of Modern-Day Pentecostalism" (1978). On several occasions, Tinney describes how large and wealthy Pentecostal organizations, such as the Assemblies of God, showed little interest in preserving the memory of those aspects of their origins implicating them in a specifically black trajectory of historical development. One organization considered purchasing the Azusa Street Mission as a historic building; they finally elected not to, claiming: "we are not interested in relics" (222). The building was torn down subsequently and the space on which it stood is today the site of the Japanese American Cultural and Community Center in Little Tokyo. (Proposals have been made to erect a memorial and mural, sharing space with the community center, but those plans remain under debate.)

Unlike the founders of other religious organizations, little basic information was available concerning Seymour's life. Tinney's biographical sketch of Seymour was intended to respond to this fact, noting, among other things, Seymour's birth into a slave family some fifteen years prior to emancipation. Tinney was uninhibited in his critique of the "silent treatment" Seymour had received; it amounted to a "veritable conspiracy [on the part of white Pentecostal institutions] to keep the facts below the surface, or at least subordinate" (215). In an aside later in the article we learn that Tinney had likely been inhibited in his own research efforts at the Assemblies of God archive in Springfield, Missouri, since payments were required to purchase copies of key documents and for the permission to quote from them. Indeed, no reprint of the image described at length in Tinney's article appeared in its published form.

Tinney's conclusions about the sources of this resistance to disclosure are insightful. "Pentecostals," he argues, "prefer to think of the movement as a wholly divine, supernatural occurrence which happened spontaneously without human intervention; and most of the available materials have been published by white Pentecostals to whom recognition of the movement's black origins would be of obvious embarrassment" (215). Whether it is a matter of eradicating physical traces of Pentecostalism's "darkey" past (to recall Parham) by allowing the building to be demolished, or by restricting access to and availability of textual and visual traces of that past, white Pentecostalism has regulated ways of "seeing" Pentecostal history.

One of Tinney's strategies of oppositional writing is a form of oppositional seeing. It pertains to a photograph from the Azusa Mission in which a seated Seymour is surrounded by four white men with various associations to the church. This image has been widely cited as evidence of the movement's early interracial character. Tinney, however, approached the scene with a different agenda. His purpose was to contend with the way Seymour had been viewed by white Pentecostals and others in society according to typical racist representations. He referred, for instance, to a *Los Angeles Times* article from 1906 whose headline read: "Weird Babel of Tongues/New Sect of Fanatics is Breaking Loose/Wild Scene Last Night on Azusa Street/Gurgle of Wordless Talk by a Sister" (Bartleman 1980 [1916]). As a typical reaction to the overt blackness of the movement, mediated by connotations of excess sexuality, violence, and madness, it is worth citing major portions of the article here:

> Colored people and a sprinkling of whites compose the congregation, and night is made hideous in the neighborhood by the howlings of the worshippers who spend hours swaying forth and back in a nerve-racking [*sic*] attitude of prayer and supplication/...*Stony Optic Defies*/...An old colored exhorter, blind in one eye, is the major-domo of the company. With his stony optic fixed on some luckless unbeliever, the old man yells his defiance and challenges an answer. Anathemas are heaped upon him who shall dare to gainsay

the utterances of the preacher. Clasped in his big fist the colored brother holds a miniature bible from which he reads at intervals one or two words—never more. After an hour spent in exhortation the brethren present are invited to join in a "meeting of prayer, song and testimony." Then it is that pandemonium breaks loose, and the bonds of reason are passed by those who are "filled with the spirit," whatever that may be. "You-oo-oo gou-loo-loo" come under "bloo-oo-oo boo-loo" shouts an old colored "mammy," in a frenzy of religious zeal...*Let Tongues Come Forth*...The old exhorter urged the "sisters" to let the "tongues come forth" and the women gave themselves over to a riot of religious fervor. As a result a buxom dame was overcome with excitement and almost fainted. Undismayed by the fearful attitude of the colored worshipper, another black woman jumped to the floor and began a wild gesticulation, which ended in a gurgle of wordless prayers which were nothing less than shocking. "She's speakin' in unknown tongues" announced the leader, in an awed whisper, "keep on sister." The sister continued until it was necessary to assist her to a seat because of bodily fatigue. (160)

The usual ingredients of antiblack racism are present here. Black performativity and expression is characterized as mad, violent, and excessively sexual. And contrary to all other known eyewitness reports from the meetings which uniformly characterize Seymour as mild-mannered, quiet-spoken and unassuming, the *Times* portrays him as the embodiment of physical and sexual aggression, consistent with well-known stereotypes of the black male as predator/rapist (Davis 1983).

It was against the backdrop of this and similar representations that Tinney sought to contest the image of Seymour as a poor, crazed, illiterate, theft-rape-or-mugging-waiting-to-happen. The photograph from Azusa Street, Tinney begins, "puts the lie to such negative descriptions," for it depicts him as "well-groomed" and "pleasing in appearance:

He was neither the stereotyped example of poverty in dress, nor the harsh taskmaster some have imagined him to be...He had a high forehead, a wide nose, and wore his hair naturale with a part near the center...A full complement of sideburns and joining beard give him the distinguished look of a scholar and gentleman. He was fully suited, and a bow-type tie was barely distinguishable beneath his modest beard. It was hardly noticeable, but he was blind in his left eye, and wore a glass eye there. (Tinney 1978: 215–216)

Tinney's oppositional strategy of seeing consisted of his effort to wed Seymour's blackness with his respectability in a social situation that militated against such associations. Thus, Tinney affirmed the Africanness of Seymour, for example, his wide nose and natural hair, while at the same time portraying him as scholarly, distinguished, composed, and well-dressed. The effect of this counter-spectatorial response to the photograph was to both rescue the black origins of the movement and to resist racist characterizations of Pentecostalism's inexorable blackness.

The true picture of the past flits by. The past can be seized only as an image which flashes up at the instant when it can be recognized and is never seen again... For every image of the past that is not recognized by the present as one of its own concerns threatens to disappear irretrievably. —Walter Benjamin

Figure 10.1 Seymour surrounded by four white colleagues associated with the Azusa Mission

Source: Photo courtesy of the Assemblies of God

Notwithstanding Tinney's relatively unknown essay, the fetishistic portrayal of multi-racial religious fraternity in early American Pentecostalism that I described before commonly identifies the photograph from Azusa Street as a self-evident point of departure. However, the mere fact (or image) of cross-racial mingling cannot speak for itself; it has to be given a meaning, a meaning which is open to contestation and which is hardly self-evident even for those involved. I would like to offer my own visual exegesis of the Azusa Street scene, which is admittedly speculative. Like Tinney, what I attempt to provide is a counter-interpretation. The point is that images always contain within them this kind of struggle over meanings, as the widely cited lines by Walter Benjamin from "Theses on the Philosophy of History" suggest (1969).

Before investigating the scene from Azusa Street it will prove helpful to briefly consider another scene similarly constructed around the politics of the pose and positionality. Edward Hopper's 1940 "Office at Night," like so many of his other paintings, distilled all the gravity and tension of everyday moments into scenes that sublimely balanced motion and stillness. The man at the desk and the woman at the filing cabinet are separated by space, attire, direction, and the gendered hierarchy of the office. But they are drawn together by their aloneness in the after-hours of the office and by what appears to be a sort of attraction in their glances toward, but not at, one another. Moreover, this tension between separation and drawn-ness is orchestrated by an otherwise insignificant detail structuring the entire space of the office like an invisible force field: the paper that has fallen to the floor. This scene has become a standard pornographic device. In the office as space of male fantasy, where women double as sexual objects and inferiors in the division of labor, the excitational point of departure will be some unintended event, like a fallen object which must be picked up, slowly. Hopper's painting interrogated (rather than exploited for male pleasure) the sexual politics of capitalism by creating a contradictory scene of desire and power in which relations between men and women are overwhelmingly organized by invisible but powerful forces of gendering and sexualization inscribed into the social syntaxes of the workplace (cf. Burgin 1986).

Is not the scene from Azusa similarly organized as a contradictory space of desire and power? Should not the invisible but structuring forces contained within the scene give us pause about peddling the image as incontrovertible evidence that race discrimination "virtually disappeared"? And how might certain details in the Azusa photograph, like the fallen paper in Hopper's painting, require us to take more seriously the likelihood that dynamics of power pervade the scene? Roland Barthes's last work, *Camera Lucida: Reflections on Photography* (1980), will assist in this effort to view the Asuza photograph in Hopperesque ways. First, Barthes thought about his own experience of being photographed and considered how the *pose* is a way of being *pos*itioned. He also imagined how the photograph never really succeeds; something always eludes its capture. Pouring over dozens of photographs, Barthes reflected on the fact that in many of them he found himself drawn to what can only be described as a puncture in the image caused by some otherwise insignificant detail. He distinguished between the image's intended effect—a product of framing, focus, context, and so forth—that he named its *studium*, and the occasional interruption into the smooth functioning production of self-evident connotation, that he named its *punctum*. The *punctum* is the cut, the rupture, the destabilization of the overall force of the image and its standard spectatorial response. The *punctum* distracts from what the photographer, camera, and community of interpreters—in short, the gaze—seek to impose.

We might ask how the image of the men at Azusa Street appears to *intend* something. How does it stage through the biracial pose the harmony of those nascent days, months, and years? It has certainly been in this evidentiary way that the image has been put to use to assure us that the Azusa Street Mission was a remarkably and rebelliously tolerant community. And to be sure the image is only one example of a much more general tendency to memorialize the early days of Pentecostalism as a sentimental space of unquestioned multiculturalism, a fetishistic scene of liberal desire. However, as I view the image I am struck, as Barthes was, by a couple of elements within the frame of the photograph that distract me; and I want to remain open to the possibility that those distractions may somehow resist the *studium* of the image.

In the first place, I am distracted by the way Seymour marks himself off from the others with a book. He displaces himself somewhat within the camera's gaze by making the book usurp the focal space of the pose. His is not the only book present. Another is visible in the pocket of a man standing behind and to his left. One book is made handy but neatly stowed, while the other is forced into the foreground of the scene. The print on the cover of Seymour's book is not quite discernible, even though he appears to have carefully positioned it within his hands so that its title would remain visible. Given the text-centricity of his tradition, it is in all likelihood a Bible, and probably the same Bible that the *Times* article creatively vilified as "clasped in his big fist" and which they (wrongly) implied he was hardly able to read. We should not, in any case, minimize what was apparently for Seymour so symbolically supplemented into the scene into which he was inscribed.

For Protestants generally, the Bible symbolizes the autonomy of the believer-reader who approaches the text assured that he or she can be inspired by its words without guidance from a priest or theologian.

Seymour's "distraction" obliges those who would be seduced by the ostensible meaning of the image to consider that issues of authority have not disappeared; thus he codified his subjection to no one but God. Would this choice have been felt compulsory were the dynamics of power and authority as uncontroversial as this image has been set to the task of proving? It would appear that Seymour viewed himself as part of an incongruous scene of the desire to surpass racism and segregation while cognizant that things remained at the level of desire, *not* its satisfaction. Did Seymour feel, in the moment this shot was "captured," that by being positioned in that way (himself seated, white men standing behind him) and having this pose encapsulated and muted, that a certain kind of visual subjugation was being risked? Was it the risk of conflating the scene of racial mingling with evidence of the "disappearance" of racism? Seymour's symbolic act quietly militates against that kind of conflation and strategically interrupts the scene as if to say "I am under the authority of no one but the Spirit."

We might also consider the way Seymour seems to be slightly removed from the scene. It is as though his presence has been retroactively inserted, giving him a slightly transcendent quality and causing him to appear mildly unengaged by the others in the picture. The man to his left is leaning away and looking at someone or something outside the frame of the image; the two men standing behind him are turned in, almost facing one another; the man standing to the viewer's far right is shoulder to shoulder with the man to his right. All of the others are turned slightly and, one way or another, engaged with someone or something in or out of the field of vision. But Seymour's position is resolutely focused, smoky eyes fixed on the camera, book squarely on his lap. In a scene cluttered with movement, contact, and gesture, Seymour's presence has a transcendent, specter-like quality. I find this interesting when read alongside Du Bois's description of double consciousness as a condition in which one feels removed from oneself, "seeing oneself through the eyes of another," and alongside Barthes's description of posing as "the advent of myself as other":

> In front of the lens, I am at the same time: the one I think I am, the one I want others to think I am, the one the photographer thinks I am, and the one he makes use of to exhibit his art... The photograph... represents that very subtle moment when, to tell the truth, I am neither subject nor object but a subject who feels he is becoming an object: I then experience a micro-version of death (of parenthesis): I am truly becoming a specter. (13–14)

Finally, if there is another distractive and truly specter-like element in the picture, it is without question Seymour's eyes. Their cloudiness halts the reflection of the image in its tracks; they refuse to return the gaze.

Their mysterious whiteness gives him, in contrast to the others, that ghost-like quality. It has already been mentioned that this was not a photographic effect, that indeed Seymour wore a glass eye. We have seen how Seymour's eyes led the *Times* to view him within the framework of a particular kind of cultural iconography, that of the "blind exhorter" or the "blind seer" who, in literature especially, has been associated with witchcraft and with African religions such as Vodou, Santería, and "conjuring."

The effect for spectators is, if only at some unconscious level, once again that of the uncanny. Seymour has been Anglicized by his inclusion into this scene of whiteness, by his enclosure by four white men and the "distinguished" suit. But something resists that enclosure. Seymour's blackness persists and resists, troubling the work of visual assimilation as much through the wide nose and natural hair as through the blind, reflectionless eye, allegory in the Western imaginary of a mysterious otherness, if not explicitly of Africa and its religions. In the attempt to visually "capture" Pentecostalism (as Parham hoped to) as a truly American spiritual phenomenon, disavowing its derivation from African sources, Seymour's eyes pierce like the return of the repressed as if to conjure the "wild," "hideous," "fanatical rites" of the dark arts and the Dark Continent right here in this otherwise respectable gathering.

In short, I see a number of things happening in this image as I attempt to view it in Hopperesque ways. It is not the self-evident verification of the multicultural fantasy common among liberal Religious Studies scholars who view religion (any religion) as the curative with which to restore national wounds. It is rather a contradictory scene of desire and power, staging a reconciliation that it abstains from fully representing. It eludes Parham's desire for a de-Africanized spiritual movement by codifying inexorable blackness. It troubles the sentimental depiction of interracial togetherness through Seymour's subtle removal from the visual organization of the scene. It haunts the portrayal of a religious Americana through the uncanny persistence of a disavowed Africa. Like "Office at Night," the scene at Azusa Street was structured by an overwhelming but barely visible politics, a politics of race, that is, dynamics of power and inequality that the image attempted to conceal with its caricature of conviviality.

And yet I do not think it will do to approach the image as either illusory or compulsory; for I also want to suggest that Seymour's complicity in the pose that he also resists is emblematic of the fact that this was not just a scene of power but also one of desire. That is to say, Seymour's participation in the Azusa Street scene needs to be understood within the framework of a longing for what one anticipates while recognizing that it has not yet arrived.

Conclusion: Pentecostalism and the Politics of Anticipation

Early American Pentecostalism has been wrongly appropriated by the nationalistic narrative of liberal Religious Studies, and this has been achieved in part by suppressing the African origins of the movement. In this chapter my concern has been not simply to reclaim the African origins of the movement (that has been done). The aggressive assimilation of early American Pentecostalism into the multicultural narrative of "American religion" necessitates an equally aggressive state of denial about the tensions that inflamed the formative histories of the movement. To parade portrayals of convivial multiracial meetings at Azusa Street as self-evident demonstrations that racial harmony flourished in otherwise racist conditions obscures the way the movement encountered and engaged rampant racism in far more complex and critical ways. The point I have wished to make is that Pentecostal ideology and practice was shaped fundamentally by the incompletion of the emancipatory goals and claims of post-abolition society; by the persistence of racialized representations; and by uneven economic conditions and social structures. Pentecostalism was born of a black- and working-class American experience of failed reconciliation and unrealized promises, an experience acknowledged at about exactly the same time by Du Bois, who insisted that abolition and reconstruction had not resolved the dilemmas of race and racism, that the color line would in fact constitute the major problem of the twentieth century (1903). Pentecostalism was a religious culture forged from the restless, unsatisfied desire for freedom and social harmony felt and expressed at the margins of American culture at the turn of the twentieth century.

Du Bois imagined that revolutionary fervor in the African diaspora did not depend on the rise of class consciousness but on cultural patterns lacking political intentionality. Illustrating his indifference to traditional Marxian ideology critique, Du Bois wrote "Slaves, even the more intelligent ones, and certainly the great group of field hands, were in religious and hysterical fervor. This was the coming of the Lord. This was the fulfillment of prophecy and legend. It was the Golden dawn, after chains of a thousand years. It was everything miraculous and perfect and promising" (1903). Du Bois was not himself all that sympathetic with the religious mindset. "The revolutionary consciousness of the slaves," Cedric Robinson once said concerning Du Bois's secularism, "had appeared to his Westernized eyes, part legend, part whimsy, part art. Yet he realized it had been sufficient to rouse the masses into resistance and had provided them with a vision of the world they preferred" (Robinson 1983: 240). Du Bois understood that nonmetropolitan forms of revolt were shaped by histories of anti-imperialist and nationalist struggles, not by industrial production; the beginnings of black resistance were mediated by precisely the sort of ideological constructions that European Marxism discredited as false consciousness. In his book on Du Bois and others in the "black radical tradition," Robinson identifies Pentecostalism and other African diasporic religions (e.g., obeah, Santería, and Vodou) as unorthodox responses to Western imperialism that routinely eluded the grasp of Western Marxism. In any case, he writes, Du Bois and the black radical tradition recognized that the political forms assumed at the margins of capitalist expansion "did not strictly adhere to the logic of working-class formation premised on capitalist exploitation" (1983: 34).

How might Pentecostal theology and expression have codified a kind of revolt, or rather a kind of critical consciousness that Marxism and multiculturalism fail to comprehend? I want to conclude by suggesting that it was a rebellion that permeated Pentecostalism with a fundamental sense of the disparity, the gap, the not-yetness of the "kingdom of God," but which longed for tangible glimpses of a world that cast an incriminating light on the depravity of the present. "Signs and wonders" have been interpreted, wrongly I would suggest, as a claim about realization and completion, about the immediacy of divine goals, about the eschatology realized in the here and now. Indeed, signs and wonders suggest the opposite of this: they served as windows into a world yet to come. They acted as interruptions in the here and now, incomplete but dramatic "signs" of how the world stands to be changed. As such, the essential characteristic of Pentecostal spirituality, which might also be interpreted as its mode of critique, its "cultural politics," was that it viewed the world from the standpoint of anticipation. The anticipatory attitude indicted the world whose perfection we still await. Early Pentecostals were as expectant as they were wary of premature claims that the fullness of God's perfect kingdom had arrived.

Paradoxically, the movement known for its gesticulations and energy was also a movement predicated on the unremitting demand to wait, to "tarry in the spirit," and to refuse to be prematurely (i.e., prior to the realization of the emancipatory aims of post-abolition society) seduced by "false idols." How might the anticipatory attitude of early American Pentecostalism help untangle some of the perplexing and underexamined aspects of its engagement with the politics of race in the twentieth century? How did Pentecostalism, like Du Bois, admonish the arrogance of a world that believed its contradictions had been resolved? How did its admonishment take the form of waiting for what has yet to arrive, the comportment of anticipation?

In the mid-twentieth century, Gordon Fee was one of the first to offer a systematic theology of Pentecostalism. He did so by locating the crucial tension in its doctrines and practices around the paradoxical condition of a heavenly kingdom which is "already" but "not yet." Signs, wonders, and speaking in indecipherable heavenly languages all testified to this desire to experience glimpses in the here and now of what was longed for but has not yet arrived. It was an eschatological standpoint not entirely foreign to those strands of post-Marxism (of which I would include Du Bois, as well as Benjamin) that await what they abstain from fully representing. Only by attending to the textured and historical nuances of this eschatology of a redeemed world still to come will we comprehend the unique revolt codified within the performative patterns and ideological constructions of a movement birthed in the unfinished agenda of the nation's egalitarian claims.

Notes

This chapter represents the compilation of years of on-again, off-again research and reflection; consequently, it has been informed by study and interaction with numerous teachers, colleagues, and relatives, with various relationships to Pentecostalism and the cultural politics of race. I would like to acknowledge the following people while insisting that all views and errors are finally my own: Del Waggoner, Gary McGee, Robert Berg, Cecil Robeck, Stan Burgess, Ben Wagner, Eddie S. Glaude, Jr., Paul Gilroy, and Angela Y. Davis. Portions of this chapter were presented at three conferences: Reshaping the Americas, University of California, Irvine, 2001; Media and Religion Consultation, American Academy of Religion, 2004; and The African Diaspora and the Study of Religion, University of Alabama, 2005. Comments from participants also informed the formulation of the final version.

Bibliography

Barthes, Roland (1980). *Camera Lucida: Reflections on Photography*. New York: Hill and Wang.

Bartleman, Frank (1980) [1906]. "Weird Babel of Tongues/New Sect of Fanatics is Breaking Loose/Wild Scene Last Night on Azusa Street/Gurgle of Wordless Talk by a Sister." In Frank Bartleman, *Azusa Street: The Roots of Modern-Day Pentecostalism*, 160–161. Plainfield, NJ: Bridge Publishing.

Benjamin, Walter (1969). *Illuminations*. New York: Schocken.

Burgin, Victor (1986). *Between*. New York: Blackwell.

Cox, Harvey (1995). *Fire from Heaven: The Rise of Pentecostal Spirituality and the Reshaping of Religion in the Twenty-First Century*. Reading, MA: Addison-Wesley.

Davis, Angela Y. (1983). *Women, Race and Class*. New York: Vintage.

Du Bois, W. E. B. (1903). *The Souls of Black Folk*. New York: Penguin.

——— (1934) [1981]. *Black Reconstruction in America, 1860–1880*. New York: Free Press.

Fee, Gordon (1996). *Paul, the Spirit, and the People of God*. Peabody, MA: Hendrickson.

Gilroy, Paul (1993). *The Black Atlantic: Modernity and Double Consciousness*. Cambridge, MA: Harvard University Press.

——— (2005). *Postcolonial Melancholia*. New York: Columbia University Press.

Hurston, Zora Neale (1981). *The Sanctified Church*. New York: Marlowe.

Jenkins, Philip (2002). *The Next Christendom: The Coming of Global Christianity*. Oxford: Oxford University Press.

Khanna, Ranjana (2003). *Dark Continent: Psychoanalysis and Colonialism*. Durham, NC: Duke University Press.

Lovett, Leonard. (1975). "Black Origins of the Pentecostal Movement." In Vinson Synan (ed.), *Aspects of Pentecostal-Charismatic Origins*, 123–145. Plainfield, NJ: Logos.

Lowe, Lisa (1996). *Immigrants Acts: On Asian American Cultural Politics*. Durham, NC: Duke University Press.

Murphey, Joseph M. (1994). *Working the Spirit: Ceremonies of the African Diaspora*. Boston: Beacon.

Nandy, Ashis (1989). *The Intimate Enemy: Loss and Recovery of Self under Colonialism*. Oxford: Oxford University Press.

Nelson, Douglas (1981). "For Such a Time as This: The Story of Bishop William J. Seymour and the Azusa Street Revival." PhD dissertation, Department of Philosophy, University of Birmingham, UK.

Raboteau, Albert (1978). *Slave Religion: The "Invisible" Institution in the Antebellum South*. Oxford: Oxford University Press.

Robinson, Cedric (1983). *Black Marxism: The Making of the Black Radical Tradition*. Chapel Hill: University of North Carolina.

Seymour, William J. (1915). *The Doctrines and Discipline of the Azusa Street Apostolic Faith Mission of Los Angeles, California*. Assemblies of God Archive: Springfield, Missouri.

Synan, Vinson (1971). *The Holiness-Pentecostal Tradition: Charismatic Movements in the Twentieth Century*. Grand Rapids, MI: Eerdmans.

Tinney, James S. (1978). "William J. Seymour: Father of Modern-Day Pentecostalism." In *Black Apostles: Afro-American Clergy Confront the Twentieth Century*, 213–225. Boston: G. K. Hall.

Wacker, Grant (1995). "Searching for Eden with a Satellite Dish: Primitivism, Pragmatism, and the Pentecostal Character." In David G. Hackett (ed.), *Religion and American Culture*, 437–458. New York: Routledge.
———. (2001). *Heaven Below: Early Pentecostalism and American Culture*. Cambridge, MA: Harvard University Press.

Chapter 11

Toward a Tradition of African American Pragmatic Religious Naturalism

Jonathon S. Kahn

Introduction

How are we to take measure of African American voices that, on the one hand, vociferously speak out against normative religious commitments—either to institutions or to traditional supernatural beliefs—and, on the other hand, invoke religious rhetoric, concepts, stories, and experiences in their moral, political, and literary imaginations? Because of their rejection of conventional theological or institutional religious strictures, too often we ignore the work that religious modalities do in the texts of figures like W. E. B. Du Bois, Zora Neale Hurston, Ralph Ellison, as well as Nella Larsen and James Baldwin. How do we make sense, for example, of Du Bois? His irreligious side leads David Levering Lewis to pronounce him a "serene agnostic" whose "religious faith shriveled in the hot breath of hypocrisy and intolerance" (1993: 65–67).[1] And yet, in *The Souls of Black Folk* Du Bois utters the call for a "new religious ideal" (1986: 505). How "shriveled" really is Du Bois's religious faith in light of his lifelong creation of parables depicting the lynching of a black Christ? And what sort of religious categories do we have to describe the religious sensibilities of Hurston's *Moses Man of the Mountain* (1991)—a text that plays with, and even disrupts, the traditional African American archetype of the Exodus as a triumphant and progressive story of God leading the slaves out from Egypt?[2] The same question about religious categories and sensibilities can be asked of the utterly remarkable but utterly neglected religious experience and sermon that presides over the opening pages of Ellison's *Invisible Man*. Finally, how do we begin to present to our students the *religious* importance of these sorts of African American texts that are marked by religious insignia, but confound normative categories of secular and religious? If our accounts of the religious significance of these texts tell us only that they reject religious convention, we have revealed only one thing: an impoverished understanding of the nature of religion in modernity. Most important, we have left the details of the texts themselves untouched and uninterpreted.

At heart, my claim for a tradition of African American pragmatic religious naturalism represents an attempt to provide a vocabulary for this strain of religious thought and a lens through which to view it. What is this category of *pragmatic religious naturalism* and how can it help us think about a particular version of African American religiosity? I will admit that pragmatic religious naturalism, with its varied roots in William James, George Santayana, and John Dewey can sound decidedly recondite, perhaps more abstruse than profound. Yet, we have the work of George Hutchinson, Ross Posnock, Paul Taylor, and Eddie S. Glaude, Jr. to tell us that American pragmatism must also be considered an African American tradition.[3] Of course, the American pragmatism of James, Santayana, and Dewey was also deeply engaged with questions of religion—most centrally, questions about what happens to religion when it is no longer understood as a source of permanent truth; when its metaphysical certainties are no longer assumed. It is time we realize that African Americans were also engaged with questions of these sorts. All the writers in this tradition use religious language, concepts, and narratives to disrupt religious traditions and norms. My very use of the category of African American pragmatic religious naturalism to characterize these texts simply follows the lights set out by Ralph Ellison who insists that America is notionally and philosophically much "darker" than it acknowledges.[4]

But even if there were not good historical reasons for conceiving of a tradition of African American pragmatic religious naturalism, I still think the category should be brought to bear. In the spirit of Paul Taylor's excellent explication of Du Bois as a pragmatist (Taylor 2004a), I claim the following: pragmatic religious naturalism is a category worth using because it provides a philosophical perspective that helps us read, appreciate, and wrestle with the religious registers of African American texts that have heretofore not been seen as religious.[5] The key question is: does using the category of pragmatic religious naturalism help us newly appreciate the state or place of religion in African American texts? I think that it does. I think this because these African American thinkers are speaking about religion naturalistically and we simply have not noticed. At the end of the day, my use of the label pragmatic religious naturalist boils down to a call to interpretation. Instead of throwing up our hands at the sound of heterodoxy in African American letters, leaving these texts at best uninterpreted, and at worst leaving them to critics who are downright unsympathetic to religion, the pragmatic religious naturalist cast of mind allows us to take some measure of ironic, combative, contrapuntal, and un-metaphysical engagements with religion.

What is pragmatic religious naturalism, then? The best critic I have found on pragmatic religious naturalism is Henry Levinson. In his book on George Santayana, Levinson speaks of how the pragmatic religious naturalists use religious modalities—biblical language, the figure of Christ, religious song, moral virtues, and spiritual experience—in ways that evade normative religious metaphysical questions (1992). These questions include: How do we make contact with the divine reality underpinning everything? How does our belief in the supernatural confirm that what we do is divinely sanctioned? Or, the more explicitly Christian question: What is the meaning of this or that worldly event in light of our knowledge of Christ as the antecedent divine truth? In more technical terms, these are all epistemic questions, and the tradition of pragmatic religious naturalism, which is to say the tradition of African American religiosity that I am concerned with, does its work by moving religion out of the epistemic arena. It challenges traditional Christological explanations that confirm that God's eye is on us. Instead, pragmatic religious naturalists hold to the stories, ways, symbols, and contexts of religion for different reasons: because they are links to the past; because they are powerful tools and narratives for shaping and envisioning life; because they can allow for a type of spirituality that emphasizes the fallibility, fragility, and power of the human-made ties that bind us to and make us dependent on each other. In other words, pragmatic religious naturalists use religion for ends having to do with exploring the angled perplexities of human finitude and not the wholeness of godly infinity. Instead of concerning themselves with God's nature, pragmatic religious naturalists find themselves using religious resources to deal with concerns such as the nature of the comic and the tragic in human existence; whether politics should ever be thought of as inspired by God; and the fixity and fluidity of sources of identity and selfhood.

These tensions galvanize the texts of this tradition of African American thinkers—think of Baldwin's *Go Tell It On the Mountain* and *The Fire Next Time*, post-metaphysical texts both. In my own work on Du Bois,

I have found that seeing him as a pragmatic religious naturalist allows us to reconcile his irreligious statements that question God and Christ with his religious compulsion to write prayers, repeatedly use the language of divinity, and make sacrifice his crucial moral virtue.[6]

The exciting part of this project is not in its defense. It is in its doing. In this chapter, I endeavor to accomplish two tasks. First, I want to position Du Bois's *Souls* as the inaugural text of African American pragmatic religious naturalism. Second, I will provide a close reading of Ellison's sermon from the beginning of *Invisible Man*. It is a passage I see as paradigmatic to this tradition of religious literature. But before I attempt these things, I want to say a little more about the hermeneutical stakes of this project in reading African American pragmatic religious naturalism.

The project will fail if it becomes simply a matter of pointing out the white pragmatist text that the African American text most resembles. An important payoff in conceiving of this as African American tradition is in coming to understand the way African American texts extend, revise, and criticize pragmatic religious naturalism. In other words, I insist that African American pragmatic religious naturalists have something new to say to the larger tradition. Taylor, I think, does not quite make this point explicit enough when he claims that reading Du Bois as a pragmatist does two things: it helps us better understand Du Bois and it helps us recall "aspects of pragmatism we might otherwise miss" (2004: 100). Both are true, and yes, African American pragmatists can be used to take us back and remind us of valuable resources originally in pragmatism. But there is a third case: African American pragmatists reveal what is *not* originally in pragmatism.

James, Dewey, and Santayana do not drain religious naturalism of all possibilities. In particular, none of these pragmatists—including Dewey—understood race. On this view, African American pragmatic religious naturalism, in working for ends only dimly envisioned by its so-called founders, changes our understanding of the tradition itself. In particular, James, Dewey, and Santayana argue over whether religion speaks to humans in their spiritual solitude, or humans in a spiritual community. To my mind, they all draw up the lines too sharply; none of them are able to fathom the way socially inherited conditions and terms can speak to the very marrow of the personal soul. For African American pragmatists, the terms of race—acknowledged very much as social and political constructs—also represent the fundamental terms of an individual's deepest personal searching.

For example, I have begun to see Hurston's Moses book—with its Freudian Moses who is not quite of the community—as negotiating the vicissitudes of what political theorist Bonnie Honig calls in *Democracy and the Foreigner* (2001) "foreign founding." As I read it, the problematics of "foreign founding" represents another way of expressing what Eddie Glaude calls African American "structures of ambivalence"—that "lingering sense of being in but not of a nation ambivalent about its own identity" (2000: 33).[7] This type of ambivalence is ramified in Hurston's writing not only as a political crisis, but also as a type of spiritual personal crisis. Not only is Hurston's Moses never really sure if he is an Israelite or an Egyptian, it is never clear if he *wants* to be either. The crucial point, however, is that Hurston constructs a notion of peoplehood out of these uncertainties. Traditional pragmatic religious naturalism has very little to say about the political ramifications of personal alienation. But, as we will see in the in the next two sub-sections on Du Bois and Ellision, the innovation of African American pragmatic religious naturalism is precisely in the way uncertainties and ambiguities become the life blood of deeply felt commitments to black peoplehood.

Locating a Tradition in *The Souls of Black Folk*

In *Souls*, Du Bois speaks as a latter-day Moses "peering from this high Pisgah, between Philistine and Amelkite, [from which point] we sight the Promised land" (Du Bois 1986: 438); he speaks as a psalmist walking low through the "Valley of the Shadow of Death" (512). He writes stunning essays on the nature of slave spirituals, the "Sorrow Songs," and he begins each chapter with a bar of their plaintive and inspirational music. At the same time, in the story "Of the Coming of John," Du Bois portrays John, the northern educated son of his community, returning home to fall into conflict with his church elders. Du Bois seems to run aground on the shoals of religious superstition. Wilson Moses, for his part, has read "John" singularly as Du Bois's depicting religion as a "power to stifle growth and development" and as "only a primitive level of struggle toward full political consciousness" (1993: 20, 246 n22).

What exactly is Du Bois doing with religion in *Souls*, using it at once to inspire and to castigate? Through his decidedly contrapuntal uses of religion, I see Du Bois asking a single question of religion. The question is not: is religion true in any deep epistemic sense? The question is: to what degree can religion negotiate the compound political crises of the color line in modernity? Du Bois's answer throughout *Souls* is sincere and searching. He does not pronounce religion a sad and sorry illusion of the unenlightened. In a variety of ways, Du Bois probes religion—its moral and social codes—for its potential contributions to a black politics of survival and criticism. In this, in his use of religion not to gain supernatural favor but as an agitating agent, Du Bois inaugurates the tradition of African American pragmatic religious naturalism.

Indeed, nowhere is this issue more salient than in the short story "Of the Coming of John," in which Moses would have us believe that Du Bois speaks univocally about religion. In fact, the story's explicit conflict between John and the church elders is crucial—*not* for the way that Du Bois disdains religion as a social and political force, but for the way it shows Du Bois actively struggling to come to terms with just the opposite: the possibility of religious community as a source for political consciousness and resource for democratic struggle. Yes, John stands as a symbol of the Enlightenment, a true *philosophe* who comes to his community with ideas of liberal rights and economic reform while disdaining religious faith. And the church elders are rooted in their religious traditions and strong sense of historical continuity. But what is momentous about John's conflict with the elders is the way Du Bois crafts it not to validate Enlightenment liberalism over religion, but *to portray, develop, and complicate the pressing uncertainties between the two*. For what Moses does not mention is that John emerges from his conflict with the elders chastened, questioning for the first time the liberal truths of positivistic analysis he learns up North. Du Bois insists that the preacher's words held a "rude and awful eloquence" for John. In turn, John "felt himself held up to scorn and scathing and denunciation. . . . He arose silently, and passed out into the night" (530).

Du Bois sees "majesty" (530) in the elders' words: in the way those words vivify the community; in the way a notion of sacredness emerges out of the religious doings of this community. John is forced to acknowledge the relevance, usefulness, and even wisdom in a religious conceptual scheme. Religion perdures; the community has long used it for ballast; and religion's historic place will not be vitiated by Enlightenment logic. In fact, the knowledge that religion provides this community is less doctrinal and theological than it is social. It is no small matter that the conflict between John and the religious elders takes place in their church. Religion is the frame through which the community takes measure of John's proposals. That the elders' conflict with John results in a scene of communal solidarity, something John could not cultivate, is an explicit example of religion providing a logic for social ethics. What I hear in the elders' rebellion, in their deep anger, is a distinct type of religious wisdom that insists that religion has long been this community's resource for addressing the very exigencies John raises: brotherhood, education, charity, spread of wealth and work, and perhaps most importantly, race relations. Through a communal rebellion against John, religion emerges as a cultural system, that is to say: an articulate language that, in point of fact, has long managed these daily affairs, despairs, and aspirations.

It is important not to overstate matters here. I am not saying that in this scene Du Bois fully renounces scientific and rationalist thinking and uncritically embraces salvation in a religious worldview. The scene is more subtle than this. The tensions are what are important. Du Bois leaves his readers at the end of this scene with a pressing dilemma. Versions of the ideas that John represents are of course needed for his community to deal with racial injustice. John's core project—updating moral and social life in light of changing political and personal desires and aspirations—remains essential. However, what John learns is that this community, this people, *his* people, cannot live without religion. It is far too rich a treasury of interpretive tools for understanding human virtues and vices, achievements and failings. At the same time, while the church elder stands as evidence that religion has in the past responded articulately to this challenge, Du Bois very much leaves it open whether or how religion will remain effective in dealing with the sorts of challenges John raises to Jim Crow. The church elder is all protest and no prospective vision: there is nothing in what he says that will help to mobilize the town for desegregation or political representation.

Though Du Bois leaves his reader with little doubt that African American religion has historically been an active social force, and that African American religion cannot be sloughed off but must in some way inform future political and social projects, he genuinely leaves up in the air how, in what ways, and with what aspects, religion is going to remain relevant to modern political and social projects. How can these religious aspects—certain religious virtues, texts, sources, and models—be marshaled, reshaped, and refashioned in order to serve interests and purposes that potentially extend beyond religion's traditional boundaries? The questions that emerge are of how to adjust, adapt, and integrate projects of democratic radicalism with the religious wellsprings his people have historically relied upon in dealing with social problems. Certainly, religion needs to be a force for social activism, but Du Bois also is acutely aware of the way in which religion represents not only the idea of tradition but also the active virtue of attending to traditions. Both, Du Bois implies, are necessary for effective social reform.[8]

Du Bois provides no easy formulae for resolving these conflicts. His engagements with religion in *Souls* represent his earnest searchings—indeed, spiritual strivings—through African American archives for "the stirring unguided might of the powerful human souls who have lost the guiding star of the past and are seeking in the great night a new religious ideal" (505). It is easy to misread this line and to assume that Du Bois thinks the new religious ideal requires losing the guiding star of the past. Instead, *Souls* itself personifies this new religious ideal by a reclamation and reconstruction of the past. The terms of that reconstruction are themselves religious ones: soul and spiritual strivings dominate his discourse. Their effect, their field of action, however, is not in the theological ether. *Souls'* concern with spirituality and soul has nothing to do with closeness to God or godly immortality. Instead, Du Bois's concerns are with the social and political realities of African American life. At heart, *Souls* transforms religious devotion from the need for supernatural succor and reality and into the need for beauty and inspiration in the sufferings and achievements of black lives. This is the wonder of Du Boisian pragmatic religious naturalism.

Religious Experience as Race-Conscious Criticism and Renewal

Invisible Man begins with its epoch-making statement on invisibility: "I am invisible, understand, simply because people refuse to see me" (Ellison 1995a: 3). Ironically, the power of this passage has rendered invisible the role that religion plays in the novel's opening struggles with how race is lived. For directly after the invisible man diagnoses and laments his state of invisibility to white people, he has a religious experience, the core of which is a stunning and remarkably complex vision of black people explicating the nature of race to each other. The contrast could not be starker: the text begins with race as a concept that abjures visibility or recognition between the races; it then turns around to address race—collaboratively spoken among African Americans and experienced in a religious setting—as a concept that deepens sense of self.

The scene goes like this: Invisible Man, high on reefer, listening to Armstrong's "What Did I Do to Be so Black and Blue?" (a breathtakingly complex title in light of the account of race to come), hears a slave spiritual being sung, and then he hears a preacher shout:

> "Brothers and sisters, my text this morning is 'Blackness of Blackness.'"
> And a congregation of voices answered: "That blackness is most black, brother, most black..."

And the preacher says,

> "In the beginning...there was blackness."[9]

The preacher here seems to establish a type of original or even essential blackness. Blackness would appear to be epistemically foundational. The battle royal, Ellison might say, is on between the sorts of white folks whose foundational views of race render the invisible man invisible and antipodal foundational views of race that lead black folks to assert that blackness is first, is original, and goes all the way down.

But in a flash, the preacher's discourse swerves and he begins to radically disrupt this racial ontology. In a stunning series of couplets, the preacher says:

> "Now black is..."
> "...and black ain't..."
> "Black will git you..."
> "...an' black won't..."
> "It do..."
> "...an' it don't."
> "Black will make you..."
> "...or black will unmake you."

And then the Invisible Man narrates:

> And at the point a voice of a trombone timbre screamed at me, "Git out of here, you fool! Is you ready to commit treason?" And I tore myself away, hearing the old singer of spirituals moaning, "Go curse your God, boy, and die."

With that final line, if it weren't already clear, Ellison unmistakably signals that the religious realm of this sermon is far from the traditional. Treason—in the form of questioning, undoing, and redoing conventional loyalties to race, peoplehood, and God—is precisely what Ellison is preparing the invisible man to commit.

This passage is in my view distinctly a passage of pragmatic religious naturalism for the way its religious bearing is, in the words of Kenneth Burke (words I learned from Beth Eddy's book on Ellison and Burke), "not about God, but rather, about the way we use our words about God on each other" (Eddy 2003: 2). And Ellison's intent here is to use his words about God not to talk about true belief, but, as he says, for treason, which is to say: to create a liminal space that unsettles and destabilizes racial essentialisms. In the ambivalence of his couplets—"black is and black ain't"—he urges us to ask what we really mean by black, or, by extension, white. Do we have control, do we need control, over these terms? More, by phrasing definitions of race in terms of what they "do" or "make," Ellison is asking: What are the effects of living according to this or that form of racial understanding? How is one's soul—and I mean "soul" in Ellison's sense as the "creative struggles against the realities of existence" (1995b: 582)—made by the meaning of the terms one uses to describe racial identity?

The relationship Ellison sees between questions of what blackness is and what blackness does or makes embodies the key epistemological insight of pragmatism. Pragmatism insists that the meaning of words and ideas is not located in some secure unchanging realm. Instead, meanings are forever disputed because meaning resides in the very rapidly changing world of human use. James famously captures the "pragmatic method... of settling metaphysical disputes" with the question: "What difference would it practically make to anyone if this notion rather than that notion were true?" (1975: 28). This line is one of the crucial antiessentialist linguistic turns of the twentieth century. And Ellison's destabilization of blackness in his *Invisible Man* sermon, by locating its meaning in what notions of race do, is the century's most profound literary statement of race pragmatically conceived.[10]

Now, if Ellison follows pragmatic principles in construing race, he resolves the uncertainties he raises in ways different from classical pragmatists. James asks questions pragmatically in order to *clarify* meaning by *reducing* ambiguity and uncertainty. If James were ever to have asked questions about race (which he did not), he would have wanted in pragmatic terms to narrow and resolve the question of what black was or was not.

And it is precisely from here that Ellison takes pragmatism in new directions. Ellison's radical questions about race reveal that once the meaning of race is released, as it were, into the world, ambiguity and uncertainty about its meaning endlessly ramify. Ellison suggests that blackness—because it is and it isn't, because it exists not as a metaphysical fact but as multiple social discourses with real world effects—is not a dispute that, in the language of James, can be settled. Instead, the *tertium quid* of Ellison's sermon is to *unsettle* race fundamentally and permanently. Ellison does this, however, not to eliminate race. He insists on race, *but in its unsettled form.*[11] Consider here the Invisible Man's response to the spiritual singer after she tells him to curse God and die: "*I too have become acquainted with ambivalence,*" I said. "*That's why I am here*" (Ellison 1995a: 10).

Living with ambivalence is, as any neurotic will tell you, not easy. And Freud called it pathological. But when it comes to living with the ambivalence of race—of facing up to the fact that this source of existence is profound and diaphanous—Ellison does not think that health, or a profounder way of living, comes from its elimination or resolution. By simultaneously insisting that race "makes" and "unmakes," Ellison brings to consciousness the way deep sources of identity are contingent, arbitrary, and perishable. This is the challenge presented by this passage of pragmatic religious naturalism. Ellison does not ask: How do we make sure that our terms of identity are firm enough to weather all encounters? Instead, he asks: What sorts of lives do we enter into (what practices do we participate in? what sorts of loves do we feel?) when we come to learn that those terms most important to us and most deserving of our devotion are also irredeemable, transient, and accidental?

What makes this a passage of pragmatic *religious* naturalism? Why can't we simply say that Ellison is speaking pragmatically about race? What does religion have to do with it? To discount religion is to ignore the obvious: Ellison chooses a religious setting and religious language in order to make this point about race. We need to ask: What is it about religion that makes it a particularly good language with which to become increasingly acquainted with this ambivalence? For Ellison, religion is rhetorically indispensable for these ends precisely because religion represents the historical grounds of two things: certainty and deep human meaning. Ellison's use of God strives to disrupt this pairing: too often certainty is considered synonymous with deep meaning. Ellison's use of God talk—with its willingness to commit treason, with its impertinence and iconoclasm—strives to replace certainty as the source of deep human meaning with indeterminacy and ambiguity. As such, Ellison turns religion into a productive source of the types of ambivalences that nurture and strengthen the soul's creative confrontation with the racial terms of its existence. Consider the impetuousness in his couplet: "Amazing grace, how sweet the sound/A bullfrog slapped my grandma down." And then consider Ellison's description of what he sees it doing: "Well, yes, the irreverence toward religious ceremonies—this is an escape valve, of which there's a large body of lore...but this lore functions to release doubt, and to give it some sort of social expression. And doubt *strengthens*" (2001: 279).

Ellison's pragmatic religious naturalism begins with an irreverent impulse, but when it leads to a doubt that strengthens, it results are a new reverence and devotion. By riffing on an African American tradition of God talk to undermine the certainties of racial identity, Ellison introduces a new dispensation: a life's work of knowing that the tools that make for the deepest forms of human meaning—and for Ellison those are the tools that make him black—are also, if held in the wrong way, tools of one's undoing. Ellison has used black religion to gain release from the drive for epistemic certainty about race; this throws him into a liminal space from which comes the possibility of spiritual transformation—a transformation rooted in a new appreciation of the finitude of race.

This is what it is to use religion in a pragmatic naturalistic fashion. Pragmatic religious naturalists do not need theological convictions to rely on religious narrative and religious symbol to help us envision the terms of human life; to give shape to the love and violence in us all. The uncertainty that Ellison presents is this: our racial selves become spiritualized insofar as they come to rely on the fast-moving unpredictable racial selves of others. Facing this sort of uncertainty is enough to make you want to curse God and die. But the African American writers I am interested in turn curses of God into a religious rebirth. They are born again, through pragmatic religious naturalism, into the conditions of human finitude. These conditions, without the supernatural, remain awe-inspiring and bring about an acute awareness of forces bigger than oneself. Pragmatic religious naturalists, African American or otherwise, reach for religious modes to express their devotion and love for the vicissitudes of our collective interdependence.

Notes

1. Exhaustive in almost every other way, Lewis's work gives short shrift to the topic of Du Bois and religion. For example, consider Lewis's description of *Darkwater* (1920), the sequel collection of essays to *Souls*. Lewis observes that *Darkwater* includes "trances, Gnostic visions, dark nights of the soul, and...other intensely religious moments." But the extent of Lewis's analysis of these features is to say they are "surprising at first to see in an agnostic and public restrained Du Bois." Lewis implies it is only *in spite of* its "hieratic language" and its "scant concession to ordinary spoken English" that *Darkwater* "sounds the emotional depth of a whole people" and thus achieves unforeseen commercial success with "working-class black folk" (2000: 22). I suggest that Lewis has it exactly backwards. Du Bois achieves the strong emotional and popular hold on his readership in writings like *Darkwater* and *Souls* on the strength of his uses of religion. He touches those emotional depths Lewis refers to because of his religious imagination.
2. For a succinct account of the archetypal role of Exodus in African American religious traditions see Albert Raboteau's "African-Americans, Exodus, and the American Israel" (1995: 17–36). Theophus Smith's essay on African American uses of Exodus is brilliant in his suggestion that the tradition is a dialectical one: Henry Highland Garnet used Exodus to resist the archetype of God delivering the Israelites/African Americans to freedom. Smith asks whether this is

"evidence of [Garnet's] advancement of, or alienation from, a vigorous and compelling tradition" (Smith 2003: 318).

3. See Hutchinson (1995), especially 35–50; Posnock (1998), especially Chapters 2–5; Paul C. Taylor (2004a); and Glaude (2000). I also place Arnold Rampersad in this camp. While Rampersad never develops a full-bodied account of Du Bois as a pragmatist, he consistently cites pragmatism's deep influence. See Rampersad (1990), especially 24–41; 174; 182.

4. For Ellison's classic statement on this topic, see "What America Would Be Like Without Blacks" (Ellison 1995b: 577–584). Also consider Ellison's 1973 response to a dashiki-ed Robert G. O' Meally who asks Ellison: "Don't you think the Harlem Renaissance failed because we failed to create institutions to preserve our gains?" O'Meally recounts: "He drew on his cigar and calmly told me: 'No.' Just before being led toward the stage, he paused to look at me with steely eyes: 'We *do* have institutions,' he said. 'We have the Constitution and the Bill of Rights. *And we have Jazz'* " (O' Meally 2001: xi, emphasis original). Ellison sets the groundwork for George Hutchinson's central claim that "studies of the (white) American cultural nationalists and pragmatists of the early twentieth century have almost entirely ignored African American writing, thus comporting with the conventional differentiation of American from African American culture, the exclusion of blackness from definitions of Americanness" (1995: 14).

5. Taylor thinks that reading Du Bois as a pragmatist uncovers parts of Du Bois that often go unnoticed.

6. My forthcoming work *Divine Discontent: The Religious Imagination of W. E. B. Du Bois* (Oxford University Press) is a full-bodied account of Du Bois as a pragmatic religious naturalist.

7. Glaude uses "structures of ambivalence," a notion he adapts from Raymond Williams's "structures of feeling," to replace Du Bois's "double life," which he finds too rigid (2000: 32–34; 174–175 n46).

8. We should not overlook the remarkable prescience in Du Bois's church scene—in Du Bois's situating the calls for social reform in religious contexts. Fifty years later, in the churches in Baton Rouge, Montgomery, Birmingham, and Greenwood, religion flew into action and mobilized African Americans chafing against Jim Crow and the color line that hemmed in them and theirs.

9. All sermon citations are from Ellison (1995a: 9–10; emphases are in the original).

10. For the best philosophical account of race pragmatically conceived see Taylor (2004b). Paul C. Taylor describes his view of race as "radical constructivism"; he encourages us to "think of it as what John Dewey might have said about race if he'd been black" (xi). See also Taylor (2000: 103–128).

11. In concluding his essay on Sammy Davis, Jr., Gerald Early similarly sees the Ellison passage I am concerned with as a statement of and for the ambiguity of race: "But Davis gave us an incredibly rich and strange

embodiment of something Ralph Ellison had one of his characters say in the prologue of his novel *Invisible Man*: 'Black is...and Black ain't' " (Early 2003: 66).

Bibliography

Du Bois, W. E. B. (1986) [1903]. *The Souls of Black Folk*. In Nathan Huggins (ed.), *Du Bois: Writings*. New York: The Library of America.

Early, Gerald L. (2003). *Where I Came In: Black America in the 1960s*. Lincoln: University of Nebraska Press.

Eddy, Beth (2003). *The Rites of Identity: The Religious Naturalism and Cultural Criticism of Kenneth Burke and Ralph Ellison*. Princeton: Princeton University Press.

Ellison, Ralph (1995a) [1952]. *Invisible Man*. New York: Vintage.

——— (1995b). "What America Would Be Like Without Blacks." In John F. Callahan (ed.), *The Collected Essays of Ralph Ellison*, 577–584. New York: Modern Library.

——— (2001). "My Strength Comes from Louis Armstrong." In Robert O' Meally (ed.), *Living with Music: Ralph Ellison's Jazz Writings*, 265–288. New York: Modern Library.

Glaude, Eddie S., Jr. (2000). *Exodus! Religion, Race, and Nation in Early Nineteenth-Century Black America*. Chicago: University of Chicago Press.

Honig, Bonnie (2001). *Democracy and the Foreigner*. Princeton: Princeton University Press.

Hurston Zora Neale (1991) [1939]. *Moses Man of the Mountain*. New York: Harper.

Hutchinson, George (1995). *The Harlem Renaissance in Black and White*. Cambridge, MA: Belknap Press.

James, William (1975) [1907]. *Pragmatism: A New Name for Some Old Ways of Thinking*. Cambridge, MA: Harvard University Press.

Levinson, Henry Samuel (1992). *Santayana, Pragmatism, and the Spiritual Life*. Chapel Hill, NC: University of North Carolina Press.

Lewis, David Levering (1993). *W. E. B. Du Bois: Biography of a Race, 1868–1919*. New York: Henry Holt.

——— (2000). *W. E. B. Du Bois: The Fight for Equality and the American Century, 1919–1963*. New York: Henry Holt.

Moses, Wilson Jeremiah (1993). *Black Messiahs and Uncle Toms: Social and Literary Manipulations of a Religious Myth*. University Park: Pennsylvania State University Press.

O' Meally, Robert (2001). "Introduction: Jazz Shapes." In Robert O' Meally (ed.), *Living with Music: Ralph Ellison's Jazz Writings*, ix–xxxv. New York: Modern Library.

Posnock, Ross (1998). *Color and Culture: Black Writers and the Making of the Modern Intellectual*. Cambridge, MA: Harvard University Press, 1998.

Raboteau, Albert (1995). "African-Americans, Exodus, and the American Israel." In Albert Raboteau, *Fire in the Bones*, 17–36. Boston: Beacon.

Rampersad, Arnold (1990). *The Art and Imagination of W. E. B. Du Bois*. New York: Schocken Books.

Smith, Theophus H. (2003). "Exodus." In Cornel West and Eddie S. Glaude, Jr. (eds.), *African American Religious Thought: An Anthology*, 309–337. Louisville: Westminster John Knox Press.

Taylor, Paul C. (2000). "Appiah's Uncompleted Argument: W. E. B. Du Bois and the Reality of Race," *Social Theory and Practice* 26/1 (Spring): 103–128.

——— (2004a). "What's the Use of Calling Du Bois a Pragmatist?" *Metaphilosophy* 35/1–2 (January): 99–114.

——— (2004b). *Race: A Philosophical Introduction*. Cambridge: Polity Press.

Chapter 12

Africa on Our Minds

Russell T. McCutcheon

> *Just an old sweet song*
> *Keeps Georgia on my mind*
>
> —Stuart Gorrell and Hoagy Carmichael,
> "Georgia on My Mind"

The study of religion's relationship to its colonial past offers a useful and complicated case study in how methodological self-consciousness actually impacts scholarship in the field of religious studies. And of all the sites from which one could draw to find ethnographic instances useful in pressing such issues, the continent of Africa—conceived either as an actual place or, far more interestingly, as a discursive space to which people can travel only in their imaginations—stands out. For, along with what was once called "New Holland" (or Australia) and "the New World" (or the Americas), "the dark continent" was a place to which our scholarly armchair predecessors imaginatively traveled as they poured over the diaries and reports of missionaries, traders, and soldiers in search of both their own evolutionary precursors as well as the origin of religion itself.

Lest we too quickly criticize our intellectual forefathers for their tendencies toward dehistoricized essentialism in their hunt for the source of the Nile, we should recognize that, even today, a variety of disembodied Africas remain the primary means by which peoples whose ancestors were forcibly spread across the world—from Brazil to the Caribbean to North America and Europe—look to find some speculative origins of their own. From the supposed ability of the pan-African colors of green, yellow, and red to represent an entire continent, to the tourist next to whom I once sat on the long flight from Atlanta to Johannesburg (who was eager to find his ancestral past in modern day South Africa), different conceptions of Africa are traded daily, for a variety of purposes, on the international market of ideas and identities.

As we have learned from several generations of myth theorists, quests for origins—whether they concern the universe, a people, or even a scholarly discipline—are far more complicated than they might first appear. For the Africa to which my companion on that jet traveled in his mind's eye was many steps removed from some stable, natural fact. Leaving aside the complexities of recovering a thing called "the past," we can at least say that the Africa of the contemporary Afrikaner is not likely to be confused with the Africa of the Nigerian farmer, the Africa of diamond mine workers, the Africa of an Egyptian businessman, the Africa of a travel agent in New York, let alone the Africa of international aide workers in an office somewhere in Europe.

Precisely this point—that there is something important at stake in too quickly homogenizing these different Africas—was nicely made in a public lecture I attended not long ago, during which the speaker was careful to caution those in attendance from too easily talking about the continent as if it was a uniform whole. Despite its apparent continuity in geographic space, a dizzying array of differences in social space (e.g., nation-states, languages, ethnic groups, etc.) quickly confounds any attempt to discuss what a previous generation of Orientalists might have summed up as "the African mentality" or "the African mind."

But having been persuaded by this caution not to overlook matters of historical and empirical difference, I was therefore struck by how quickly the lecturer, who hailed from Africa though was trained in Europe and worked in North America, then set about to describe the key traits of this thing known as "the cosmos of African traditional religions" (e.g., ancestors, healing rituals, etc.). This was accomplished in a manner that would strike a European phenomenologist of religion from a generation or two ago as thoroughly familiar. What happened, I wondered, to the caution about the perils of homogenization? Is anything gained by studying a "cosmos" rather than a "mind?" Simply put, how did matters of empirical difference so quickly give way to such metaphysical uniformity?

Moreover, as one of our undergraduate seniors in the religious studies department asked during the question and answer session that followed the lecture, how was the lecturer able to use such colonial era terms as "myth," "ritual," and "religion"—terms that rose to prominence in eighteenth- and nineteenth-century Europe—to describe authentic patterns of living that, or so we were told, predated the colonial era? A sharp question, for it hinted at the problems associated with too quickly assuming our ability to do a little dreamy time traveling, despite never leaving the lecture room in Alabama. The answer that our student received amounted to being told that we had no choice but to use such Greek and Latin-based English terms because, were the lecturer to call these things by their local or indigenous names, well, none of us attending the lecture would understand what was being talked about. This was, however, a rather unsatisfying answer, for, much as with Shakespeare's Juliet asserting the self-evident nature of the rose's sweet smell regardless what it was called, a philosophically idealist presumption was apparent, suggesting that names are just arbitrary labels that we apply to stable realities already existing in the world. This is nothing but the old "you say 'to-*mae*-to'; I say 'to-*mah*-to'" view of classification; apparently, regardless what we call it, we all know what to put into a salad or onto a sandwich, not to mention what religion is and is not. This is, in fact, Mircea's Eliade's well-known (and often criticized) assertion that, whether you call it religion or not, and whether you know it or not, everyone is religious because it is, as he phrased it, a structure of human consciousness.

What struck me as particularly interesting was that this answer to the student's question seemed to satisfy many who were in attendance. Perhaps it is not surprising that people are quite comfortable assuming that their local words, concepts, and grids, are in a one-to-one correspondence with reality, presuming that—much like manufacturers who produce the same basic product for different distributors, each of whom use their own unique labels and packaging—only one map exists despite the different ways it is folded and used. However, I have a sense that those in attendance at this lecture would likely not have been persuaded if they had been told that there was this actual thing in existence known as *amandla* (a Zulu term) which we, in the English-speaking Euro–North American world, simplistically call "power." Unbeknownst to us, therefore, *amandla* is really what we are all talking about when we talk about power; what we are all manipulating and exchanging; that it derives from ancestors, healing, powerful figures in the sky, and so on; and, through careful historical study, we might be able to recover our indigenous, precolonial sense of *amandla*. Because of the difficulties imagining a taxon local to distant people being adopted here at home as a name for a self-evident aspect of reality, the ease with which the audience universalized their own local classifier (i.e., "religion") ought to strike scholars as curious.

So, instead of starting off with a self-flattering idealism that finds in each new social world's essence what we knew to be there before ever coming across it, perhaps a better way to begin to answer our student's question is to take a little more seriously the act of naming itself. For naming is nothing more than the act (and please note: it is an *action* of specific people in specific locales) of establishing and regulating what some group sees to be relationships of significance. In so doing, we would highlight the sort of methodological self-consciousness referenced in my opening sentence.

Now, by methodological self-consciousness I have in mind something once written by Jonathan Z. Smith: "The student of religion," according to Smith, "must be relentlessly self-conscious. Indeed, this self-consciousness constitutes his primary expertise, his foremost object of study" (1982: xi). Why? Because, as he memorably stated on the opening page of the Introduction to his influential collection of essays, *Imagining Religion*—in the lines immediately preceding the above quoted admonition—"Religion is solely a creation of the scholar's study.... Religion has no independent existence apart from the academy."

Some have criticized Smith's famous lines for apparently missing the fact that people outside the ivory tower routinely talk about religion and act in ways that they themselves understand as religious—indicating to such critics that Smith has overlooked that scholars are not alone in thinking that they have some categorical prerogative when it comes to this term. But I think that such critics have missed Smith's point entirely. For in my reading of his work Smith argues that the term "religion" is used as a name for a universal, experiential trait which, owing to the fact of the varying historical and cultural sites of its public expression, comes in a relatively small number of more or less stable varieties (today known as "the world's religions"). If indeed this is the case, then we have little choice but to conclude that this modern concept "religion" was originally developed in that laboratory we call the early modern academy, during that time we once euphemistically knew by such names as "the Age of Discovery" and "the Enlightenment"; the concept was later honed during what we know simply as the colonial era. For this is when reports from abroad meant that Europeans were confronting human novelty of an order previously unknown. "Religion," for those busily reworking their society's epistemological and sociopolitical grids in light of the previously unforeseen and unknown, became a handy indicator of intangible likeness in the face of sometimes seemingly overwhelming empirical difference.

As such, we find from this era great scholarly debates about whether this or that practice was religious (think no further than, at the height of modernity, Emile Durkheim's efforts to distinguish religion from magic). "Religion," then, became shorthand for the degree to which "they" were or were not like "us." If they were like us, then the question was just how much we were alike (i.e., are they an early version of us, frozen in amber? Or are they a degraded form of us, thereby functioning as an early warning sign of what we might become?). If they were not like us, then a host of other designators was at hand for naming the newly found alien peoples, along with some of their beliefs, behaviors, and institutions—apostasy, paganism, superstition, and magic—all come to mind as useful examples. (Today, we could easily add cult, fundamentalism, and extremism to this list.)

Religion, then, as a designator of a domain shared, to varying degrees, across cultures, that names a social space separable from other sorts of spaces (such as the political or the economic), is indeed a creation of the scholar's study; moreover, recognizing the double entendre of "study" in Smith's sentence (understood both as disciplined practice [i.e., method] as well as a room or an office) means that we who today study religion or religions, whether in our offices or out in the field, whether near or far, may not be all that removed from our predecessors seated in their comfortable armchairs. For—much like the ethnographer seated on the woven porch in the photo that graces Jim Clifford and George Marcus's *Writing Culture* (1986)—we too have little choice but to use familiar, local, and thus comfortable imaginative constructs to chart that which strikes us as distant, unknown, unfamiliar, and thus uncomfortable. That the scholarly category "religion," used as an indicator of social affinity or distance, then takes off so successfully outside academia's hallowed halls—such that today, as identified by those who, in my opinion, use this observation to critique Smith, we cannot help but find it used worldwide as a preferred self-designator, such that many people have no difficulty identifying this or that as their religion in contradistinction to other seemingly stable and self-contained domains of their life—is therefore the thing that we ought to be studying. To rephrase: rather than studying the spread of religions, perhaps we ought to consider studying why naming part of their social world *as* religion has caught on so widely among diverse human communities.

All this is merely to say, rather inelegantly, what Smith said so plainly twenty-five years ago: self-consciousness about our use of categories ought to comprise a scholar's primary expertise, for the knowledge we gain from putting into practice the rule of our field is premised on the assumption that but one culture's folk category (i.e., the Latin-based term "religion") can be effortlessly elevated to the status of a cross-cultural universal, thereby naming an essential feature of all humankind. Of course, using the local *as if* it were universal, and doing so for *our* analytic purposes, to satisfy *our* own curiosities and *our* interests, is the inevitable situation in which we find ourselves inasmuch as we, as scholars, are situated human beings with no choice but to grapple with issues of familiarity and strangeness, similarity and difference, nearness and distance, etc. However, doing so because of our confidence in the universal reach of these purposes, curiosities, and interests is best understood (at least to my way of thinking) as that form of ideology that goes by the name of imperialism.

To see some of this in action we should return to an example derived not from Africa—as if there is such a uniform place in the empirical world—but, instead, from the study of Africa (which is but one site of what we might as well just term the discourse on Africa). So consider, for example, David Chidester's book, *Savage Systems: Colonialism and Comparative Religion in Southern Africa*—winner of the American Academy of Religion's book prize in 1997 (in the analytic-descriptive category). Rather than being simply an historical study of the ways in which others were classified and thereby managed by each successive wave of colonial administration, in the background of Chidester's book there is a rather harsh indictment of the European failure or outright refusal to, as he puts it in his opening, "recognize the existence of indigenous religions in southern Africa" (1996: xv). In other words, instead of seeing the classifier "religious"—no less than such other classifiers as superstitious and savage—as an historical tool once useful in creating a cognitively and socially habitable world, one whose varied uses came in handy for a dominant group's interest in ranking and managing diverse populations so as to create certain types of "civility," Chidester, too, employs the classic idealist set of assumptions regarding the universal presence of this thing some of us happen to know as religion. It is on the basis of this assumption that he indicts our predecessors for the "mistakes of the past" (Chidester 1996: 259). Furthermore, to avoid committing the sins of our intellectual fathers he advocates toppling the formerly canonical sense of what constitutes a religion, such that more things can now be entertained as religion (hence his support for polythetic, openended definitions, such as those commonly known as family resemblance definitions). The failure to recognize indigenous religions for what they really were and are, and instead seeing them either as savage precursors to, or degradations of, the normative European world, is therefore the basis of the present's judgment against the failures of the colonial past.

But recalling our interest in proceeding more self-consciously, we must ask, is this best understood as a *failure* on the part of our intellectual predecessors? Although for a host of reasons I wish not to reproduce their particular approach, using their specific tools (e.g., unilinear social evolutionary theory), must I conclude that they are culpable for generating knowledge by means of a classification system removed from their object of study? If so, then by what standard are they culpable? Have we, their latter-day judges, finally arrived at the end of history, such that we now know what things really are and how they really ought to be studied? In fact, being far more timid in my confidence with the current classifications that we use, I think that a different book would *not* have portrayed the eventual discovery that "they" indeed had religions just like "us" to have been a triumph but would have seen this judgment instead as evidence of the tremendous victory of the European map of the world! That is to say, there may be no better evidence of the success of a hegemonic power than what we find in those who—like the lecturer of whom I spoke earlier—deploy the colonialist's terminology in a postcolonialist effort to recover the pre-colonial heart of authentic Africa. For finding authentic religions out there may constitute sufficient evidence that there's nothing particularly "post" about our postcolonial world.

As suggested, a different study—one working to be self-conscious of the historical nature of the concepts by means of which we, like our predecessors, inevitably create knowledge about the world—would have problematized this now taken-for-granted classificatory development (i.e., "religion") and examined, for instance, the last century's preoccupation with cultivating a type of politically and theologically liberal interreligious dialogue in step with the interests of liberal democracy and market-driven capitalism (i.e., what are the relationships between the invention of private property and the invention of discourses on private religious experience?). This could have been accomplished by mapping the use of the classifier "religion" onto the long history of management techniques used to ensure a specific sort of identity and social organization among potentially competing and conflicting identities—whether in modern Europe (where difference of belief and opinion helped to establish the uniformity of behavior and organization) or its many peripheries. Only then would we be serious about engaging the history of our field and its relations to a colonial past, for we would cease treating our term "religion" as a natural kind; instead, we would be open to scrutinizing the sociopolitical worlds that it helped, and still helps, to make possible and persuasive.

Keeping in mind the overly confident presumption of earlier scholars to have transcended their own cultural boundaries—much like science fiction movies about either the past or the future that cannot help but look like the time in which they were made—the use of "religion" to single out essential, transhuman traits therefore constitutes evidence of the failure of scholars to be self-conscious about how it is that they go about their own work. For when were are told about such a thing as the precontact sacred African cosmos, such scholars fail to recognize that their presumption that this long past world quite naturally had a religious heritage that is somehow distinguishable from the messy world of insidious politics is itself a historically specific management technique, projected backward in time, and whose use outside its original domain in the European world is evidence of its tremendous utility. In fact, that people the world over now routinely understand themselves to have an active, inner religious life that is distinguishable from their outer political activities is evidence, to me, of the success of the dominant systems that such scholars think they are overcoming by spinning nostalgic tales of the past.

The invention and perfection of the distinction between religion and politics was useful in creating a specific type of order in the European world several centuries ago. It relates, of course, to such other useful distinctions as belief/practice, intention/interpretation, experience/expression, myth/ritual, and, finally, private/public. But this seems to be of no relevance to us today; instead, like many before us, we not only self-impose but also export these distinctions to distant shores and distant times, as if all groups naturally understand themselves in just this manner, and as if all groups know what does, and what does not, count as the real significance beneath the changeable appearances. Much like the current young generation's inability to imagine a world in which there are no microwaves, no CD players, and no Internet, scholars who imagine religion to be lurking around every cultural corner cannot imagine "religion" to be our historical invention, able to satisfy our intellectual (and political) interests.

While I am not trying to suggest that, like a golden egg resting comfortably beneath a fairytale goose, some authentic, indigenous self-understanding awaits the careful conservator who has cleaned all the surfaces of some exotic artifact of its accumulated residue, I *am* suggesting that recognizing that all we have are discourses by means of which banal stuff become such things as artifacts, will help to dispel the rush to culpability and the search for complete understanding that drives so much of our work as scholars in our post-colonial world. In place of this quest for the authentic heart of Africa (or of India; or of pre-Christian Europe; or of Native American spirituality; etc.), I suggest that we become a little more self-conscious about what it is we do when we do this thing we call scholarship. Such an adjustment in our practices will help us to retool our field as the cross-cultural study of contesting classification systems and the differing identities and social worlds made possible by the simulation of permanence that human beings often find nowhere but in their mind's eye, lurking somewhere in our peaceful dreams. For, if we are really interested in the relations between intellect and power, as evidenced in the ongoing interplay of colonialism with the study of religion, then we must be prepared to

> reveal and examine the prejudices of previous generations as unsentimentally as future generations are likely to reveal and examine the prejudices that we, in our supposedly greater wisdom, labor under. (Mishra 2003: 36)

Note

Portions of this chapter are drawn from McCutcheon (2003a and 2003b). My thanks to the editor for his very helpful comments.

Bibliography

Chidester, David (1996). *Savage Systems: Colonialism and Comparative Religion in Southern Africa*. Charlottesville: University Press of Virginia.

Clifford, James and George E. Marcus (1986). *Writing Culture: The Poetics and Politics of Ethnography*. Berkeley: University of California Press.

McCutcheon, Russell T. (2003a). Filling in the Cracks with Resin: A Response to John Burris's "Text and Context in the Study of Religion," *Method & Theory in the Study of Religion* 15/3: 284–303.

———— (2003b). "The Jargon of Authenticity and the Study of Religion." In Russell T. McCutcheon, *The Discipline of Religion: Structure, Meaning, Rhetoric*, 167–188. New York: Routledge.

Mishra, Pankaj (2003). "The Way to the Middle Way," *The New York Review of Books* 50/10 (June 12): 34–37.

Smith, Jonathan Z. (1982). *Imagining Religion: From Babylon to Jonestown*. Chicago: University of Chicago Press.

Conclusion

"Africa" in the Study of African American Religion

Eddie S. Glaude, Jr.

Introduction

Studying religion is a perilous endeavor. We need only think about the inherent ambiguity in the field's central term of art, "religion," and reflect on the multiplicity of traditions and practices that complicate what can be said about religion(s) to get a sense that the subject matter is fraught with difficulties. Those of us who study religion often find ourselves in what Samuel Beckett called "the mess" (the messiness of faiths, beliefs, doctrines, rituals, of modern prejudices, and of the practices of a scholarly community with its own standards of excellence and failure). Like Beckett, our task as scholars has been, and continues to be, to find some way to accommodate this mess that is, in part, our own doing.[1] And many of us recognize, even as we stumble about, that much is at stake.

An informative body of literature has been written about the difficulties in the study of religion.[2] My aim in this brief chapter is not to take up the particulars of those debates. I do hold the view, however, that many of the concerns evidenced in these conversations are interestingly complicated when the term religion is described by the adjective black or African American. I hold this view, because the adjectives bear the unusual burden of an enormously complicated history that colors the way religion is practiced and understood. Indeed, on their own, both terms generate enormous debate. Distinctions between "being religious" and "doing religion" or concerns about whether races are real or not animate conversations throughout the academy. But what happens when we think about them in tandem? What do we mean when we describe certain African American practices as religious practices? What work is the adjective doing here? And, how do our answers to these questions inform our histories of African American religion?

I will not be able to take up these rather broad questions in the context of this chapter, but they frame how I examine the vexed issue of the place of "Africa" in the study of African American religion. Indeed, uses of the trope of "Africa" in many accounts of African American religion help us understand the potential meanings that follow from thinking about the terms together—particularly, in the manner in which the trope registers histories of violence and displacement that capture the distinctive entrée of African Americans into the modern world.[3] Indeed the distinctiveness of African American religion is often located in its African origins—a place that simultaneously marks a condition of living prior to the fateful encounters with white Europeans and one tragically disrupted by them as well. That disruption, in some ways, necessitates (at least for some of us) a narrative insistence on the centrality of Africa and its place in the beliefs, choices, and actions of the continent's descendents. Africa and, in some instances, its diaspora, stand then "as a principle of narrative and historical uncertainty, the site of an imaginary order disrupted by profane history that speaks of a destiny resulting from that disruption" (Ernest 2004: 9).

In this sense, constructions of African American religion that take seriously questions of African origins and dispersion accentuate issues of black agency, resistance, and freedom precisely because those constructions take shape amid the destruction and ruin that followed Europe's encounter with Africa. Robert Orsi has it right when he says that "the history of the study of religion is also always a political history, just as the political and intellectual history of modernity is also always a religious history" (Orsi 2005: 178). The history of the study of African American religion is no different. It is always a political history of sorts—distinctly signifying on discourses about religions and religion in the "West"—and, of course, the trope of Africa is one its central tools.

The Problem of Beginnings

Uses of "Africa" in the histories of African American religion do a certain kind of work in narratives of recovery, redemption, and resistance. These kinds of stories announce that the lives of Africa's children do not begin with the transatlantic slave trade; that these individuals exhibit in their daily living the presence of Africa in their worldviews, in their conceptions of life and death, and in the moral and ethical principles that guide them as they negotiate their circumstances. Within these narratives, black agency is central because the very presence of African Americans acting on their own behalf betrays the lie that white supremacy has reduced them to mere pawns in the doings of white men. Of course, the "fact" of Africa-descended peoples "acting for themselves" taking on *this* significance, as opposed to some other, involves a kind of "poetic troping of the facts," which gives them the quality of heroic self-assertion, a sense of commonly shared experience, and a singularity of reference and meaning that come to signify the essence of a people engaged in struggle.

Such stories are not necessarily bad. The violence of America—physical and epistemic—easily warrants such a narrative technique that emphasizes the "unifying experiences of African peoples dispersed by the slave trade" as well as efforts "to locate a single culture with singular historical roots" as a basis for emboldening those persons to resist their subjugation (Kelley 2002: 126). Moreover, in light of the grand narratives of American religion and history that marginalize the presence of African Americans, such narratives constitute important interventions and corrections: they reveal the bodies buried beneath the pristine histories of the American nation-state. But we need to understand these stories as *constructions* that attempt to do a certain kind of work—not simply as *the* account of the *origins* of African American religion. There are indeed other ways of *beginning* the story.

Of course, a distinction is to be made between origins and beginnings. Beginnings constitute a first step in the production of meanings about a given topic as well as a means of differentiating between competing views: I begin this way as opposed to that. Origins, some would believe, are not subject to such choice; they reflect the fact of the matter. We can not begin the story otherwise.[4] My aim here is to recast this concern about origins in light of the overall question of narrative. What are the implications of "beginning" the story in this way, and holding the view that this beginning as opposed to another constitutes *the* beginning of the story of African American religion? Edward Said writes of beginnings:

> A beginning suggests either (a) a time, (b) a place, (c) an object, (d) a principle, or (e) an act—in short, detachment of the sort that establishes distance and difference between either a, b, c, d, or e on the one hand and what came before it on the other.... *My* beginning specializes still more, but the moment I unconditionally speak of *the* beginning, knowledge is theologized.... Once made the focus of attention, the beginning occupies the foreground and is no longer a beginning but has the status of an actuality; and when it cedes its place to that which it has aimed to produce or to give rise to it, it can exist in the mind as

virtuality.…Paraphrasing both Hegel and Vico, we can say that formally the
problem of beginning is the beginning of the problem. (1985: 42, emphasis
added)

Stories of African American religion that posit Africa as *the* beginning
generate particular problems that need to be made explicit. Not so much
because knowledge is theologized. Said is justifiably skeptical of the processes by which historical claims are mapped on to the very order of
things—an order that stands apart from the actual doings and sufferings
of people. I take it that his characterization of such processes as the "theol-
ogizing" of knowledge is consistent with his thoroughgoing secularism.
One need not embrace, however, his overall suspicion of "religion" to take
seriously his insights about "the problem of how to *begin* to grasp the relationship between the past and the circumstances and exigencies of the
present" (42). We can in fact begin to do some of the work of making these
problems explicit by isolating particular dimensions of the narrative of
African American religion such a beginning has produced.

We should be mindful when we write or invoke history as historians,
philosophers, or as cultural critics, that we are not engaged in a dispassionate detailing of facts or a mere representation of the record. Rather, we
actively work in shaping the narrative, in singling out certain events and
particular characters; and we do so with purposes and interests in mind. In
writing such histories, we find ourselves negotiating the authority of tradition, the constraining power of conventions, *and* encountering the limits
of narrative form. History then is always written, even when not explicitly
acknowledged to be so, from a self-consciously critical point of view and in
full awareness of the temporal distance between the historian and the
subject(s) about which she writes. As Thomas Tweed writes:

[T]he stories that fill history textbooks are important because they negotiate
power and construct identity. They situate us in society and tell us who we are.
Historical narratives often reflect, and shape, the social and economic order:
individuals and groups excluded from narratives are excluded from more than
stories. Those who do not find themselves or their experience represented in the
most widely told stories engage in struggles—private and public, quiet and
noisy—to make sense of themselves and locate their place among others in the
wider society. Historical narratives, then, never are just history. There always is
a great deal at stake for narrators and readers, always much to gain and lose in
power and meaning. (1997: 2)

For a subject people, this insight takes on added significance. Their
subjugation not only involves their actual bodies, but also the colonization
of history and the forging of a regime of truth that often relegates them

beyond the margins. This account not only removes the slave, for example, from history, but denies her moral standing as a result. As such, history becomes a critical battleground, often resulting in a "theologized history" upon which issues of meaning, identity, and resistance are addressed (Glaude 2007: Chapter 3). And, for black folk, "Africa" stands as a crucial site of contestation.

In his brilliant book, *Afrotopia* (1998), Wilson Moses delineates popular traditions of African American historiography that reflect this political and existential reality.[5] Both the historiography of decline (a historical narrative that begins with the greatness of an African past that has been displaced by the brutality of the West) and the historiography of progress (a story that posits a progressive evolution toward improved conditions for African Americans) engage in a battle around meaning and identity. Both historical accounts take up the importance of Africa as a site for regeneration and recovery of meanings lost in the face of the brutality of white supremacy. Both stand as different examples of a kind vindicationism, or "the project of defending black people from the charge that they have made little or no contribution to the history of human progress (1998: 21) What is interesting about Moses's account, for my purposes, is the extent to which he captures a general tendency in African American religious historiography: how we account for the African presence in African American religion; how we understand its power in the religious imagination of African Americans; its influence on the form and content of black religious expression; and its centrality to a conception of black identity forged in the struggle for freedom in the New World.

W. E. B. Du Bois: A Beginning—of Sorts

W. E. B. Du Bois's classic text, The *Souls of Black Folk*—and particularly his chapter "Of the Faith of Our Fathers"—inaugurates these sorts of concerns in the formal writing of African American religious history (1969: 210–225). I read "Of the Faith of Our Fathers" as one of the first treatments of African American religion as an object of inquiry. Du Bois does not take himself to be explicating the faith claims of a particular religious denomination; rather, he sets out to examine the social history of "the Black Church" and its then current role in African American life. As such, many of the concerns that preoccupy contemporary studies of African American religion can be found in Du Bois's account.

Three important tendencies stand out. First, Du Bois foregrounds the social function of black churches and draws on the distinction between otherworldly and this-worldly religion (between accommodation and protest) that has defined so much of the literature on the subject. (This emphasis on black churches also reveals the decidedly Christian bias in much of the work done on African American religion.[6]) Second, Du Bois refuses to ghettoize his account of African American religion; he understands it within the larger context of American religious history—prefiguring Sydney Ahlstrom's claim that the recovery of African American religious history serves as a paradigm for the recovery of American religious history. Du Bois's account of African American religion functions then in the context of *Souls* as a synecdochic account—where to tell the story of African American religion is to tell, in part, the story of American religion. Lastly, Du Bois attempts to account for the place of Africa in the history of African American religion. In fact, he answers the question—what have been the successive steps of this social history?—with the claim that the foundations of African American religion are found not in America but in Africa. Du Bois writes:

> First, we must realize that no such institution as the Negro church could rear itself without definite historical foundations. These foundations we can find if we remember that the social history of the Negro did not start in America. He was brought from a definite social environment—the polygamous clan life under the headship of the chief and the potent influence of the priest. His religion was nature worship, with profound belief in invisible surrounding influences, good and bad; and his worship was through incantation and sacrifice. (1969: 215–216)

Drawing on the "bad" anthropological descriptions of Africa that circulated at the time, Du Bois offers a description of a form of life that, in fact, informed how African-descended peoples negotiated the devastating implications of New World slavery. He describes the violent disruption of forms of life and claims that although it was a horrific social revolution, "some traces were retained of the former group life, and the chief remaining institution was the Priest or Medicine-Man" (216).

I am not interested in vindicating Du Bois's claim about the continuity between the medicine-man and the black preacher. What interests me instead is that his move to "Africa" as foundation must be understood within the context of writing history against History, a form of writing bound up with a struggle against white supremacy. To highlight the trope of African beginnings in the construction of his story, then, is to read Du Bois's use of the trope as part of a discursive battle to redeem African Americans. And, given that I am figuring his study as paradigmatic for African American religious history, his *beginning* sets the trajectory of how the story has been told ever since.

One can see this way of beginning the narrative in the extraordinary ferment of the 1960s and 1970s when so many of our now "classic" texts in the field were written. These histories sought to recover and redeem a past long neglected in mainstream American religious history. Albert Raboteau, reflecting on the time, writes:

> [F]or many of us studying in those 'movement' years, the attempt to research and write about African American history had a personal significance and a political impetus. I felt that in the recovery of this history lay the restoration of my past, my self, and my people. In this context I chose to write about the history of the religious life of slaves. (2004: 325)

I think this view captures much of the moment, particularly the sorts of debates about slave agency and religious commitments. Many wrestled with "the question of what, if anything, was distinctive about slave culture." The question of distinctiveness was answered, by many, with appeals to African survivals: slave religion was not a mere replication of the master's religion; slaves were not reduced to Sambos by the peculiar institution; rather, they had the resources to forge a self amid the absurdity of their condition. Those resources were African, and the scholarly work aimed to demonstrate this connection and continuity.

I point your attention to this work not to belittle it or to call its scholarship into question. Far from it. I only want to highlight the way "Africa" has been emploted in the story in light of a broader context within which histories of African American religion have been written—histories in which certain motifs, characters, plots, and settings orient the reader and locate her in a particular terrain and social space (see Tweed 1997: 1–23). And, perhaps most importantly, the narrators themselves—those who write the histories—are situated within particular political/historical moments and write their histories in light of the challenges such moments present. Indeed, representations of "Africa" reflect choices made in these contexts.

Conclusion/Another Beginning

To be sure, African American religious historians have relied on certain motifs to tell their story of African American religion. More often than not the stories are framed within a liberatory or progressive model (even narratives of declension stand as a prelude to liberation). I have tried to show that uses of the trope of "Africa" are central to such efforts. Indeed, beginning the story of African American religion with the question of African origins orients the narrative in a particular way. The result has been an affirmation of a certain kind of black subjectivity and, too often, an evasion of the particulars of the vast continent and the complexities of its relationship to the New World. In other words, "Africa" in the service of a particular story of recovery, redemption, and resistance often obscures more than it illuminates. It blinds us to the "fact" that "Africa is neither a figment of New World imagination, frozen in time, nor the sole birthplace of modern African culture" (Kelley 2002: 129).[7] Instead, the actual doings and sufferings of African-descended peoples constantly reshape, recast, and transform Africa and its diaspora.

The stories I have alluded to mattered and continue to matter, but we can and must insist on a different beginning (in part because these older stories make it possible to *begin* anew). "Africa" can now be approached without the justificatory burden of black agency and the weight of resistance. We can take up the extraordinary richness and diversity of its landscape not simply to establish continuity and connections, but to explore the beliefs held, the choices made, and the actions taken in the context of an ever-changing world. We have certainly seen some good work in this regard. I am thinking about the tremendous scholarship of John Thornton and Michael Gomez, the work of David Eltis and David Richardson,[8] and the ongoing work at Amherst College with *African American Religion: A Documentary History Project*,[9] as well as the work in and around the Black Atlantic that is not so caught within national histories (in fact, the work seems to disrupt such accounts).[10] We can now see much more of the complexity of the relationship of African ethnic enclaves to their New World destinations, and see somewhat clearly their cultural effects.

But even Thornton and Gomez, for example, ironically fall into some traps. As Philip Morgan has argued, they tend to overreach their evidence and claim a cohesive and coherent African identity for many slaves that, in his view (and I would agree), downplay cultural creation, adjustment, and adaptation that characterized the efforts of diverse Africans on this side of the Atlantic (1997: 122–145). One might wonder if the question of black agency has been recast here.

My primary purpose in this brief chapter has been to call attention to how our beginning of the story of African American religion shapes the history of the study of African American religion. To my mind, there is much more to the story of African American religion than the issues of resistance and agency. Important concerns though they may be, neither exhausts the myriad narrative possibilities evidenced in the extraordinary religious imaginations of these New World peoples. To begin the story differently, I am quite confident to say, will return us to that mess with which

I began this chapter. And, like the artist to whom Beckett refers, and like those scholars who have come before us, we too must find a form to accommodate it.

Notes

1. I refer to Jonathan Z. Smith's rather provocative formulation: "There is no data for religion. Religion is solely the creation of the scholar's study" (1982: xi). Beckett said famously: "To find a form that accommodates the mess, that is the task of the artist now" (Driver 1961).
2. Just to list a few, McCutcheon (1997); Masuzawa (1993); Asad (1993); Kippenberg (2002); Orsi (2005); Taylor (1998); Braun and McCutcheon (2000).
3. My use of trope follows Hayden White in his essay, "Narrative in Contemporary Historical Theory" in *The Content of the Form* (1987).
4. A great example of this can be seen in Mechal Sobel's book, *Trabelin' On: The Slave Journey to an Afro-Baptist Faith* (1988). The first section of the book explores "The African World View and Its Enslavement." Sobel writes
   The current reevaluation of the changing nature of black American culture in the seventeenth and eighteenth centuries brings into question the broadly accepted view that the American context is sufficient to explain the content of black Christianity. The African component of the earliest slave cultures was so overwhelming that, with growing awareness of it, it has become impossible to explain black religion in American without exploring continuities with African understandings. (xix)
   Sobel goes on to suggest that "a quasi-African body of values functioned in almost every African household in America" (xxi).
5. John Ernest does a wonderful job of debunking Moses' easy dismissal of popular histories in the name of "a truer historical sense." Ernest states that his operating assumption is that visions of a 'true historical sense' or an objective ideal of scholarship aside, conceptions of historical truth are culturally generated and necessarily reflect struggles for cultural authority—struggles that inform Moses's book as well as those popular or folk historians that he studies and sometimes critiques. (2004: 2–3)
6. Anthony Pinn takes issue with this decidedly Christian bias in his many writings. See, for example, Pinn (1998).
7. Here Robin D. G. Kelley refers to J. Lorand Matory's wonderful essay, "The English Professors of Brazil: On the Diasporic Roots of the Yoruba Nation" (1999: 72–103).
8. I am thinking of John Thornton's major work (1998); Gomez (1998); Eltis (2000); and Eltis's coedited volume with David Richardson (1997).
9. The documentary project at Amherst seeks to provide a comprehensive history of African American religion and it begins with the extraordinary encounter of

race and religion along the West Coast of Africa in the mid-fifteenth century. The project aims not only to uncover origins but also to draw out the complexities and nuances of this particular beginning on how we think about African American religion.

10. Here I am thinking primarily of Brent Hayes Edwards's work (2003).

Bibliography

Asad, Tala (1993). *Genealogies of Religion: Disciplines and Reasons of Power in Christianity and Islam.* Baltimore, MD: Johns Hopkins University Press.

Braun, Willi and Russell T. McCutcheon (eds.) (2000). *Guide to the Study of Religion.* New York: Cassell.

Driver, Tom T. (1961). "Beckett by the Medeleine" [interview], Columbia University Forum IV (Summer).

Du Bois, W. E. B. (1969) [1903]. *The Souls of Black Folk.* New York: Penguin.

Edwards, Brent Hayes (2003). *The Practice of Diaspora: Literature, Translation and the Rise of Black Internationalism.* Cambridge, MA: Harvard University Press.

Eltis, David (2000). *The Rise of African Slavery in the Americas.* Cambridge: Cambridge University Press.

Eltis, David and David Richardson (eds.) (1997). *Routes to Slavery: Direction, Ethnicity and Mortality in the Transatlantic Slave Trade.* London: Frank Cass.

Ernest, John (2004). *Liberation Historiography: African American Writers and the Challenge of History, 1794–1861.* Chapel Hill: University of North Carolina Press.

Glaude, Jr., Eddie (2007). *In a Shade of Blue: Pragmatism and the Politics of Black America.* Chicago: University of Chicago Press.

Gomez, Michael (1998). *Exchanging Our Country Marks: The Transformation of African Identities in the Colonial and Antebellum South.* Chapel Hill: University of North Carolina Press.

Kelley, Robin D. G. (2002). "How the West Was One: The African Diaspora and the Re-Mapping of U.S. History." In Thomas Bender (ed.), *Rethinking American History in a Global Age*, 123–147. Berkeley: University of California Press.

Kippenberg, Hans G. (2002). *Discovering Religious History in the Modern Age*, trans. Barbara Harshay. Princeton: Princeton University Press.

Matory, J. Lorand (1999). "The English Professors of Brazil: On the Diasporic Roots of the Yoruba Nation," *Comparative Studies in Society and History* 41/1 (January): 72–103.

Masuzawa, Tomoko (1993). *In Search of Dreamtime: The Quest for the Origin of Religion.* Chicago: University of Chicago Press.

McCutcheon, Russell T. (1997). *Manufacturing Religion: The Discourse on Sui Generis Religion and the Politics of Nostalgia.* New York: Oxford University Press.

Morgan, Philip D. (1997). "The Cultural Implications of the Atlantic Slave Trade: African Regional Origins, American Destinations and New World Developments," *Slavery & Abolition* 18: 122–145.

Moses, Wilson J. (1998). *Afrotopia: The Roots of African American Popular History*. Cambridge: Cambridge University Press.

Orsi, Robert (2005). *Between Heaven and Earth: The Religious Worlds People Make and the Scholars Who Study Them*. Princeton: Princeton University Press.

Pinn, Anthony (1998). *Varieties of African American Religious Experience*. Minneapolis, MN: Fortress.

Raboteau, Albert (2004). *Slave Religion: The Invisible Institution in the Antebellum South*, Updated Edition. New York: Oxford University Press.

Said, Edward (1985). *Beginnings: Intention and Method*. New York: Columbia University Press.

Smith, Jonathan Z. (1982). *Imagining Religion: From Babylon to Jonestown*. Chicago: University of Chicago Press.

Sobel, Mechal (1988) [1979]. *Trabelin' On: The Slave Journey to an Afro-Baptist Faith*. Princeton: Princeton University Press.

Taylor, Mark (ed.) (1998). *Critical Terms for Religious Studies*. Chicago: University of Chicago Press.

Thornton, John (1998). *Africa and African in the Making of the Atlantic World, 1400–1800*, 2nd ed. Cambridge: Cambridge University Press.

Tweed, Thomas (ed.) (1997). *Retelling U.S. Religious History*. Berkeley: University of California Press.

White, Hayden (1987). *The Content of the Form: Narrative Discourse and Historical Representation*. Baltimore, MD: Johns Hopkins University Press.

Contributors

Afe Adogame holds a PhD in the History of Religions from Bayreuth University, Germany, where he was a senior research fellow in the Department for the Study of Religion and the Institute of African Studies for a decade. He teaches at the Divinity School of the University of Edinburgh, Scotland. His research interests include: the African diaspora, new African religious movements, and religion and globalization. He is the author of *Celestial Church of Christ: The Politics of Cultural Identity in a West African Prophetic-Charismatic Movement* (1999). He is also the coeditor of *European Traditions in the Study of Religion in Africa* (2004) and *Religion in the Context of African Migration* (2005).

Christine Ayorinde received her PhD in history from the University of Birmingham in 2000. She was awarded a postgraduate studentship from the Arts and Humanities Research Board of the British Academy and has held a postdoctoral research fellowship with the UNESCO Nigerian Hinterland Project at York University, Canada. Her recent publications include: *Afro-Cuban Religiosity, Revolution and National Identity* (2004) and chapters in *Identity in the Shadow of Slavery* (2000); *Contesting Freedom: Control and Resistance in the Century after Emancipation in the Caribbean* (2005); and *The Yoruba Diaspora in the Atlantic World* (2005). Research interests include African and diaspora religions and comparative studies in race and ethnicity.

Angela N. Castañeda received her PhD in Cultural Anthropology from Indiana University. She is assistant professor of Anthropology and Latin American and Caribbean Studies at DePauw University in Greencastle, Indiana. Her research interests focus on issues of identity, festivals, religion, and expressive culture among communities of the African diaspora in Latin America and the Caribbean. With research and field experience in various Latin American countries including Brazil and Colombia, her dissertation, entitled "'*Veracruz tambien es Caribe*': Power, Politics, and Performance in the Making of an Afro-Caribbean Identity," was based on field research in Mexico.

Fatimah Fanusie is a doctoral candidate in American History at Howard University. Her dissertation, "Fard Muhammad in Historical Context: An Islamic Thread in the American Religious and Cultural Quilt," explores the Indian Ahmadiyya background of Fard Muhammad and the early history of the Nation of Islam (NOI) through a comparative Islamic framework. Ms. Fanusie's research interests include American religious history; twentieth-century Islamic development in America; and comparative historical Islamic development. Her studies and research in Egypt, India, and the United States have focused on the use of syncretism as a tool to introduce "normative" Islam to unlettered populations.

Eddie S. Glaude, Jr., is a professor in the Religion Department at Princeton University. His research interests include American pragmatism—specifically the work of John Dewey—and African American religious history and its place in American public life. He is the recipient of numerous fellowships and awards, including the 2002 Modern Language Association William Sanders Scarborough Prize for his book *Exodus!: Religion, Race, and Nation in 19th Century Black America* (2000). He is also the editor of *Is It Nation Time?: Contemporary Essays on Black Power and Black Nationalism* (2002) and, with Cornel West, *African-American Religious Thought: An Anthology* (2004). His most recent book is *In a Shade of Blue: Pragmatism and the Politics of Black America* (2007).

Kelly E. Hayes received her PhD in the History of Religions from the University of Chicago. Her work is ethnographically based and centrally concerned with issues of gender, sexuality, marginality, and morality in the context of Afro-Brazilian spirit possession religions. She is assistant professor of Religious Studies at Indiana University Purdue University Indianapolis.

Jonathon S. Kahn received his PhD from Columbia University and is currently an assistant professor of Religion at Vassar College. He has published essays on Du Bois and religion in *Philosophia Africana* and *The Souls of W. E. B. Du Bois: New Essays and Reflections* (forthcoming, 2009). His current book project, *Divine Discontent: The Religious Imagination of W.E.B. Du Bois* [2008], unearths Du Bois's distinctive religiosity—a decidedly black faith that is in constant tension with traditional Christian metaphysics.

Maha Marouan is assistant professor in the Religious Studies Department at the University of Alabama. She completed her PhD in African American literature at the School of American and Canadian Studies, University of Nottingham, England. She is currently investigating the constructions of religion and history in Toni Morrison's *Paradise*, David Bradley's *The Chaneysville Incident*, and Maryse Condé's *Moi, Tituba, sorcière Noire de Salem*. Additional interests include Afro-Caribbean Literature, postcolonial literature, comparative literature, and African American religions.

Russell T. McCutcheon is professor of Religious Studies and chair of the Religious Studies Department at the University of Alabama. Among others, he is the author of *Manufacturing Religion* (1977); *Critics Not Caretakers* (2001); *The Discipline of Religion: Structure, Meaning, Rhetoric* (2003); and *Studying Religion: An Introduction* (2007). He is also the editor of *The Insider/Outsider Problem in the Study of Religion* (1999) and coeditor with Willi Braun of *Guide to the Study of Religion* (2000).

Wilson Jeremiah Moses is Ferree professor of American History and senior fellow of the Arts and Humanities Institute at the Pennsylvania State University. He has been Fulbright senior lecturer at the Free University of Berlin and Fulbright guest professor at the University of Vienna. He has written five books and published three others as a documentary editor. Recent publications include: *Creative Conflict in African American Thought* (2004); *Liberian Dreams: Back to Africa Narratives from the 1850s* (1998); *Afrotopia: The Roots of African American Popular History* (1998); and *The Wings of Ethiopia* (1990).

Merinda Simmons is a PhD candidate in the Department of English at the University of Alabama. Her research interests and areas of emphasis include African American literature and theory, postcolonial literature, and Third Wave and transnational feminist theory. She is currently working on a dissertation tentatively entitled, "Mary Prince and Her Sisters: Gender, Labor, and the Formation of 'Authenticity' in Afro-Caribbean and African American Women's Migration Narratives."

Maboula Soumahoro is a doctoral candidate and teacher in the English Department at the Université François Rabelais. She is currently completing her dissertation entitled "Black Peoples, Black Gods: A Comparative Analysis of the Early Ideologies of the Nation of Islam and the Rastafari, 1930–1950." She has been a visiting scholar in the History Department and the Institute for Research in African-American Studies at Columbia University, New York; she has also lectured and delivered papers in the United States, the Caribbean, and Europe.

Theodore Louis Trost is associate professor in Religious Studies and New College at the University of Alabama. He received his PhD from Harvard

University in American Religious History. He is the author of *Douglas Horton and the Ecumenical Impulse in American Religion* (2002) and, with Carolyn M. Jones, the coeditor of *Teaching African American Religions* (2005). In 2005, he was awarded a Louisville Institute "Religious Institutions Grant" to study the United Church of Christ's television advertising campaign.

Matthew Waggoner received his PhD from the History of Consciousness Program at the University of California, Santa Cruz, where he specialized in critical and cultural theory and the study of religion. He has served as visiting assistant professor of Religious Studies at Yale University and is currently assistant professor of Philosophy and Religion at Albertus Magnus College in New Haven, Connecticut. Dr. Waggoner has published articles and reviews for *Culture and Religion* and *Journal of Cultural and Religious Theory*. He is also coeditor of the forthcoming *Readings in the Theory of Religion: Map, Text, Body* (2007).

Regennia N. Williams is associate professor in the Department of History at Cleveland State University and the founder and director of The Initiative for the Study of Religion and Spirituality in the History of Africa and the Diaspora (RASHAD). She has designed courses for Cleveland State University on "The History of Blacks through Sacred Music" and "Collective Survival in the African Diaspora." Her published works include "Reading Writing, and Racial Uplift" in *Education and the Great Depression (2006);* "Mother to Son" in *Montage of a Dream: Essays on the Art and Life of Langston Hughes (2007);* "'Race Women' and Reform" in the *Proceedings* of the Ohio Academy of History (2002); and entries in *The Encyclopedia of the Harlem Renaissance.* Her current projects include a biography of photographer Allen Cole and a history of Cleveland's African American community.

Index

Entries in *italics* refer to illustrations.